a Tear in the Soul

AMANDA WEBSTER was born in Kalgoorlie, where her father and his father before him were doctors. She attended school with Aboriginal children from the local Kurrawang mission. After an early career in medicine, Webster earned an MFA in creative writing. She has published essays in several literary journals. Her first book was *The Boy Who Loved Apples*. *A Tear in the Soul* is her second book.

Dedicated to the memory of

Elizabeth Ugle and Beverley Joy Noble (Owatta).
May their grandchildren's grandchildren
know their names.

a Tear in the Soul

Amanda Webster

A NewSouth book

Published by
NewSouth Publishing
University of New South Wales Press Ltd
University of New South Wales
Sydney NSW 2052
AUSTRALIA
newsouthpublishing.com

First published 2016

10 9 8 7 6 5 4 3 2 1

National Library of Australia
Cataloguing-in-Publication entry
Creator: Webster, Amanda, author.
Title: A tear in the soul / Amanda Webster.
ISBN: 9781742235134 (paperback)
9781742247984 (ePDF)
9781742242552 (ebook)
Subjects: Webster, Amanda—Childhood and youth.
Children, Aboriginal Australian—Western Australia—Kurrawang Mission.
Stolen generations (Australia)—Western Australia.
Aboriginal Australians, Treatment of—Western Australia—History.
Reconciliation.
Kurrawang Mission (W.A.).
Dewey Number: 920.720994

UNSW
AUSTRALIA

Design Josephine Pajor-Markus
Cover design Vivien Valk
Cover images TOP A stockman from Moola Bulla Station, pictured with family and friends. The station and nearby Hall's Creek Mission run by the Australian Inland Mission housed many members of the Stolen Generations. Photo taken by Ava Margaret Cook, circa 1949; BOTTOM Marcus Garrett / Arcangel Images

Aboriginal and Torres Strait Islander readers should be aware that this book may contain mention of people who have died.

Contents

The Question

A late-model station wagon, washed-out blue like the sky, makes a sharp turn into the Kalgoorlie Regional Hospital car park and pulls up before a brick-walled building. A thin bespectacled man steps out. He leans down, pokes his head through the open front window. Instructs his six-year-old daughter in the back seat: 'Stay here. I won't be long.' Straightens up and wheels around. Stethoscope in hand, pockets bulging with Minties, he hurries along an open walkway, his leather soles slapping the bare concrete. The girl waves at her father's retreating back. She's small for her age, thin with dead-straight hair, cut pudding-bowl style with a fringe. She looks around. The front passenger seat – the *death seat* in an accident – is forbidden territory when the car is moving; stationary it's fair game. She clambers over the seatback, her shoe buckles scraping the vinyl. She plonks herself down. Grasps the metal window handle and winds the glass up and down. Her gaze wanders to the driver's seat. She slides over, raising a small cloud of red dust and dog hair, and wraps her hands around the steering wheel. Tugs it this way and that. Rubbers her lips to make brmming noises. She fiddles with the indicator, and clicks her tongue, *Ticaticaticatic*. Black flies buzz inside the windscreen. Outside, eucalyptus leaves tumble over the bitumen. The air so thick with sulphurous fumes from the mines you could cut it.

Does a group of barefooted Aboriginal people straggle by, swatting at the flies and calling out to each other in words familiar yet incomprehensible? Does the little girl stare at their dark skin and then at her own eggshell-pale arm? Do a million small observations of difference and of how white people treat Aboriginal people coalesce into one burning question that falls out of her mouth the minute her father opens the car door: 'Daddy, are Aboriginals people?'

My father likes to repeat this story of a moment I've long since forgotten. For him, my childhood question belongs to a cherished compendium of such questions, no more significant than one from my novel encounter with a lift in a department store during a visit to Perth: 'Why are those people in a cage?' His remembering is similar in intent to me keeping my children's baby teeth, their effusive handwritten cards to 'the best mum in the whole wide world', their reluctantly surrendered dummies.

But for me the question has been like a lesion tucked away on a difficult-to-get-at part of the body, festering, pestering, irremovable, at least by simple means. Wishing I had never asked such a horrible question wouldn't make it go away. I needed to look at the question's root causes – was it a product of my own imagination, or did it come from a more general conditioning? – before I could decide its significance and what to do next, a similar process to my father lancing a boil so he could examine its suppurating contents and choose the appropriate antibiotic.

My father never relates his answer, might not remember. In any case, sometimes the question matters more than the answer. Sometimes the questions behind the question matter even more.

Molokai

Quiet writing time ended on the first full day of our retreat on the Hawaiian island of Molokai in 2009, and preparations for dinner – 'potluck' as the other eight women, all American, called it – got underway. In the kitchen, two of the women sliced bread, boiled pasta and chopped and sautéed eggplants and tomatoes. My mouth watered at the smell of the fried vegetables; I hadn't realised how hungry I was. I helped another couple of women set the table, glasses here, cutlery there, jugs of water in the middle. We uncorked bottles of wine, folded paper napkins and distributed salt and pepper shakers.

By dinner time, confidence boosted by vodka shots beforehand, we were ready to tackle the world's problems. The volume ratcheted up a few notches. Discussion turned to ObamaCare. The Americans leapt in, some for Obama's changes to healthcare, one against, others uncertain. I took a sip of wine to moisten my lips and cleared my throat.

'You Americans need better welfare, like us,' I said, beating a self-righteous path through the thicket of voices.

Obama's critic glared down the length of the wooden table at me.

'You've no right to hold the Australian system up as perfect when you have a second-class society.' Her angry words fell into a room gone strangely silent.

My pulse raced, and I could feel my face burn with the blood rush. The silence lengthened, broken only by the scrape of knives against plates, the jangle of cutlery against glasses. *A second-class society? What does she mean?* My thoughts caromed like squash balls around the inside of my head. The women around me studiously tended to the task of eating.

Suddenly one clear thought spun out from the chaos: she meant Indigenous people. My insides twisted and my face burned hotter. I knew the problems: shortened life spans, alcoholism, diabetes, heart disease, deaths in custody, illiteracy, rural communities torn apart by glue- and petrol-sniffing and drugs, poverty and violence. How many times had I read the reports and studied the statistics? If not in newspapers, then in lecture notes or a textbook years before in medical school. By and large, my 'better welfare' comment did not apply to Aboriginal people. Yet how easily I had dismissed them from consideration, a consequence of their relatively low numbers, perhaps, and their underrepresentation in public forums. Or a consequence of how easy it was to ignore the plight of people beyond one's personal sphere, as had become the case for me as an adult. Whatever the reason, Obama's critic was right – the health and living circumstances of our Aboriginal population were no advertisement for our so-called universal healthcare. I slugged a few mouthfuls of wine.

'I guess you mean Aboriginal people. It's difficult in remote areas, where so many of them live …' I faltered, aware of how feeble my excuse sounded. Aware, too, of how there had been a time when Aboriginal people were a big part of my life.

Did anyone mention parallels to Native Americans? I no longer remember. The room buzzed with alcohol-fuelled volatility, and the woman's accusation looped in my head. The other women, a nurse and a teacher among them, professed support for free healthcare and welfare for the less fortunate. Their comments once more provoked the ire of Obama's critic – free universal healthcare would encourage welfare bludgers, she declared. Her concern brought to mind a cartoon from my medical school years that mocked white paranoia about 'undeserved' handouts. The cartoon depicted a bike-riding Aboriginal university student with children: the ultimate and unlikely welfare recipient at a time when Aboriginal people rarely made it through school and still endured segregation in many situations. One of the women argued that bludging was uncommon, that people on welfare were generally in need. Another that a certain amount of bludging was the necessary price for a safety net for the disadvantaged. I agreed and subsided into silence, wary of attracting a repeat of the earlier vitriol. The women shifted the conversation to a more neutral topic. The books we were reading – Edwidge Danticat's *Brother, I'm Dying* and Barack Obama's *Dreams from My Father,* books that discuss racial politics. I barely noticed. Let their voices wash over me. Pushed my plate to the side.

I tried to anchor my mind in the present, to the hard smooth stem of the glass, the American voices rising and falling, 'r's rolled and vowels drawn out. But the wine turned sour in my mouth and I sweated under the the lights. Two images from my past, images I'd reviewed many times, kept bobbing to the surface, like driftwood in a storm.

One of a scrawny white girl in scuffed Mary Janes, a kilt and a home-made cardigan, deep emerald green, unlike any green in her landscape. In an instant I was once again that girl playing elastics with the other white girls, desperate to fit in. It's my turn to jump, but one of my two left feet hooks the elastic and I fall. I untangle myself, stand, rub grazed knees and bolt across the concrete towards the only tree and a group of Aboriginal girls from Kurrawang Mission, 10 miles from town.

'Mandy, Mandy. Come here, Mandy,' a voice calls, welcome as a summer breeze: Bronwyn, one of my best friends, has seen me. She draws me into the circle of Mission girls. Slings an arm around my shoulders, her deep brown skin warm. She wears a faded cotton dress (brown and white, my memory stubbornly insists). She's taller than me, and fleshier. When she smiles, her cheeks form soft mounds. Her scent reminds me of red dirt and the subtle, floral smell of the bush, whereas mine smells like soap from last night's bath.

Another Aboriginal girl, straight hair parted down the middle, threads her fingers through my hair. Dead straight for years, it has recently sprung into curls – I ate all my crusts, which I'm beginning to regret. The girl winds a stray ringlet around her finger. I relax, sunning myself in the attentive glow, happy for the spotlight on something other than my clumsiness. I want this moment to last forever, until next Christmas at least. The bell summons us, the Aboriginal girls to their classroom, me to mine.

As an only girl with two male siblings, I envy the Mission girls as a group, envy their closeness, their entwined lives outside of school that resembles, to me at least, an extended sisterhood. I have to make do with Tessie-bear. Even though I cherish her faded pink fur and the surgical patch Mum knitted for her neck where the intensity of my love had worn her hair thin, it isn't the same. Not even close. Nightly, tucked into my bed under the window of the sleepout that serves as my bedroom, I petition God to breathe life into Tessie-bear, to grant me a sister. When my prayers go unanswered, I figure I've overreached God's abilities. Switch to praying for Bronwyn to come and live with us. God continues to turn deaf ears my way. My mother grants me the next best thing: Bronwyn can come with us to our holiday house in Esperance, for Christmas. I can't wait. I'm still young enough to believe the world revolves around me, so I never spare a thought for Bronwyn's family.

Around me, the American women emptied and refilled plates and glasses. I examined a second mental image, twin to the first. From a distance of 20 metres, Tony Ugle, a Kurrawang boy, smiles back at me as he leans over the tap at the water tank. Boys and girls have separate playgrounds. We're in strife if we stray, so I never get to play with Tony. Sometimes we pass each other in line for class. I like the way the consonants leapfrog the vowels into his surname when I repeat his name quickly: *Tony Ugle, Tony Ugle, Tony Ugle.* And of course I love the openness of that smile. I think Tony is Bronwyn's brother, but I'm not sure why I think this. I don't remember talking about him with Bronwyn.

Raucous laughter erupted from my writer friends, their earlier tensions discarded like the dregs from a wine bottle. I knew I should relax too. I should lighten up, talk, laugh, be one of the gang. Fit in. I wanted to. But couldn't. I nursed my bruised feelings and glass of wine. Contemplated leaving in the morning to escape my shame. As soon as I could, I fled the dinner table.

In my unlit room, I mulled over my extreme reaction to the woman's accusation. Why had her words hit so hard? I thought about how Tony and Bronwyn's names had stayed with me all these years, even though we hadn't seen each other since the age of 11. I'd intended to find them, to try and renew our friendship, but had never got around to it. Now, for all I knew, they were card-carrying members of my writer-friend's second class citizenry.

If they were even alive. A valid concern, I knew; even though life expectancy figures had recently improved, Aboriginal people still died younger than non-Aboriginal people – 11.5 years younger for the men, with a life expectancy of 67.2 years, and 9.7 years younger for the women, with a life expectancy of 72.9 years, I would later learn from a 2005–07 Australian Bureau of Statistics study. If they were alive, my childhood friends, like me, would be gaining fast on their mid-fifties. A sense of time running out struck me, of having betrayed my intentions, of letting my former friends down.

Another memory, recurrent as a migrainous aura, came to mind.

Grade Six at Kalgoorlie Central, the top-streamed class, determined by ability. Forty white children paired behind rows of desks, with wooden lids and inkwells and pencil slots. Dust motes drift in a stream of sunlight. If I paid attention, I'd catch a whiff of sweat, wet grass and flatulence.

A knock on the door interrupts a lesson. The school nurse enters. We stand. Parrot a greeting. Flop down on our seats. Fidget and rock while the two women talk. The teacher announces a head lice check. Her face scrunches up and she says 'head lice' carefully and precisely, as if holding the words at arm's length, the thumb and a finger from the other hand squeezing her nostrils. 'Now get on with your work!' The nurse makes her no-nonsense way to the rear of the classroom. We return to our work.

The year is 1970, and colours rain from night skies as fireworks explode. Australians – not all, I was yet to learn – are celebrating the bicentenary of Lieutenant (as he was at the time) James Cook's arrival on the *Endeavour Bark*. He declared the east coast of *Terra Australis Incognita*, as the country was known to Europeans, to be *Terra Nullius*, or 'nobody's land', and claimed it for England's King George III, naming it New South Wales. No one mentions the subsequent demise of many of the estimated 500–700 Aboriginal nations. Or that only three years have passed since the 1967 referendum achieved the highest 'yes' vote ever – 90.77 per cent, giving Aboriginal people, including my school friends, the 'right' to be governed by the Federal government, which gave them access to social security benefits, the war pension and child endowment among other things, and to be counted in the official population census. No one discloses that in all Australia, my hometown Kalgoorlie recorded the highest 'no' vote.

When the nurse reaches me, she uses a knitting needle to lift the hair behind my left ear, and asks me to lean forward. I obey, flushing under the imagined gaze of 39 pairs of eyes. The nurse's breath on the side of my face is like the tickle of feathers. My own breath comes quickly, in short gasps. For a doctor's daughter, being found to have head lice would be even worse than having been caught with wet pants and a puddle beneath my chair in Grade Two. And that memory still gave me the willies.

The nurse presses the sharp point of the needle against my scalp. After the longest moment, she straightens. She smiles kindly and moves on to the remaining heads. I slump in relief, and feel my face cooling. Before long the bell rings.

Play-lunch flies by, a flurry of biscuits in greaseproof paper or a piece of fruit, a few swigs from a plastic flask of fast-melting frozen raspberry cordial or a Tetrapak of warm milk from the canteen. The bell rings and we hurry inside and find – and this is the moment that haunts me – a group of Aboriginal children huddled in the hall near our classroom. News spreads through the school as surely as lice between heads: the Mission kids have 'nits' and are being sent home by bus. Relieved to avoid such humiliation, I fail to notice if my friends are among the group.

Inside my classroom, I look around. No empty seats. No white kids have head lice. The rest of the day passes without incident. When the final bell rings, we leap up, push our chairs in and stand behind them. The teacher dismisses us. As I file past her, she pulls me, and only me, from the surging tide of children. She waits for the room to empty and slips a folded sheet of paper into my hand for me to give my mother. Without a second thought, I tuck the note in my leather satchel and tear out the door.

At home, my mother reads the note. She extends a hand and lifts my hair, as the nurse had done. Peers intently. Tells me I have head lice and to wait while she goes to the chemist. 'Back in a jiffy.' Dad's surgery is open at the front of the house and my brothers are somewhere, so I won't be alone. I nod; having avoided public humiliation, I'm more interested in getting my grubby mitts on some biscuits. My mother unties her apron and picks up her car keys and handbag. The back door clicks shut behind her. Shortly afterwards the engine of her Mini Minor thrums as she reverses down the driveway.

On her return, my mother shoos me into the bathroom. She douses my hair with a pungent-smelling lotion, to remain on for 24 hours. My eyes water, my nose runs, and despite being a big girl, I'm crying as the comb drags at my tangled curls.

I retreat to my bedroom, which is a mess of toys and books. Cross-legged on my bed, I inspect Barbie with the new short, spiky haircut I've given her for head lice. No creepy-crawlies. No need for a note to take home.

No folded notes for the Aboriginal children either, I think. I'm old enough to recognise kid-glove treatment when I see it, and I'm fairly sure the reason is my father's position as a doctor. Which means he's clever and rich. Which makes him a VIP. Me too, as his daughter. Which isn't fair.

I also think my special treatment has something to do with being white. Somehow this puts me a cut above Aboriginal people. I'm not sure how I know this. I just do.

It might be because Aboriginal people speak faster and pronounce their words funny. Or perhaps it's because of how they live. All the children I know live on the Mission, which means they must be orphans; otherwise, why wouldn't they live with their families? As for the grown-ups, they live in the bush in humpies, not great big houses like ours with a brand-new kitchen. The government started building the Opera House before we even knocked down our old kitchen, but we beat them to the finish and had a Grand Opening Party. No one drank beer because my mother is a teetotaler. Because drinking alcohol is a slippery slope. Which is another thing – some of the Aboriginal people get drunk in the street, and that's *disreputable*.

But the biggest difference of all, as far as I can see, is that Aboriginal people have black skin. Apart from her black skin, though, none of those rules count with Bronwyn, who is a very important person to me. I hope she wasn't one of the kids in the school hall.

In the morning, my hair clumped and stinking, I beg for a sick day to avoid teasing. But *you don't want to act like you've got tickets on yourself, do you?* My mother packs me off to school.

Outside my Molokai room, the wind clamoured at the shutters. I thought of my donations to Indigenous causes here and there, my earnest debates with like-minded medical school friends, my participation with my husband, our three children and my father in the May 2000 Sydney Harbour Bridge Walk for Reconciliation. Of how, rugged up against the wind, I soaked up the happy atmosphere and the winter sunshine as we plodded along the bitumen beneath the steel girders. Of how I smiled at an Aboriginal woman leaning against the bridge railing near the train line, but didn't speak to her or any other Aboriginal person.

Frocked up in liberal opinions, I'd been waltzing through life, mistaking symbolic gestures and puffed-up speech for sufficient contribution to the process of reconciliation. It had taken a foreigner a long way from home to show me just how inflated and inadequate, how limited my largely academic responses to correcting the inequality had been to date. As if I existed at a remove from the problem when, unlike many Australians, I had grown up around Aboriginal people and had friends among the Mission kids. My so-called 'orphans' – another belief I had yet to challenge.

My mother might, intentionally or otherwise, have sparked my belief in benevolent missionaries rescuing Aboriginal children from God-knows-what. After leaving school at 14, my mother cared for her Great Aunty Maude. According to my mother's sister, my mother fell under the spell of Maude's Victorian principles and, in a religious fervour, wanted to save the 'heathen' Aboriginal people. She became a nurse and, before she married my father, found her calling with the Australian Inland Mission in the Kimberley, among Aboriginal people.

In turn I fell under the spell of my mother's stories of her missionary work; memories of the warmth in her voice if not the content remain. Did she view her young Aboriginal charges as either orphaned or saved from poverty and perdition? If so, perhaps she simplified the possibilities to orphanhood for her impressionable daughter, a bookish girl, who may have fancied herself as a missionary of sorts when she befriended the Aboriginal girls at school.

That impressionable girl's Sunday School teachers at Wesley Church, on the nearest street corner, must also have influenced her. Gussied up in her Sunday best, and more than a little fervid herself, that young girl in her innocence cleaved to the message of spreading the good word and doing good deeds.

In 'A Letter to My Nephew', African-American James Baldwin writes of white people, 'It is the innocence which constitutes the crime.' 'Innocent' people were those who did not know – or want to know – the harm they had done to African-Americans. By which Baldwin means people can't do something wrong and pretend they didn't, or dress it up as something else. Again in Baldwin's words, it was 'not permissible that the authors of devastation should also be innocent'. As a child, I knew the Aboriginal children with head lice were treated unkindly; I saw the inequality on the streets and I was part of the system that allowed all of this to happen, but didn't see that I was – or refused to. As an adult, I didn't see that the Aboriginal people I'd known would have been just as susceptible to the terrible treatment and statistics we all knew of. I hadn't connected them with the need for reconciliation. It was high time I did.

After a restless sleep, I decided to stay on for the remainder of the retreat. What would come next was unclear. I knew I would look for Bronwyn and Tony, ask for the real story of their childhoods, see if we could re-establish friendships.

I also knew I wanted to learn more about Kurrawang. What I didn't fully comprehend at this stage was that, despite everything a life of white privilege had taught me, it wasn't all about me and my feelings of shame.

The Skin Divide

My paternal grandparents hankered after retirement in Esperance, on the south coast, where they holidayed with their children in the 1930s and 40s. They camped on deserted beaches, the water so glassy my grandfather could keep watch from the granite headland. If he yelled 'Shark!', my father and his sisters scuttled out of the water, until Grandfather sounded the all-clear. No need to get all het up: the ocean belonged to sea creatures, after all.

When a buyer for Grandfather's medical practice in the front rooms of his house failed to materialise, my father resigned from his position at Royal Perth Hospital, bought out my grandfather for a relatively small sum because Kalgoorlie was considered 'on the way out', and returned to his childhood home, his new bride reluctantly in tow. The year was 1957.

In making the move, he assured my brothers and me of a very particular childhood, in many ways more similar to his than our peers'. I might never have scrabbled in a gravel street after rain, searching for washed-out alluvial gold as my father did, but two populations co-existed along a cultural divide in the bitumen streets of my youth as they had in my father's – Aboriginal and non-Aboriginal.

The commonly used measure of belonging was skin colour. Decades later, the Molokai suggestion of a second class of society forced me to consider the mark left by such a town on its inhabitants. Was the question my child-self asked of my father in the hospital park an anomaly, and therefore irrelevant? Or was it confined to my family and therefore hardly more relevant? Or was it symptomatic of a more widespread malady, like bacteria in the water, and therefore let's-get-to-the-bottom-of-this relevant?

Let's start with my family, so you can better understand my role in this story, so I can better understand my role. Start with memory fragments I've examined many times over the years, and with family documents. Vestiges of my mother's response to relocation linger in what she refers to on the front cover as her 'Memoirs' (handwritten in blue ink on 14 pages torn from an exercise book). She writes of inheriting 'cupboards full of out-dated equipment, horrible paintings by grateful patients, and mementoes of the Great War and other high points.' 'A little bit snarky, your mum was,' says my son when I read him the excerpt.

The memoirs go on to document a true high point the following year – my older brother's arrival, on a day the temperature soared to 102°F. My mother describes my brother as beautiful, but records no details of his birth, which was likely a frightening and mortifying experience for a woman who protected her modesty with sensible layers – underwear, girdle, petticoat. Instead, she notes that through holes in the roof of her hospital room, she could see 'tiny patches of sky' and on the walls, if she cared to, she could read old copies of the *Kanowna Herald*, the newspaper from one of several ghost towns to Kalgoorlie's east.

Eighteen months later, I presented 'a severe feeding problem requiring much care and patience'. Of her hospital stay for my younger brother's birth three years later, my mother says: 'I often wondered whom I shared a bathroom with and one day we met – a bush native placed in the other private room because she couldn't speak English at all and was shy and scared of all things civilised.'

My father adamantly testified to a different version of the story, when recently asked. Mrs Stokes (the 'bush native') lived in town with her husband, a hospital orderly, also Aboriginal. They were two of his favourite patients. Both spoke English. My father delivered Mrs Stokes of her baby son the same day my mother gave birth to my younger brother. Both boys were named Geoffrey.

This version sounds familiar from previous retellings, and I'm inclined to believe my father. He has a prodigious recall of detail, a natural advantage in medicine. I would like to blame my mother's mistake on confusion induced by twilight-sleep anaesthesia, in vogue in obstetrics at the time. I suspect she made assumptions based on skin colour and prejudice.

My mother's narrative skips forward, leaving me to fill in the missing years. True memories commingle with memories of lost photographs. Mostly I can tell the difference. True memories tend to carry extra weight, often burdened by a fraught subtext such as 'the Mission kids with head lice were treated worse than I was', whereas memories of photographs tend towards the benign, and I'm left to wonder who captured the image of, say, me attempting to apply lipstick to our dog Rex, and what significance the moment had to the photographer.

Everything about my mother showed she meant business. She eschewed makeup other than lipstick and, after dabbling in hair dye, let her black curls become steel wool. At home, she tied an apron over her house dress and laid down the law: elbows off the table, cover your mouth if you cough, use a hanky and don't answer back. *No one likes children who are too big for their britches.* She taught us to say *you* not *youse*, and *children* because *a kid is a baby goat.* She dispensed fluoride tablets for our teeth and egg flips to build me up; I was a sickly child. She taught us to hospital-corner the bedsheets, and *if a job's worth doing, it's worth doing properly.* She answered the phone *Mrs Webster speaking*, a habit she would retain until a stroke eroded her memory, and insisted people she considered socially inferior – tradesmen, shop assistants and probably Aboriginal people – address her as Mrs Webster too. I married the first boyfriend to refuse.

To an extent I'm grateful for her habit of formal and correct address: she spared me a measure of shame by teaching my brothers and me never to use the hateful names for Aboriginal people in common usage at the time, names too awful to repeat.

My mother's hoity-toity ways failed to disguise her dirt-poor roots. The hut she lived in with her great-aunt Maude was made of wattle-and-daub and had no plumbing or electricity. The Great Depression never left my mother. She spanking for misdemeanours like swinging on the Hills Hoist or giving cheek.

Other times, he read to us (Captain Hornblower was a favourite), taught us 'The boy stood on the burning deck' parodies and, one winter, woke us early each morning for 'physical jerks' – star jumps, sit-ups and a short run up the back lane and home past Wesley Church. Most prized were his invitations to 'come for the ride' to the local hospitals for ward rounds or, on Saturday afternoons, to the archery club to retrieve his scattered arrows after target practice. ('Near the old aerodrome?' I ask my father in the car one day. 'No, near the old dairy. Its owner was a member of the club. Another member was called Mr Archer.' With that, his mind races away, chasing down a thread that twists and turns, veers suddenly to the left and doubles back through memories as labyrinthine as underground tunnels. If you need to know how the Kalgoorlie Archery Club fared when it competed against the Boulder Golf Club in the 60s, or how the main runway of the old aerodrome was recycled as the main street of a new suburb, call me. Does my urge to record all he remembers represent my belief in the value of each nugget from the past, or is it a variation of my mother's habit of hoarding? Or something else? And how unreliable a child's memory is if it can so easily relocate an archery club. It seems only associated feelings can be trusted.)

More specific memories survive from when I was no more than four or five. One places me with my brothers early one morning, leaping from paver to paver along the side pathway beneath a canopy of vines that in summer bore vast quantities of sour purple grapes we disliked. Our destination: the red metal seesaw with horse-head handles on the front lawn. My older brother leads the way. Tall and lean with prominent ears and crooked teeth, he is always in the vanguard. My younger brother, who calls me 'Sis', trails after me like a puppy. His frequent thunderstorm looks, when he lowers his eyebrows and sometimes hits out, disappear as swiftly as they arrive, to be replaced by a cheeky grin as he gets up to monkey business. He's Mum's favourite and my life's goal is to steal that crown.

As we round the corner of the house we encounter a group of people, instantly identifiable by their black skin and their speech as Aboriginal. The absence of empty beer cans means they are waiting for the surgery to open rather than recovering from what Mum refers to as a beer party. We ... what *did* we do?

Here my memory wavers. I want to stick to my usual ending, where three non-Aboriginal children have warm fuzzy feelings around the Aboriginal people they've grown up with. I like that ending; it allows me to feel good about myself. Not one iota of racism in my bones or past!

But that ending can't be true. My mother inoculated us young with a healthy dose of stranger-danger fear, and her stranger category included Aboriginal people. Desire to see myself in a certain way has obscured my vision, like steam on glass. When I wipe the glass, I'm pretty sure I see three barefooted children in pyjamas hightailing it back down the side path.

A later memory fragment from when I was nine seems to confirm my suspicion. Exiting our front gate, on the way to highland dancing classes, I see a group of Aboriginal people up the street, on the other side. They sprawl on the kerb, lean on the fence or stagger between the two. Sticking to my side of the street, I set off. As I draw near, I see the scruffy clothing, the bare feet. Some of the grown-ups drink what I know to be beer from brown-paper-bagged bottles, the complex reasons for the drinking as yet unknown to me. The Aboriginal people yell at each other and at the scrawny dogs scavenging in the gutter. At Wesley Church on the corner, I cross over and hurry past the group, avoiding eye contact. No one bothers me.

I'm willing to bet on my next memory. It places my mother at her knitting machine, a waist-high structure resembling a keyboard. Ignoring her warnings of chilblains, I huddle close to our kerosene heater and watch.

The knitting carriage clatters, like an old-fashioned typewriter, as Mum coaxes it along the metal bed. She stops. 'Ruddy thing,' she says. She clenches her jaw. Hunches over to untangle wool from shiny silver teeth. Knitting, like everything else, makes her angry. She's making two cardigans to go with the red and green kilts I am to alternate at school, a surefire way to prevent me from looking like we have *more than others*. She doesn't want me to be one of those rich children who *skite* about how much they have.

A linked memory comes to mind: in the school yard, a girl in line behind me asks, *Why do you always wear the same thing?* I shrug. I can't for the life of me figure out the point of my limited wardrobe. Mum doesn't want my clothing to stand out and make other people feel uncomfortable.

Instead, she's making me stand out in a different way that makes *me* feel uncomfortable. All the kids with less money have more clothes, shop-bought clothes, than me. Even the Mission kids. I'm unable to see her actions for what they are: my initiation into the fruitless world of her guilt at becoming the adult version of one of the more affluent girls she'd envied as a child.

Memories from my latter Kalgoorlie years are more short film than fragment. In one, I'm in a child-sized marquee, in my neighbour's back yard. Barry is a year younger than me, dark-haired and amiable, with a tan that never seems to fade. We're in and out of each other's yards, hauling ourselves over our shared picket fence instead of using the gate. By Barry's back shed, a 44-gallon drum rests sideways on a wooden rack, a real saddle on top. Most days, I hoist myself into the worn brown leather, gather the reins and giddy-up. I'm a cowboy chasing Indians like on *F-Troop*, my favourite show, now Kalgoorlie finally has television reception. I'm yet to encounter the concept of racist stereotypes.

Today my brothers and some other kids have showed up. From inside the marquee, we push and poke at an empty powdered milk tin on top of the canvas roof, aiming to keep it out of the gutter formed where the roof sags to meet the metal rods running along the top of the four walls, our invented variation of volleyball.

My older brother ducks outside. Circles the marquee, trying to snatch the tin. The rest of us tumble and squeal, a pile of sweaty, squirming bodies, each struggling for the pleasure of smacking the tin into the air. I clear out from under the pack, leap up and poke the tin hard. A clunk follows and Graham yells. I run outside. Blood drips from a gash on my brother's forehead. At home, a wide-eyed gaze for my mother. *It wasn't me.* My lie like an ulcer in the pit of my stomach.

Years later, in the house my parents retired to in Perth, my mother and I reminisced. Late afternoon sun slanted in low through the window behind her armchair, casting her olive features in shadow. Opposite, on the floral sofa, my feet firmly planted on the floor because *chairs aren't for putting feet on,* I mentioned Barry.

'He was part-Aboriginal, of course.' My mother spoke in a conspiratorial voice, as if I were finally old enough to be privy to this secret.

'What?'

The new information slammed into my consciousness.

I remembered Barry's skin, darker than mine, except in summer when I acquired a dark tan.

Later, thinking of my reaction, I drew what seemed the obvious conclusion – my close friendship with Barry meant I missed the difference in our skin colour. Gold star material, right? Wrong.

In a number of ways. For starters, I *had* noticed that Barry's skin was darker than mine, but I also saw it as lighter than that of the Aboriginal people in the street, and I didn't know that Aboriginality wasn't defined by the depth of skin colour. Or that respect for and understanding of racial difference might be preferable to not noticing, with its implied *I didn't even see the flaw.* Even as recently as a few years ago, none of us knew that race itself is a flawed concept. Genetic studies reveal more similarities between 'races' than differences.

But if my mother had confirmed a social hierarchy she'd introduced me to as a child, I'd found no evidence to suggest she or my father taught me to question the humanity of Aboriginal people. And while their attitudes weren't always the most enlightened, they taught me to care.

Christmas, the year I turned 10, old enough for life to lay down more complete tracks in my memory, Dad detoured down the Eastern Goldfields Highway on our way to Esperance. After what seemed like an age, he turned right onto a dirt track towards Kurrawang and bumped across the pipeline from Perth. Ahead, I saw a house, not fancy but well-maintained, surrounded by garden. I was jumping out of my skin with excitement: the long-awaited holiday with Bronwyn had arrived. Dad pulled up in front of the house and Mr Sercombe, the boss of Kurrawang, came out. Dad told us to stay put and got out. Behind the house, scattered buildings with corrugated roofs reminded me of houses in what I knew to be the poorer parts of Kalgoorlie, seemingly wobbly as a domino stack but surprisingly able to weather the elements.

Several small Aboriginal children appeared. Wraithlike, they peeped from behind tall, skinny trees that seemed to crowd in on us, obscuring our view of the setting sun. The sky seemed drained of warmth and colour, and the wind whistled and moaned through parchment-like leaves, a mournful sound that made the hairs on my arms stand on end.

Bronwyn carried a plastic bag of clothes. I swung the door wide for her and told my brothers to make room on the mattress on the laid-back seat. Bronwyn climbed in. Suitcases and Tupperware containers of home-made slices surrounded our tangled limbs.

Like migratory birds, every time we visited Esperance, my brothers and I returned to our favourite haunts. Bronwyn willingly joined in. We hid out in the old chicken coop. Discovered secret 'moss gardens' in the vacant acreage across the road. Ambled down the hill and past the railway yard to the public library to borrow plastic-covered books. From a bed of self-sufficient plants at the back of the house overlooking the ocean, we crushed lavender to make perfume. From the trellis outside the front door, we picked orange nasturtiums from a vine we nicknamed Galloping Gertie, after a great-aunt I never met, with a name as fascinating a relic as the old bottles we found in the bush. If Mum wanted Dad to 'get them out of my hair', he drove us to Twilight Cove and we slid down sand hills, the coarse white grains abrading our skin as the wind whisked our screams out to sea and the gulls wheeled and shrieked overhead. We shimmied into our bathers and swam together in the curling clear waters of the Southern Ocean, and it was not so much the colour of Bronwyn's skin that impressed me as the strength of her legs, so unlike my own spindly limbs. Some nights, near the old jetty, we fought like seagulls over fish and chips wrapped in newspaper, and poked sticks at the bloated bellies of dead blowfish on the jetty landings where fishermen baited hooks. Other nights, we ate tea in the kitchen, windows open to dispel the smoky warmth of the slow combustion stove, and then bathed in the tub in the small, cement-floored bathroom. Exhausted, we fell asleep in the living room on divans that doubled as couches by day.

At holiday's end, we returned Bronwyn to the Mission. She waved and was gone, swallowed up by the gathering hoarded everything from plastic bags to empty takeaway containers, buttons and scraps of fabric, even bath water, insisting my brothers and I take turns in our ration of two inches. She mashed the leftover slivers of soap most people would discard into a technicolour, misshapen lump for us to wash our hands with. My impulse towards bountiful extravagance at home and excessive generosity (if such a thing exists) in donating to those in need doubtless stems from my desire to become my mother's negative image as much as any genuine kindness, although it must be said that my mother donated regularly to the church and other 'good causes'.

We all inherited our mother's curly hair – my older brother Graham a bouffant mass of black curls, shorn into submission; my younger brother Geoffrey a helmet of cropped corkscrew curls, and me a mop of loose brown curls, frustratingly slow-growing, so much so I sometimes made a wig from Mum's pantyhose. I stretched the pants over my head and twisted the legs into a braid down my back that I swung from side to side until it felt like my head would fall off. Only Geoffrey has my mother's olive skin, which she claimed to have inherited from an African ancestor from St Helena who was partnered by a Dutch ancestor, migrating to South Africa. I happily bought into a legend that seemed to have only an exotic upside.

My father's presence in our home was more of an absence. As far back as I can remember, his working day began before we rose and more often than not stretched long into the night. My brothers and I both feared and worshipped him. Second-in-command to my mother, he was tasked with delivering punishment in the form of a dusk and those tin-roofed buildings, by what I thought of as her comfortable, happy life, not that I ever asked or she ever told. I went home to my bedroom and my books and my bride doll Valerie and my play-clothes and my special occasion outfit: a blue cotton, lace-edged dress with a matching parasol. I went home with my brothers and my parents.

Ghost Town

On the balcony railing outside my study, a pied currawong trills the sound of his name – two ascending notes followed by a downward flourish. He's a handsome fellow, coal-black plumage with a smattering of white feathers, yellow eyes and a dark beak. He stands a good hand high. The currawong may well have lent his name to Kurrawang.

I started my search for Bronwyn and Tony and for information about Kurrawang by asking my father. For the past few years, he has lived a street away, in an apartment. His lively intellect finds pleasure in crosswords, televised sports and books on subjects as varied as botany and plane crashes; he enjoys days of retired leisure, in stark contrast to his Kalgoorlie days.

In the first 15 years or so, before my father formed a group practice, he treated up to 100 patients a day, by necessity. If a hospital ward round took him away from his surgery in the evening, he would return around 11 p.m. to a row of cigarettes glowing in the dark. He served as a flying doctor, took part in mine rescues, delivered babies, administered anaesthetics and performed operations. Someone always needed him. My father loves to tell stories of that time.

I thought my father's repertoire might include Kurrawang stories. But he said he was never called out to Kurrawang, although he did hold one treatment session at Cundeelee Mission, a community of under 300 people, mostly indigenous, east of Kalgoorlie, and never wanted to return, happy to leave the task to other flying doctors. He dredged up memories of rusted corrugated iron, flies and poor hygiene.

'There was something wrong with the water supply,' he said, frowning. 'The place was dirty.' A problem of government neglect, he thought.

I returned to my glass-topped desk, a cup of chamomile tea steaming within reach. Under the intermittent, watchful eye of the currawongs, I continued my online search. I found nothing on Bronwyn or Tony, but several references to Kurrawang turned up. The WA Goldfields Firewood Supply Company established the settlement as their headquarters in 1897, alongside the state-run railway from Perth. The company built a large private network of narrow gauge rails – the timberlines – that splayed out from the settlement into wooded areas, mostly of salmon gum, mulga and tuart. Felled wood was sent to Kalgoorlie to fuel the mines and supply the electricity company. When one wooded area was depleted, the rail structure was shifted to another.

In 1910, the township of Kurrawang was officially gazetted. The same year, Perth's *Sunday Times* condemned the itinerant 'bumboats' – small two-wheeled spring carts that required drivers to sit on top of the goods to control the draught horses, one for each cart – that brought illegal 'purge and swankey' (beer, stout and whisky of inferior quality) to the 'Kurrawangians – cutters, loaders, drivers, and line-repairers … ' for the men to get drunk on. Nothing could stop a man, or 'beer walloper', with sufficient 'boodle', or money, often a month's pay, from 'shickering up until his back teeth are submerged under a throbbing ocean of foam-flecked swankey'. While under the influence, these men of splendid muscular proportions were preyed on by 'harpies … with the relentless ferocity of a den of starving tigers'.

But it was rising costs and diminishing wood stocks, not alcoholic orgies, that forced the company to relocate nearly three decades later. Approximately 70 wooden houses, a store, a school, a hall and a post office were loaded onto wagons and transported by rail 24 kilometres south. Almost overnight, Kurrawang became a ghost town.

By November 1952, when the government was scouting for a suitable site for a 'native reserve', Kurrawang was a ghost town with a substantial infrastructure – a water supply, courtesy of the pipeline from Perth, as well as the original government railway and roads. William Sharpe, a Brethren missionary, who with his wife Marjorie was ministering to sick Aboriginal people in Kalgoorlie, was an obvious choice to superintend the reserve. He received the title of Honorary Aboriginal Protector.

According to a Department of Native Affairs report from 1953, Sharpe was a member of the Gospel Brethren, a description which another Kurrawang missionary would in time dispute. In the decade between Sharpe's arrival and that of the second missionary, Sharpe might well have realigned his position within the Brethren. He was in any case a member of the Open Brethren (as distinct from the Exclusive Brethren, who have a cultish reputation), although he was undoubtedly at the more conservative end of the spectrum. The Brethren Gospel Assemblies set up a controlling trust. Before long, members began to squabble: mission status would pave the way for a residential program that included Christian education for children, whereas the proposed reserve status would restrict the site to temporary accommodation in accordance with the guidelines as outlined by the Commissioner of Native Affairs in his 1953 report:

a) Care of hospital ex-patients and repatriates awaiting transport.
b) Rationing of indigent aborigines native to Kalgoorlie.
c) Camping facilities for transient aborigines between terms of employment.
d) Camping facilities for tribal aborigines who visit Kalgoorlie for ceremonial purposes.

Faced with the threat of the project's collapse, the Brethren regrouped. A new controlling trust reached a compromise with the government: Kurrawang would operate as a reserve while being registered as a 'native mission'.

A foot in the door, really. Within a few months, Mr Sharpe was encouraging Aboriginal people to settle permanently at Kurrawang. His motives are easily read as self-serving – permanent residents would offer a captive congregation of heathens, ripe for conversion, and would allow greater control over any welfare payments. Perhaps

I'm revealing my bias here; perhaps Sharpe's motives were more humane than I've allowed. Either way, his actions earned him a rap over the knuckles from the Department of Native Affairs, who had their eye on him and reiterated the order to offer temporary sanctuary only. A few months later, after noticing the alleged enthusiasm of Aboriginal parents in response to the Sharpes' apparent sincerity, the department had a change of heart and decided 'to permit the Gospel Brethren to proceed with institutional Mission activities on the native reserve'.

My ongoing research turned up a reference to the presence of several state wards at the Mission by 1968. As I had as a child, I naively considered the possibility that the state wards were orphans. I had yet to accept that members of the Stolen Generations might have lived at Kurrawang, the kind of failure of imagination common when one has held a fixed belief. How could the world be round when it had always been flat?

Like many Australians, I learned of the Stolen Generations in the 90s through newspaper and TV reports. Aboriginal children removed from their families by virtue of the *Aborigines Act 1905*. Now I learned the background to the Act.

From the outset, driven by fear and contempt, British settlers sought to exclude Aboriginal people from society by either death or legislation. The timing and exact nature of the relevant legislation varied from state to state. Western Australia wasted no time with early legislation like *An Act to prevent the enticing away [sic] the Girls of the Aboriginal Race from School or from any Service in which they are employed 1844*. A more muscular attempt at removing children from parents came with the *Industrial Schools Act 1874*. Aboriginal parents could voluntarily send their children to these schools, but in so doing surrendered them to the government until the age of 21.

The British government stepped into the fray with the *Aborigines Protection Act 1886*, ostensibly to protect Aboriginal people from malignant whites, many of whom were, after all, descendants of British convicts. Protection in this instance often meant removing children and sending them away to work.

The Western Australian government wrested control of Indigenous affairs from the British with the *Aborigines Act 1897*. The Act allowed for an Aborigines Department, of which Henry Thoby Prinsep was appointed Chief Protector. Born in India to English parents, Prinsep shows his hand: '... we must not forget they are savages ... they can never hope to have the same status as a white man ...'.

When he first arrived in Western Australia, Prinsep managed family estates around Bunbury. He went on to marry Charlotte Josephine Bussell, whose family were important pastoralists in the region. His association with Aboriginal people in this context would shape his policies as a Chief Protector.

Prinsep regarded Aboriginal people as an essential and cheap labour force, belying his supposedly humanitarian concerns regarding their possible extinction. Further, their 'immorality', as evidenced by venereal disease and the birth of 'half-castes,' would, he believed, cause 'damage to both races'. On this 'nauseous' subject, he writes regretfully, 'The present law only gives power to expel natives from towns when they are not decently clothed from neck to knee …'

Prinsep wanted wider powers to expel Aboriginal people from towns, where the Aboriginal men could live off the earnings from sex work of the women, and force them back to their essential work on rural stations. Prinsep's wish for greater control was granted with the 1905 Act. It was passed for the supposed protection of Aboriginal people from their own 'indolence' and from white 'injustice, imposition, and fraud'. To achieve this outcome, the Act gave legal authority to the Chief Protector and bestowed on him sweeping powers. He was the 'great white god' who dispensed food, clothing and medicine to Aboriginal people in need, and supplied work permits for Aboriginal people of working age – one year for working on the land, eight months for a ship. He was able to 'cause any aboriginal to be removed to and kept within the boundaries of a reserve'. With a wave of his protectorial wand, he could demolish those reserves or alter boundaries or force Aboriginal people to relocate to another area, even beyond their traditional land.

In *Henry Prinsep's Empire: Framing a distant colony,* historian Malcolm Allbrook describes how, under the Act, Prinsep was able to isolate Aboriginal people infected with venereal disease, most notably in the Lock Hospitals of Dorre and Bernier Islands off the coast of Carnarvon. In many cases, unqualified people such as police and station owners brutally examined Aboriginal people in camps. Those identified as sick were neck-chained, marched to the coast and taken by boat to the islands. On hearing of complaints about neck-chaining, Prinsep replied that it 'has not a pleasant sound and perhaps that is the worst part of it'. Over 600 people were incarcerated on the islands; 170 died.

If you wanted to control and isolate Aboriginal people and 'half-castes' to preserve their health and lives and thus maintain a cheap workforce, who better to target than the children?

> By my report of last year I showed that there were now growing up in the State probably more than 515 half-caste children under the age of 16; very few of these are being taught in any way, and, unless action is taken, will grow up to be as wild, lazy, and dirty, and probably more criminal, than the aborigines hitherto dealt with.

To this end, another clause in the Act made the Chief Protector the guardian of 'every Aboriginal and half-caste child to age of 16 years'. This was the clause that permitted the Chief Protector to authorise the removal of these children from their families 'to be sent to and detained in Aboriginal institutions, industrial schools, or orphanages'. This was the clause that meant Aboriginal mothers hid their children or darkened the skin of their 'half-caste' children with dirt or boot polish to escape detection by government officials and police, who arrived in jeeps to search the camps. When the Chief Protector's title changed to Commissioner of Native Affairs in the 1930s, the power remained unchanged. From the late 1800s until the early 1970s, according to the Australian Human Rights Commission's *Bringing Them Home* report, between one in three and one in 10 Aboriginal children were removed from their families. Bronwyn and Tony both entered Kurrawang Mission in the 1960s. It was entirely possible that they were members of the Stolen Generations.

The only other references to Kurrawang my research turned up were a few photos of Aboriginal children with white adults, and mention of Kurrawang's current status as a Christian Aboriginal community. For an institution that had existed for almost two decades, the Mission had left remarkably little trace.

I hit the bookstores and found *Rene Baker File #28/E.D.P.*, co-written by Aboriginal woman Rene Powell and Bernadette Kennedy, Powell's white friend. Powell spent time at Kurrawang in her teens. Of a return visit years later she writes, 'My feelings were not good there and I wanted to leave straight away.' I read her comment with a sinking heart. My childhood fantasies of motherly women tucking their freshly bathed and contented charges into bed with a kiss on the forehead were as illusory as a desert mirage.

I found no other books relating to Kurrawang. Back at my computer, I continued to research, a slow and laborious process. Day after day, I typed in various keyword combinations. I searched Aboriginal websites, state records, museum websites and library catalogues. Many times I wished for more expertise. Yet in a way my rookie status was the point. Sure, my grammar and punctuation were mostly up to scratch and sure, I possessed a defunct medical degree, but I wasn't a historian. Nor had I received formal training in anthropology or race studies. For the purposes of this work, I was simply an Australian woman wanting to understand the past and look to the future. If reconciliation was truly an ongoing partnership, there had to be something more I could and should do than walk over Sydney Harbour Bridge.

One day, a particular keyword combination yielded a report of a family of nine children, placed in the Mission as state wards for reasons including 'Parents inadequate'. This, I knew, was how the Chief Protector's henchmen went about their business: find evidence of parental neglect (which, let's face it, included Aboriginality). Fail to take into account their displacement from country by white settlers and the subsequent loss of food sources. Ignore their inability to draw equal welfare benefits. Show no compassion and offer no treatment for any alcohol dependencies developed through trauma, poverty and despair. Remove the children and assure everyone including yourself they would have *a better life*.

I leaned back in my chair. Stared at my computer screen, my desk by now cluttered with fiction by Aboriginal writers and academic texts on Aboriginal history and life. Outside, the currawongs continued their surveillance. I remembered the comforting weight of Bronwyn's arm, the rapid-fire way she called my name, the earthy smell of her skin. I pictured Tony's wide smile. Had they been forcibly removed from 'inadequate' parents?

One day, I tried to imagine Tony in a neat suburban house, complete with white picket fence and freshly mown lawn. Tony, not Bronwyn, because this was a fantasy, in which to weave magic. Life expectancy was shorter for male than female Aboriginal people; if I was waving my wand, I might as well wave it hard.

Within seconds my magic failed me. The odds of Tony spending his weekends pushing a lawnmower were low. The odds of him even being alive were poor. If he was alive, he might despise this white Australian utopia I had tried to conjure for him. After all, what did I know of his life before the Mission? Had his family lived in the bush in a humpy? Or had they, like many Aboriginal people, lived an urban, if poor, life?

Perhaps if he was alive, instead of living the white picket fence dream, he might have become someone I would, and perhaps should, fear. In *Dreams from My Father*, Barack Obama writes of his rage when he observes his white mother's fear of a black homeless stranger, but comes to understand she has good reason to fear because the black homeless stranger has good reason to hate.

I stumbled upon the story of an itinerant Aboriginal couple, Bowee and Gidum, or 'Tommy' as white people called him. Unable to clothe and feed their son and daughter, the couple 'voluntarily' relinquished the children to Kurrawang. It sounded like the simple outcome of domestic economics. No money equals can't feed the kids. The couple went on to have two more children.

Mary Bennett, an activist in the fifties, saw things differently. She saw the regulations surrounding welfare payments as a thinly disguised ploy to encourage parents to relinquish their children. She wrote to the Minister for Native Affairs regarding Bowee and Gidum's family: 'While the two older children of this family of four are allowed to have Child Endowment because they live in a mission, the mother is refused Child Endowment [for the younger children] because the faithful soul moves around with the father in his struggle for employment.'

Sadly, the younger children died, one aged three from septicaemia, the other aged two from gastroenteritis. Both potentially preventable deaths. Then in 1967, the year I turned seven, Bowee died in Kalgoorlie's main street, mere blocks from my family and me in our comfortable house. Bowee was 39. She lay in the gutter for three days before someone reported her death.

Given the parents' poverty, the younger children's deaths and the existing legislation, I wondered if the Mission had indeed offered the children, who had been renamed Beverley Joy and Ron Noble (no mention was made of their Aboriginal names) their best shot at survival. Then I wondered if the Mission represented the best chance for Bronwyn and Tony too. I couldn't just assume that the Mission did more damage than good. I had to know for myself. I had to find Beverley Joy and Ron as well as Bronwyn and Tony.

Layers of Skin

At some point during the 9000 anaesthetics my father administered as a general practitioner, he apprehended his talent for sending people to sleep. The unrelenting demands of life as a country doctor and my sickly health were the deciding factors: a year after the Esperance holiday with Bronwyn, my family moved to Perth for my father to undertake specialist training in anaesthetics. This meant I would attend the private girls' school they had chosen for a 'good' education as a day rather than boarding student. Convinced by my parents' enthusiastic marketing of the big city and thrilled that the school's uniform included a boater hat, gloves and elastic garters for my socks, I greeted the move with enthusiasm and barely noticed the loss of contact with my Kalgoorlie friends, both Aboriginal and white. In fact, in the move to an affluent, largely white suburb, I scarcely noticed my complete loss of contact with Aboriginal people. In a disturbingly short period of time, even neighbour and friend would become stranger and other.

After high school, in keeping with family tradition, I signed up for medical school. Sometimes on my way to ward rounds in East Perth I passed Aboriginal people on street corners. As in Kalgoorlie, their loud voices and drunkenness unsettled me. Or was it something else? Did I already sense a flaw in the tale I'd spun for myself about my childhood friends and the missionaries? Was that why I dug my hands deeper into my white medical student's coat and hurried, eyes blinkered, across the street, up the stairs and through the glass doors into the hospital's cool interior with its comforting smells of polished linoleum, lunch trolleys and disinfectant?

During my fourth year, our studies included skin. Skin, it turns out, is the largest organ in the integumentary system. A soft and pliable covering, it contains you within your identifiable shape and functions as a protector and an insulator – the polyurethane or fibreglass panels of the body. If I were to skin you, I would harvest roughly two square metres depending on your size, enough for a small rug.

In laboratory classes, I discovered there's more to skin than meets the naked eye. Seated on tall stools at metal benches, white coats unbuttoned, pages of glossy illustrations spread open at our elbows, we peered down electron microscopes and came to grips with the five layers of the epidermis or outer covering. The bottom layer, or *stratum basale*, we learned, contains melanocytes, the cells that produce melanin, a brown pigment and natural sunscreen.

Nature, in one of its more egalitarian moments, endowed everyone with a similar number of melanocytes. The amount of melanin each melanocyte produces is a different matter and is determined genetically: switch the order of nitrogen bases in the relevant genes and your skin is a different colour.

Back then, I still associated Aboriginality with dark skin. And Aboriginality, I was learning, carried with it the slew of health and related problems I would remember in Molokai – greater incidences of diseases like diabetes and heart disease, shorter life expectancies, overrepresentation of young Indigenous people in the prison population, lagging literacy rates. Not that I ever thought of my former school friends in terms of those statistics.

As a new graduate in the 80s, I interned in a large public hospital. During a vascular surgery rotation, I regularly assisted the surgeon in abdominal aneurysm repairs. These marathons lasted upwards of five hours. With the unconscious patient buried beneath sterile drapes, my primary task was to retract the layers of skin, fat and muscle to ensure the surgeon's view was unobstructed. Under the lights, in my theatre greens, I grew hot, sweaty and faint from maintaining a single position for so long, but I was struck, always, by our generic appearance beneath the surface no matter our skin colour: yellow fat, red muscle, glistening white tendons and red blood amid a treasure trove of organs.

Much as I liked being able to witness the wonder of the human body and learning how to treat illnesses, other aspects of medicine I disliked, the long hours and stress among them. All things considered, I was relieved to abandon my medical career to raise three children while my businessman husband worked 14-hour days and travelled overseas for weeks at a time. But fragments of medical knowledge would come in handy in other ways. In helping me care for our eldest child while he was seriously unwell, for example, and in writing the story of his recovery to make sense of an experience that had reduced life to survival terms. And now, as I seek to understand the genetic basis of skin colour and how we've allowed those arbitrary differences to dictate our relationships.

In the process, writing has become a midlife career, a second chance to carve out an independent identity, an opportunity I only partly recognised as privileged when I started out. I enrolled in literature and grammar courses at a public university; when the commitment proved too great for my family, I switched to online writing classes. One of my teachers organised a retreat, which was how I ended up in Molokai.

To date, I had failed to find any information about Bronwyn or Tony. From time to time, I fed their names or 'Kurrawang' into a search engine to see what it spat out. I had almost given up when, in 2011, after the umpteenth search, a new result appeared – *Forced Exile*, a newly released, self-published book by Gregory J Ugle. I checked the preview. The word 'Kurrawang' leapt off the screen. My throat tightened. Gregory was surely Tony's brother. Finally, after all this time, a lead! Then my breath caught and my stomach knotted as the horror inherent in the title sank in, leaving no room for doubt. I leaned back in my soft leather desk chair and stared at the image of a grim-faced, silver-haired man with dark brown skin. Behind him, a small white church, a dying eucalypt and the sky, a washed-out blue that sang to my heart. I placed an order.

Forced Exile

When I lifted the padded brown envelope from our letterbox, I felt the shape of a book. Inside, at my desk, I ripped the package open and saw Gregory Ugle's grim visage. It was late afternoon, time to start preparing dinner for my husband and the two kids still at home – a son at university and a daughter in year nine. Instead, I opened the book's glossy blue cover, and started to flick through the pages, until a list of siblings caught my attention. Sixth down of 10 names was Anthony – Tony, my former school friend. I scanned the rest of the list. And again. No mention of Bronwyn. I looked up. Removed my glasses. Thought for a moment. Had I remembered Bronwyn's surname incorrectly? Or, worse, had I somehow invented her? Not intentionally, but through memory's plasticity. I replaced my glasses. Another name on the list, Delphine, was familiar. Was she the girl I remembered as Bronwyn?

I set the question aside and turned to chapter 1. Greg, as I would come to know him, writes about life on a 'native' reserve in a three-roomed tin hut. It had blankets to screen doorways. Tin pots for the leaky roof. A fire for warmth and to heat a camp oven. A Coolgardie safe to keep flies from the food. A Tilley kerosene lamp to provide light.

Not exactly the lap of luxury but there were compensations, such as after-school lessons from the old men on the reserve: how to trap and cook galahs and other birds – a 'good feed' – and to hunt and clean kangaroos.

Work dried up for Greg's father, John Jackamarra, forcing the family to move many times over the next few years. His father sought work 'as a farm hand, sometimes as a railway worker, wherever work could be found'. Several more children were born. Their arrival made it harder than ever to make ends meet. John Jackamarra and his partner Elizabeth Ugle took to drinking and fought frequently in the lead-up to what would be the last night the Ugle children spent as a family:

> On a late February night in 1965 Dad comes home from jail, drunk and starts an argument with Mum. Dad punches her hard a number of times she hits the floor. We the children, start screaming and crying. I see June grab Susan and Robbie and rush outside. We keep shouting, 'Dad – stop it'. With blood streaming down her face Mum pleads for him to stop. He stops the bashing, but carries on with the verbal abuse. Mum gets up and goes to the cupboard and finds a medicine bottle of Purple Paint and drinks the whole bottle. The Police arrive and arrest Dad. The ambulance turned up to take Mum away to the hospital. The next day we head down to the Police Station to see Dad to work out what to do. Our little baby sister is taken away to the hospital at Konunoppin, then transported to Northam by the Native Welfare without telling us

> where she was or where she was to go. Then the Welfare came for the rest of us. We were taken to Northam where we spent the night in jail awaiting our future.

Apart from Susan, the youngest at six months, the children's future was, of course, Kurrawang Mission. And the Ugle siblings, I realised, were the nine children I'd read about when I first started looking for Greg's brother Tony. Greg was 10. Robbie, the youngest to be placed in the Mission, was 18 months old. Baby Susan was placed with a couple at the Native Reserve in Northam. All the children were made state wards until the age of 18.

In the growing darkness, I continued reading. Greg missed his parents. It felt like he'd been spirited away to another country – the missionaries, the bunk beds in the dormitory, the services in the white wooden church where boys sat with boys in order of age and the girls with the girls, the lunches of soggy tomato sandwiches and grapefruit, all were foreign to him. He was never allowed to speak to his sisters, and he barely saw Robbie, who lived in a separate house for the littlest kids and attended kindergarten at the Mission, a cloistered life. Even when Greg saw Robbie in church, he wasn't allowed to touch or speak to him. Before long, Robbie would pass Greg without recognition. He would reach his mid-teens before he knew he'd had older siblings in the mission.

In time, Greg, a Noongar boy from the southwest coastal regions, learned Wongi to get along better with the Wongi boys, losing his own language in the process. Not that they were allowed to speak anything but

English. I also note that, unlike me, restricted to English, Greg is bilingual.

I studied his address and phone number inside the book's front cover, surely inviting communication. Much as I wanted to talk to him, and to ask after Bronwyn and Tony, I couldn't bring myself to make the call. Why would he want to meet a random white woman, with no official associations and a privileged lifestyle? What's more, I hadn't spoken to an Aboriginal person in years and, like anyone else, was a product of time and place. I'd already uncovered instances of racism in my memories, and I suspected there was more, scattered like cancerous metastases. Greg was my only lead in finding Bronwyn and Tony. I didn't want to blow it.

In the weeks while I procrastinated over the phone call, I returned to copies of official documents I had glossed over in my first reading of Greg's book. One stated that on 24 February 1965 Greg, 10, and his siblings were charged in the Bencubbin Children's Court with being neglected children.

A police officer and a Native Welfare Officer tendered the following evidence regarding the family:

1 Poor and substandard living conditions.
2 Continuous bad behaviour of both parents.
3 Inadequacy of parents to support children.
4 Unbalanced state of mind of mother.
5 Mother conducting herself for monetary gains.

6 Prison record of each parent.
7 Medical record of youngest child.

The document gave no other information. There was no evidence of psychiatric or social assessments or of the prosecution bearing any burden of proof, not even for the accusations regarding the mother's supposed sex work and state of mind. No one, it appeared, spoke on behalf of Greg's parents, John Jackamarra and Elizabeth Ugle. He was in jail. She was in hospital, awaiting jail. No one spoke on behalf of the children. Greg, I would later discover, remembers being in court but has no memory of being spoken to or of speaking himself.

I can imagine the scene easily. The judge swats at flies and fans his face with a sheet of paper. Even with the windows open, the courtroom is an oven. 'Speak up, son,' he says to the police witness. Not that he really needs to listen: he's heard it all before – the drunkenness and the fighting. He peers at the children. Clothes all ragged, bare feet, snot streaming from their noses. Skin not too dark. Half-castes probably, he thinks. Poor little blighters. They'd be better off being brought up like white people, in a mission away from their parents, who would be stuck in their Aboriginal ways. They could learn to be civilised, have a bit of training, then they'd have a fighting chance.

The policeman finishes up. The judge blinks. Clears his throat. He adjusts his glasses, his hands red and bloated in the heat. The children fidget on the bench in front of him. The judge gazes sternly at them. Sighs. Hands down his decision: he finds the children guilty – the actual word used – of being neglected and therefore, according to the

Child Welfare Act, 1947, he henceforth declares them State Wards, no chance of parole. He slams his gavel. Jots down a quick note. Moves on to the next case on his docket. The policeman and the Native Welfare officers spirit the convicted children – the *criminals* – away.

White Stranger

Six months passed before I finally developed enough psychological muscle to lift the receiver and dial Greg's number. I wanted to arrange a meeting. In Perth, a tenor voice answered.

'Hello.'

'Is that Gregory Ugle?'

'Yes.' He sounded cautious.

I introduced myself, told him we'd gone to the same school, congratulated him on his book and said I was a writer. Stumbling over my words in my enthusiasm, I launched into a longwinded explanation of wanting to understand what it meant to grow up alongside someone without knowing the reality of his life. I might even have said I wanted to know what it *really* meant.

'Uh-huh,' Greg said.

I decided to try a different tack. I asked if the Tony of my memory was his brother. I held off on asking why Bronwyn's name wasn't on his list of siblings. If I'd remembered it incorrectly, or if she'd never existed, I wasn't ready to know. Nor did I want to alienate Greg by giving the impression that my interest was only in Bronwyn and Tony.

'Yes, Tony's my brother.' He spoke in blunt syllables, a sound so entwined with my formative years it seemed to resonate within my cells. 'Whadidja say your name was?'

I repeated my name and told him three generations of my family had lived in Kalgoorlie, forgetting this made us brand spanking newcomers in comparison to Aboriginal people, whose ancestors had lived in Australia for 60 000 years.

Greg told me a little of his experience in the Mission. I made notes.

'I did nothing wrong yet I was punished,' he said. 'I was deprived of me family connections.'

As in his book, he emphasised his removal from his family's Noongar land to Wongi land. He spoke of bullying by some of the older Wongi boys, being forced to clean their shoes, tidy away their belongings, make their beds. Horrible as the bullying sounded, something in the tightly controlled anger in his voice, the guardedness of his tone, made me suspect that there was more of the story to tell. But first I had to earn Greg's trust.

'I always felt different. I was always an outsider.'

Greg spoke of leaving the Mission with a dependent mentality. Of having to make his way as an adult without the necessary skills such as how to cook or maintain a house. As he spoke, I noticed that while he seemed happy to answer my questions, he didn't volunteer any additional information. I wondered if he simply lacked trust in me, a stranger, which would hardly be surprising. Or if this was another legacy of a mission childhood – being discouraged from voicing his opinions.

'I'd like to come to Perth to meet you,' I said.

A slight pause and then a careful, 'Sure.'

We settled on a date a couple of weeks away, in early May, first thing in the morning, and arranged to meet at the War Memorial in King's Park, an easy and obvious place, at my request. Then I hung up and booked a flight.

I flew into Perth on a cool, sunny day, rented a car at the airport and set off. My brother Geoffrey and sister-in-law Connie had invited me to stay. My call to them had been brief and I hadn't thought to mention the reason for my visit. They lived in the house my parents had bought for their retirement, before my mother's stroke, before my parents moved east to live with me, before my mother's gradual decline and the blessing of death. A house I'd never lived in and had visited rarely.

Geoffrey is my younger brother, by three years. He left school before final year and worked in an auto spare parts shop, a job he enjoyed. Geoffrey was eight when we left Kalgoorlie. We'd never discussed our memories.

I parked my car in the street and carried my bag up the long driveway to the house, on a subdivision behind an older house. I let myself in with the key Geoffrey had left out, put my bag in the spare room, and after turning the kettle on, wandered from room to room. Wherever I looked I could see traces of my parents, especially my mother – photos, furniture, recipe books, knick-knacks.

Within an hour Geoffrey arrived, without Connie, as pleased as ever to see his big sister. We hugged and he poured glasses of wine that we sipped at the kitchen bench. I shared my plan to meet Greg. Said he'd lived at Kurrawang and was a member of the Stolen Generations. I admitted my hope that this interview might lead to a book. It would be a story of personal reconciliation, with my former school friends and our shared past, I said. I was yet to finesse my elevator pitch.

Geoffrey rested his glass on the kitchen bench, crossed his arms over his chest and eyed me intently from beneath thick, dark eyebrows, one of his old thunderstorm looks.

'You don't know this man. He's a stranger, sis. Could be anyone.'

He thought he remembered a newspaper article about a Ugle in some kind of trouble with the police. Could it be Greg? I said I thought it unlikely.

'You don't know.' Geoffrey uncrossed his arms.

Putting my wine glass down, I offered to show him the list of community boards Greg had served on, intending to reassure my brother but unwittingly revealing one of my biases: if you look good on paper, you're good. I fetched Greg's book from my room and opened it to the relevant page, pointing out that Greg had served in more volunteer positions than Geoffrey and I put together.

'We're meeting in broad daylight. At the King's Park War Memorial. I won't be alone,' I said.

A car pulled up in the carport and my sister-in-law let herself in through the screen door. She worked long hours and I didn't want to drag her into our discussion, so I switched the conversation to takeaway menus and Geoffrey poured her a drink.

My mother's old stranger-danger warnings probably explained Geoffrey's reaction. A proposal to meet with an unknown white man would have provoked a similar reaction. But over the years, we'd also heard stories of alcohol and violence among adult Aboriginal people who lived on the streets, stories that likely left an impression.

In one, my father arrived home from the hospital at around 7 p.m. He lingered at the front gate, under a jacaranda tree, relishing a few undisturbed moments. It must have been winter, he says, because he remembers clear night skies and the smell of sulphur in the air (as the sun rises after cold, still winter nights, the layer of air next to the earth warms and rises above the cold air, trapping the sulphur plume from the gold-ore treatment process close to the ground, which makes the smell stronger).

He became aware of an Aboriginal man with his wife and three children – all under six – walking down the street. They stopped right across the road. Without warning, the man grabbed the woman by the wrist and elbow and jammed her forearm down, hard, on the top railing of the wood and steel-mesh fence behind them. The woman screamed. Unconcerned, the man led her across the road, the two of them reeking of alcohol and unwashed skin, for my father to examine the fresh injury. Later that night, my father operated on the woman to repair her fracture.

In another story, a woman fell asleep on the railway track at the top of our street. Neither the sound of an approaching train nor the vibration of the tracks woke her, and the train wheels amputated an arm. Witnesses notified my father. He rushed to the scene and found the woman bleeding heavily yet in little apparent pain, effectively anaesthetised by alcohol. Nearby, unaware of the commotion and equally drunk, her husband slumbered on.

Sure, my father told stories about white people too, like the man he helped the health department evict from the empty cyanide drum he inhabited. In a mining town, there must have been heavy drinking and violence – domestic and otherwise – among the white population as well. In the 1990 Royal Commission into Aboriginal Deaths in Custody a Justice of the Peace writes of Kalgoorlie:

> ... it's fairly obvious that there is a problem in the white community with respect to alcohol abuse as well as there is in the Aboriginal community. In that respect it's not only confined to Aboriginals at all. I think that in a town such as this there is a heavy dependence on alcohol.

But drinking in the white community was much less spoken about. The drinking and violence among the Aboriginal population, on the other hand, was out in the open, on the streets, a product of myriad socioeconomic problems – the loss of land, livelihood and family structure and the resulting trauma, and welfare inequities and racism that made finding a job difficult. But few saw those intangible causes. The results were far easier to see.

By the time Connie and I had finished cleaning up after dinner, the two-hour time difference had caught up with me. Yawning, I said goodnight and retired to the spare bedroom. I wanted to be in good shape for the meeting with Greg.

On Noongar Land

I woke early to a silent, dark house. With an eye on the clock and my mind on peak hour traffic, I rose and dressed. I slipped a notebook in my bag and stole out, shutting the front door quietly so I didn't disturb my brother and sister-in-law.

I turned the heat up in the rental car and set off, navigating streets that looked familiar yet unfamiliar, distorted by memory and progress: new skyscrapers needling the skyline, a train track slicing traffic lanes on the Kwinana Freeway, the Swan River lapping higher against newly reinforced concrete retaining walls. Despite the heavy traffic, I pulled into the War Memorial car park early, before 9 a.m. I parked and emerged into the damp morning air. At the Memorial, high above the tracery of roads below, there was no sign of the man pictured on the front cover of *Forced Exile*.

I wandered for a while, past pink salmon gums and beds of boronia with their bold floral scent. At 9.15, I returned to the War Memorial. Still no sign of Greg. It looked like he would stand me up, always more likely than any risk of violence to me. I rang him. He answered. Skipped a beat at my name. Sounded surprised, as if he'd forgotten or had never intended to meet. 'I'm at home. Give us another twenty minutes.'

I spotted him easily with his silvery nimbus of hair, the only dark-skinned person in sight. He faced away from me, towards the endless flat sprawl of Perth's suburbs and the sinuous brown spread of the Swan River, the Darling Ranges a low purple smudge on the horizon. Noongar land, a new thought for me: Greg's traditional land. Nearby, a group of uniformed men gathered near the cenotaph. I hurried across the dew-frosted grass.

'Greg?'

He swung around and met my gaze with a slight smile.

'Hello, Amanda.'

I extended my hand. He shook it firmly, his skin soft and warm, and agreed to my invitation to adjourn to the nearby café. Taller than me and with a muscular build, he walked with a fluid, loose-limbed gait. I thanked him for agreeing to meet. Greg nodded. Said nothing. I babbled about the weather and changes in the city.

In the café, I placed our orders and asked Greg to find a seat while I paid. Despite the cold wind, he chose a small outside table, away from other customers. For the fresh air or to escape prying and possibly hostile white eyes? I was unsure. I took a seat, and because I had yet to discuss the possibility of writing a book, left my notebook burning a hole in my bag.

As we spoke, Greg barely moved. Next to him I fidgeted, aware of having more at stake in this meeting. Sole stakes, really. We talked traffic, weather, Perth, until a waitress delivered our coffees and my scone, her interruption seeming to signal a natural end to our somewhat stilted small talk.

In the trees near our table, currawongs warbled, and a light breeze scattered fallen leaves. Greg waited. The tragedy of his early life was far beyond my experience: I didn't know where to start. I worried about retraumatising him with my questions, even if he had spent – survived – many hours reliving past events in his writing.

'So where do you live?' I said, the best I could come up with.

'With my son,' he said. 'My wife passed away recently.' The lines around his eyes deepened.

'I'm sorry,' I said. 'You must miss her.'

He nodded. Pursed his lips, hands crossed in his lap, and turned away. He stared into the distance. I took his body language to mean he had no wish to discuss her.

I broke off another piece of scone and ate it. I wondered if Greg thought me rude, eating in front of him. He had refused my offer of food.

'Were you really never allowed to talk to your sisters in the Mission?' Was this safe ground?

Greg heaped several spoons of sugar into his untouched coffee. Mesmerised, I watched as he stirred. He swallowed a few mouthfuls. Looked up at me.

'That's right. They separated us. Made sure boys didn't go near girls.' His voice lifted at the end of the sentence, in that typically Australian way. He relaxed his posture, and the muscles around his eyes softened, giving me the impression the story of his distant past was comfortable territory.

'Never?'

'Never.'

With the occasional prompt, Greg went on to describe a world that had existed alongside mine but about which I was ignorant. He spoke in a detached and monotonal voice, as if delivering an oft-repeated narrative, its edges smooth as river stones. He was unable, when asked, to elaborate on events in his book, making me suspect a degree of traumatic amnesia. Or perhaps it was just too long ago. Or he had no wish to reveal more to a stranger.

On Wongi Land

The boy wakes early, as the watery dawn light washes through gaps in the curtain and pools on his bed. For a moment, before he makes out the ceiling a foot or so above his head, he thinks he's at home, in the tin shack, not a top bunk in the boys' dormitory. The realisation hits him like a fist in the stomach and tears spring to his eyes. At first he'd liked the top bunk, his own little domain, but the novelty quickly wore off. He missed the warmth of his brothers and sisters' flesh, the small sounds they made in their sleep, the gamy smell of kangaroo meat from dinner. The boy made a fist, rubbed his eyes. Years later, he would describe the way four of the older Wongi boys scared him, their skin so dark all you could see was their eyes and teeth, so different to the people in his land. If the boys saw him cry, they'd call him a sook. Why were they so mean? Why did they make him … The boy shivers, pulls the thin scratchy blanket up under his chin. He doesn't want to think about that now.

Soon, the missionary man enters. 'Rise and shine. Time to get up.' The boy climbs down. Shivers in the early morning air. 'Hello, Daddy,' he says, just as the missionary man taught him. The man is not his father, has white skin. The boy selects a shirt, pants and a jumper from his drawer in the dresser. Hand-me-downs donated by good white church people from town. The generator hasn't been going long, so the water is only lukewarm and the sand soap scrapes rather than lathers on his skin. They never have shampoo to wash their hair. The boy washes swiftly and gets out to dry and dress.

The boy climbs back up to his bunk and tries to straighten the sheets. The missionary man will inspect later and the boy doesn't want a caning. Leaving the dormitory, he passes the missionary woman in charge. 'Hello, Mummy Sharpe,' he calls. His black school shoes kick up fine clouds of red dust as he runs to breakfast in the girls' dormitory. That's another thing he misses – sinking his bare toes into sandy grey soil.

At breakfast, the boy joins the other boys at the table next to the girls' table. If he reached out, the boy could touch the warm brown skin of one of his sisters. He wants to; he wants to more than anything, but it's against the rules. He's not even allowed to speak to his sisters. He wants to ask when his parents will come for them. He misses his parents. Don't they love him? He's starting to forget the shape of their faces and the sound of their voices. The missionaries never talk to him about his parents. He doesn't even know if they're still alive.

A missionary starts the morning prayer. The boy closes his eyes and presses his hands together, fingers pointing heavenwards, bony elbows sticking out. When the missionary finishes, they all murmur 'Amen'. Then they stand and line up, girls first and then boys, to be served porridge at the counter separating the room from the kitchen. Back at the table, the boy, like the others, picks out as many weevils as he can and puts them on the side of the plate or on the table. He tries to eat the porridge but it still contains weevils. When he pushes the plate to the side, a missionary scolds him for being ungrateful and wasteful. The boy takes a slice of cold, hard toast from the plate in the middle of the table. He spreads the toast with raspberry jam. Dry crumbs cling to the jam on his knife. The boy reaches for the jug of cold powdered milk one of the big boys mixed and fills his white china tea cup. When he's a big boy, he'll graduate to a mug. The milk smells like sick. The boy gags on lumps as he swallows.

After breakfast, they line up at the school bus stop. Mr Sercombe, one of the missionaries, inspects their shoes. Some of the boys get in trouble for cutting the leather to make shanghais or slingshots to shoot stones at targets. They have no other toys. The boy has yet to work up the courage.

The bus pulls up and the missionary supervises the boarding process – bigger boys at the back, then the little boys and then the girls. Once the bus gets going, the bigger boys kick the smaller boys out of their seats so they can sit behind the girls they fancy. Stuck in one of the back seats, the boy still can't speak to his sisters.

The boy doesn't speak to his sisters at school, either. They are in different classes, and at play-lunch and lunch, they hang around in the girls' playground, while he plays footy in the boys' playground. Occasionally he catches sight of June's dark hair or hears Gloria's voice pitch skyward, but for the most part it's as if they don't exist.

When he started at this school, they put him in a class with kids a year younger, the second-stream class with the slower white kids. None of the Aboriginal kids are in a top-stream class with the smart-alec white kids. Each day, the boy takes his place with the other kids in a single line, or Indian file as his teacher says, to go into class, white kids at the front of the line, Aboriginal kids at the back. In class, the Aboriginal kids must sit up the back. Sometimes, on the way to his seat, one or other of the white boys he passes whispers, 'You stink.' The boy showers each day, so he knows he smells fine. The white kids just want to make him mad.

Some of the other Aboriginal kids have glue ear. The teacher's voice reaches them as if through red mud. The boy is one of the lucky ones with good hearing. Not that it helps much – at the Mission, no one ever listens to him read or supervises his other homework, so what's the point? He soon falls behind with the work. Anyhow, the teacher treats all the Aboriginal kids like they are slow learners. When it's time for play-lunch, the teacher lets the white kids out before the Aboriginal kids.

The Aboriginal boys get their own back in the playground – they run rings around the other boys when they race or play football. The boy's sporting prowess increases over the years to the point where, in the annual athletics carnival, he sets a new record for high jump and wins the title of champion athlete for the oldest boys in primary school. His chest swells with pride when he feels the flimsy weight of the trophy in his hands. The Aboriginal boys fight better too; over the years, at least eight different teachers on playground duty catch the boy with his fists up, socking another boy in the guts or the face to pay him back for something or other. The teachers send him to the headmaster for the cuts. The headmaster puts all his strength behind a wooden ruler and brings it down across the boy's knuckles. It hurts like billy-o but the boy never cries.

The boy's father, John Jackamarra, visits Kurrawang once, a couple of years later. Mr Sharpe, Kurrawang's superintendent, grants Mr Jackamarra a few hours with the boy, his two older brothers Alfred and Adrian and younger brother Tony. The girls and Robbie see their father separately. Later the boy will remember little of the visit, just the feeling that his father had become a stranger. He thinks his father's drinking and violence is to blame for all of them being in the Mission.

One day, the boy and his friend Greg Newland slog 12 miles into town, along the railway line. They sneak into an outdoor cinema, where *South Pacific* is playing and find empty seats up the back. But someone calls the police, and the boys get to cool their heels in a prison cell for an hour or so before being carted in a paddy wagon back to the Mission where old Sharpey gives them the cane.

Until the age of 16, the boy is considered government property and must live at the Mission. The minute he turns 16, he's given his marching orders. By then, the Mission feels like home, and the boy doesn't want to leave, especially as his brothers and sisters are still there. At the Kurrawang train station, a ticket to Perth in hand, his few belongings shoved into a small suitcase, the boy feels an ache inside, like hunger pangs. The missionaries and all the Aboriginal kids have come to see him off. The train rumbles into sight, spewing smoke. It stops. The boy boards, grabs a window seat. Outside, the barefooted children spread out along the length of the train, which coughs back into action. The boy presses his nose to the window. He waves furiously at the kids. Some of them start to run alongside the train, smiles as wide as footballs on their faces. The missionaries start to sing 'Kumbaya'. Without prompting, the Aboriginal kids join in with the farewell anthem, a song they've sung many times, and the sound swells, until it seems to surge up inside him. The young man swallows hard as the train bears him away.

Heart Bypass

Wait a minute!

Do I hear you protest? Do you think I've crossed the line in attempting to imagine myself into the story, inside the thoughts, inside the skin of an Aboriginal boy? You wouldn't be the first – or the last – to level the charge.

Let me describe our meeting: conversation, as it had on the phone, lurched from question to answer to the next question. We fell into awkward silences as vast as Australia's interior. And as arid. Greg seemed happy enough to talk to me, but his story skimmed the surface like a stone skipping water. Or as if no words existed to really convey what his life was like back then. Or perhaps as if there was no way I could understand.

I floundered, mentally scrabbling for my every move. The currawongs mocked me from above. The coffee grew colder. The sugar from the scone and jam fizzed in my veins, making my heart race and my head pound. Greg's words reached my ears but the mechanics of the conversation were so difficult they gained little purchase in my heart.

I wanted to understand how his life felt back then. I wanted to *empathise*. In medical school, we practised empathy in role-playing classes. We learned to reflect back what we'd heard. 'The pain keeps me awake at night, Doctor.' 'The pain keeps you awake at night? That sounds terrible.' That technique worked well to make a patient feel understood, but I'm not sure it ever really helped me understand the patient. It didn't even begin to do the job of helping me to understand Greg's life. Reading Greg's book helped, of course, but the reader must be an active participant in any book he or she reads. You remain an outsider, looking in, unless you make the leap and imagine yourself into the life of whomever you're reading about. Greg's story-telling, both written and spoken, might have been short on emotion but it was vivid and full of sensory details; it would never be possible to know exactly what his life had been like, but I could at least try to imagine my way in through his descriptions.

When Greg finished with his story, we fell into yet another awkward silence. I reminded him I had met Mr Sercombe, one of the missionaries, father of one of my brother's best friends.

'I still visit old Mr Sercombe.' Greg's face lit up. 'He was the boss. Took over when Sharpey left. He lives in Coolgardie.'

'You visit him?' This was a turn-up for the books. 'Why? The missionaries kept you from your parents.'

'I treat him as family. Him and his sons and his old girl, his wife.'

There was an unmistakable tone of affection in Greg's voice, which confused me at first. But the missionaries were the only adult family figures – parents, aunts, uncles – Greg knew through his teenage years, and although complicated, those relationships likely represented a measure of stability and security, at least for a while.

A currawong swooped onto our table and attempted to steal a piece of my scone. I squealed and flapped a hand over my plate. Greg laughed and the bird flew away. Somehow the air between us seemed to lighten.

'I remember a girl from the Mission called Bronwyn Ugle,' I said, carefully. 'She was my friend. I thought she might be Tony's sister, but you didn't mention her in your book.'

'You mean Bronwyn Newland.' Greg's recall was instant, as if Bronwyn was indeed a family member rather than just another Mission inhabitant.

'Ah. Of course. Newland.' As if it had been there all along, waiting to be recovered from beneath the weight of decades of memory. 'Was she Stolen Generations?'

Greg shook his head. 'There were eleven Stolen Generations children at the Mission: nine Ugles and two Garletts.'

I nodded, barely breathing, as I considered my next question.

'Do you know where she is?'

'I think she's in Kal.'

Bronwyn was still alive? The blood whooshing in my veins belonged once more to a nine-year-old girl, her scrawny shoulders encircled by Bronwyn's warm brown arm, in the shade of a playground tree. Then I noticed Greg's sombre expression. I took a deep breath.

'How is she? What's her life like?'

'She's had a hard life. Been in trouble with the police.'

I nodded. Paused to let that piece of news sink in.

An image flashed on my retinae of a tall, dark-haired girl plucking orange nasturtiums from a vine.

'Has she done jail time?'

'I think so.' Greg spoke slowly.

I nodded again. Thought of asking why but didn't. It was all too much to process, like watching unrelated movies, running simultaneously, side-by-side.

'She got kids?'

Greg frowned, as if trying to remember.

'Seven or eight.'

'Any of them been in trouble?'

'A couple of the boys.' He spoke with effort, as if the words cost him.

We fell silent again. The cold coffee I sipped turned to stones in my stomach.

Suddenly there was a thunderous roar overhead. An airforce flyover. The noise faded. Greg and I swapped banal comments on the planes. I steeled myself to ask my other long-preoccupying question.

'What about Tony? What's he doing these days?'

'He drives a bus in Kalgoorlie. For the Aboriginal medical service. Been doing it for three years.'

'How's his health?'

'He's not well. He's got diabetes, hypertension and heart disease.'

I sensed a finality in his voice. Case closed. Was he being protective – stay away from my brother? Or was I imagining his reluctance? More silence. Greg seemed perfectly at ease now, just sat there, looking ahead, hands resting on the table in front of him. Waiting.

'I haven't asked about your health.'

'I've had the heart bypass operation and I got diabetes and high blood pressure,' he said. 'I blame the missionaries. They never taught us how to eat properly.'

I nodded, wanting to agree, but I found myself thinking *that's passing the buck*. Greg gazed off towards the War Memorial. He was one of the stillest people I'd ever met. I wondered if he'd acquired the habit in the Mission, to stay out of trouble from both the missionaries and the Wongi kids. And I thought, with shame, that I'd likely underestimated the amount a child learns about diet from a parent, in the supermarket and in the kitchen, and I remembered how alone Greg had been when he left the Mission with only a small suitcase of clothes. Greg turned to me.

'We used to be classified as flora and fauna.' He frowned, his eyes wide open, giving him a look of indignation.

His claim was news to me. He looked as if he expected a response, so I muttered something like 'outrageous', which it was, if true. I asked if he'd received compensation for being a member of the Stolen Generations.

'The amount we was paid depended on how long we was in the Mission, and whether we was subject to any abuse.' Greg paused. Glared at me. 'I got $13 000. I believe we was ripped off.'

I asked after his plans for the future. He said his current truck-driving job would end in a month. He would head to Kalgoorlie to see Tony.

'Me and me brother, we'll go walkabout for three to four months.'

'Where will you camp?'

'By the side of the road. It's Crown land. Covered by Native Title. We'll go gold prospecting and hunting.'

'Kangaroos?'

Greg nodded.

'What will you hunt with?'

'Guns.'

Although no gun enthusiast, I felt a rush of excitement, something to do with the thrill of danger and the primal nature of a hunt, followed by a sudden sense of longing. For Kalgoorlie. For the bush. For my fantasy childhood. I felt a sudden irrational urge to join Greg and Tony on their walkabout. I would like to say that my understanding of the cultural inappropriateness of such a desire held me back from asking, but I would be lying. It was simply that I knew the answer would be 'no'. Greg, I was beginning to understand, had his own idea of what stranger danger looked like. It was coloured white. And my being a woman didn't help.

I turned to historian Russell McGregor's *Indifferent Inclusion: Aboriginal People and the Australian Nation* to understand Greg's claim about being classified as flora and fauna. McGregor takes the reader through the early Protection legislation, before Federation. He then describes how, in the late 1800s, with Federation approaching, people began to wonder what the new nation would look like, and how paranoia about race swept across the country.

Alfred Deakin, Attorney General of the new Federation and future second prime minister, sought to reassure future constituents:

> The Aboriginal race has died out in the South and is dying fast in the North and West even where most gently treated. Other races are to be excluded by legislation if they are tinted to any degree. The yellow, the brown, and the copper-coloured are to be forbidden to land anywhere.

Even if British settlement hadn't already decimated the Aboriginal population, the white populace needn't have worried. The Constitution included two specific and repressive clauses relating to Aboriginal people: Section 51 allowed for special laws to cover Aboriginal affairs, and Section 127 excluded Aboriginal people from being counted in the population census. For the most part, Aboriginal people were denied the vote.

Control of Aboriginal affairs continued to reside in State departments. In Western Australia, where a senator described the Aboriginal person as 'a horrible, degraded, dirty creature', the Aborigines Department directed Aboriginal lives. Then in 1909, the Aborigines Department amalgamated with the Fisheries Department to become … the Aborigines and Fisheries Department.

Perhaps being lumped in the same department as fish, along with exclusion from the population census, contributed to the belief held by Greg and others that Aboriginal people were officially counted as flora and fauna. In reality, they weren't counted at all. As for how non-Indigenous Australians treated them … with a history that included neck-chaining, segregation and control over every aspect of their lives, no wonder Aboriginal people thought they were considered less than human.

Whither Should They Flee?

The day after my meeting with Greg, I came across *What an Experience*, a booklet by Kurrawang's founders, William and Marjorie Sharpe, in Western Australia's JS Battye Library. The Sharpes write of their decision to heed God's call and leave their ministries in Queensland to spread the good word elsewhere. Elsewhere turned out to be Kalgoorlie, which the Sharpes describe as equally famous for its gold and beer, omitting the third arm of the town's holy trinity: sex work. Knowing Greg's story, I wanted to find fault with the Sharpes. My hackles rose at their devout tone, the presumption of moral superiority, of being 'chosen'.

A serious flu had apparently gripped the Aboriginal population. The Sharpes ministered to the sick from their van as best they could. I had to concede that instead of cowering behind a pulpit, the Sharpes walked the talk, risking infection themselves. They freely admitted to considering Aboriginal people uncivilised, but did more than most to assist them when they were sick.

The Sharpes go on to write about the government's 1952 request that they scout around for a site suitable for a 'native' reserve and a rations depot, and their eventual choice of Kurrawang. According to them, the Mines Department surrendered a square mile. The Sharpes galvanised voluntary Brethren labour from as far afield as Melbourne. They trucked in abandoned buildings over corrugated roads from Kanowna, another ghost town in the area, the one whose newspapers had lined the walls of my mother's hospital room after my older brother's birth. Converted, the buildings served as dormitories. But ongoing funding dried up. The Sharpes complain of government threats in response to requests for funding for furniture. They don't elaborate on the nature of the threats and I've come to believe they were, in fact, related to the Sharpes' desire to run a residential mission rather than a 'native reserve'. In neutral language, the Sharpes note that they weren't required to register Aboriginal births or deaths. Mentioning the situation might have been a protest in itself.

Towards the end of the memoir, the Sharpes write, 'The Aboriginal Dreamtime, alas was only a "dream time", it had done nothing to lift them up.' The Sharpes believed Aboriginal people needed to get away from 'dreaming' and face reality. They write, 'Whither should they flee?'

My hackles stood to attention again. The reality the Ugle siblings had to face in the Mission was a white-engineered nightmare of separation from everything and almost everyone dear to them.

The Sharpes claimed that despite a welcome from the white teachers and children, the Mission kids still experienced difficulties:

> A lot found their way hard going – for it was from one world into another. Most felt that they could not catch up with their white brothers and sisters …

> the gap was too great. Some attempted to run away, but kindness and perseverance helped many to win through.

I was unable to completely dismiss the Sharpes' summation. Sure, their description of the children's reception at school bore little resemblance to Greg's, and they had applied a smooth veneer to Mission reality with their comment 'kindness and perseverance', but they were right about the different worlds and may well have been some of the first to identify the 'gap' that politicians now promise to close.

After a few more pages of exuberant reflections in what was essentially a glossy paean to the Brethren church, Marjorie Sharpe concluded: 'See a clean Aborigine walking down the street, and in most cases you can be sure that they are mission trained.'

It seemed a horrible distinction – clean or unclean. I didn't want to think about Greg in those terms at all. I packed my notes and returned to Sydney.

Taped to the wall above my desk was a hand-out from the grammar class I'd taken at an Australian university in 2005, a couple of years before the Molokai writing retreat. An exercise in the art of sentence construction, it demonstrated different sentence positions for descriptive phrases and, for the grammatically adventurous, offered routes to compound or complex sentences. Intent on expanding my skills to something more than subject and predicate, I'd studied the sheet a million times without paying attention

At the Australian Institute of Aboriginal and Torres Strait Islander Studies in Canberra, a week or two after my Perth trip, I came across my former primary school headmistress's 1961 Teachers Higher Certificate thesis. Margaret Bull wrote the thesis four years before the Ugle siblings were forcibly removed to Kurrawang.

A plump, straight-backed figure at the front of the hall during school assemblies, Mrs Bull offered guidance in firm but kind tones to squirming rows of children, who sat on the wooden floor and stared longingly at the rectangles of sunshine framed by the open side doors. In the same tone, her thesis argues against forced removal of Aboriginal children from their families. Instead, Mrs Bull recommends Aboriginal parents be encouraged to *voluntarily* relinquish children to the Mission for the duration of their schooling, but argues that they should still have access to them. Such a situation, she concludes, would overcome the problems that inevitably arose when children went bush with their parents: they picked up foul language and came back unwashed, poorly groomed, and shabbily dressed; sometimes they even had no shoes. *See a clean Aborigine walking down the street, and in most cases you can be sure that they are mission trained.*

Daddy, are Aboriginals people?

Aboriginal Names and Aliases

On the State Records Office website, I came across a list of Aboriginal names and their aliases, widely used by police, farm owners and missionaries in Western Australia during the early to mid-1900s. Some aliases stood in for a number of different Aboriginal names; in many cases the Aboriginal name was not recorded:

Male		**Female**	
Balarabar	Jimmy	Bimering	Mary
Dungallah	Jimmy	Balnah	Mary
Gillanda	Jimmy	Cabbilya	Mary
Boogardiessonie	Publichouse	Eiljelan	Mary
Yarragally	Monday	Billilia	Nellie
Urrmaring	Old Monday	Coongie	Nellie
Illgidy	Looking Glass		
Kolongulla	One Eye		
Unknown	Sugar bag		

Greg had told me the nurses in Mogumber Mission, where he was born, told his mother to choose an English name. As a child, I'd been completely ignorant of the fact that my Aboriginal friends might have had Aboriginal names. More recently, I'd struggled to catch the names of Aboriginal people I'd met, and had let embarrassment prevent me from asking a second time. The element of racism inherent in not bothering to learn foreign-sounding names was obvious to me, but in *The Protectors*, lawyer and university lecturer Stephen Gray argues that other influences came in to play, 'The names were a social register, a way the missionaries had of distancing themselves from danger ...'.

The danger, perhaps, of having to see themselves as equal to 'savages'.

A Homecoming

I peered out the window on the flight between Perth and Kalgoorlie, only an hour or 600 kilometres in distance, but another world in other ways. It was mid-2013 and I was visiting my hometown after an absence of nearly four decades. Below, a black, arrow-straight road cut through miles of bush, monotonous from this height with the terrain flattened and the trees all sage-green, the only other visible colour the orangey-red soil.

I'd rehearsed this moment many times, expecting to feel a tug of recognition somewhere deep within my marrow. Instead, I found myself fighting off the urge to weep. The landscape looked alien, the vivid dirt almost cartoonish, the vegetation parched. I'd been away too long; it didn't feel like a homecoming.

The plane was far bigger than I remembered from the occasional flight to Perth in the 60s, an indication, I guess, of the renewed importance of gold mining in the region. Australia may have ridden on the sheep's back in the past; these days the country rides in the massive dump trucks and bulldozers of its mines.

Next to me, my 15-year-old daughter Louise had her head in a magazine. She was leaving for boarding school in the US in a few weeks. Her experience of living away from home would be far different to Greg Ugle's life in the Mission. Louise was older, had chosen to go, grabbing independence with both hands. Or an independence of sorts. We would be footing the bills, and she was going to a comfortable dorm room with one roommate, well-equipped bathrooms, a nutritious and varied diet and a smorgasbord of interesting subjects. Louise could call home whenever she wanted.

My husband Kevin and I had given her our blessing. I'd grown up with a father who had fond memories of boarding school, and was disappointed when my family's move to Perth made boarding unnecessary. Although I would miss my daughter, I knew she would be safe and was well-equipped to make the most of her opportunity. And we could visit whenever we wanted. Before she left, I wanted her to see where I had come from, to know my story and understand my connection to this dry, red country on which we were soon to land.

Greg sat a few rows behind. Less than two months had passed since we met. In the interim, he'd landed work as a truck driver, so his proposed walkabout with Tony didn't eventuate. Knowing he'd be able to smooth my way in Aboriginal communities and perhaps introduce me to Tony and help me find Bronwyn, I'd asked him to accompany me to Kalgoorlie as a guide. We agreed on a figure I would pay to compensate him for his time and effort. By now he knew I wanted to write a book. We'd agreed that all proceeds would go to Aboriginal people whose stories would be part of the book. I had yet to fully comprehend the complexities inherent in this decision.

The flight attendants patrolled the aisle in preparation for landing, collecting rubbish, checking seatbelts and seatbacks, urging recalcitrant passengers to turn off electronic equipment. The engine whined as the landing gear descended with a few shuddering jolts. The plane banked. I craned forward to catch a glimpse of the Super Pit, Kalgoorlie's most recent gold mining foray, a 3.6-kilometre gaping maw in the ground, right up the road from where I'd lived. The mine started where the houses stopped. From the air, the town looked in danger of being swallowed right up. Behind the pit, slime dumps rose abruptly to form ranges whose oddly symmetrical flat-tops betrayed their man-made nature, formed from excavated dirt and waste from the gold extraction process. As we came in low over rooftops, the mine disappeared from sight and we landed smoothly. The airport was new, a modern building in a field of fake grass, a lush emerald-green at odds with the glaucous leaves of the gum trees.

As I walked across the tarmac, I could almost feel the sulphur from the mines permeating my skin and filling my lungs. We collected our bags. My daughter raised her eyebrows at our rental car – iridescent blue with airfoils, a car for young revheads, not a middle-aged mum. Greg was going to stay with Tony, so I drove him to a small fibro house in the back blocks of Boulder, Kalgoorlie's twin town. Greg didn't invite me in, and I didn't want to assume Tony would welcome me, so I stayed in the car.

Louise and I continued on, up the 'top end' of Kalgoorlie, passing alongside the Super Pit. Ahead loomed the Mount Charlotte head frame, or poppet head as we called it, like an overgrown tripod, towering above the to the content. The day I typed up my notes from my interview with Greg, the clauses and phrases leapt out at me, and I examined them with renewed interest:

> Captain James Cook died – or rather was murdered – at Kealakekua Bay, Hawaii, in 1779.
>
> Bleeding profusely, Captain James Cook died because he turned his back on natives: his body may have been eaten.
>
> Swiftly, unexpectedly, horribly, James Cook, illustrious navigator, died violently, gruesomely; in fact, he was butchered by natives.

Exemplary sentences, the glut of adverbs aside, they contain the indisputable fact that James Cook was killed, an event that took place a short island hop from my Molokai writing workshop. But I saw now how easily and insidiously language slants the facts, in a university no less, and how easily I – and other students (there was no outcry) – had overlooked the bias: the assumption that Captain Cook was a victim rather than an intruder in an occupied land; the pejorative nature of the language pertaining to 'natives'; and the suggestion – unproven – of cannibalism. If a 21st-century university could disseminate printed material containing embedded racism without causing a ruckus, what had a 60s rural primary school, consciously or otherwise, imprinted on its younger, more impressionable students, including me?

shaft, several storeys high. Poppet heads house pulleys and a cage to transport men down or up the mine shaft as they start or finish a shift hundreds of feet below ground. This one was a bright orange framework of massive steel girders, not the brown wooden structure of my childhood.

I turned into the main street – Hannan Street – and encountered another sign of the personality change my town had undergone: Montgomery's, where my mother had taken me to buy scratchy plaid slacks to wear after school in winter, where the shop assistants put your money in a tin and sent it along a wire to the cashier in a mezzanine office, where linens lay in neat piles on tables, had been abbreviated to Monty's, a 24-hour café/pool parlour. The conversion of both name and service seemed sacrilegious to me. In my day, only the hospital, the Boulder Block Hotel and the brothels (which I didn't know about until my father enlightened me as an adult) kept those hours.

My father had also told me that the underground tunnels of all the old mines used to form a vast network, linking up with each other under the surface and ending in the Boulder Block Hotel's basement. No matter the time of day, a miner coming off his shift could slink off for a drink without his missus knowing. One more subterranean world to escape my notice as a child.

My father, not a drinker, had more to do with the brothels than the hotels. On one occasion, after noticing a spike in gonorrhoea cases, he wrote to the council health inspector, asking him to investigate the brothels as the likely source, holding the women responsible as was common practice in the 60s. The man reported that the police, who 'managed' the brothels, refused him entry. The assistant commissioner of the Western Australian Public Health Department, in response to my father's next letter, said brothels were illegal and, as far as he was concerned, none existed in Kalgoorlie. Another example of the state looking after the 'interests' of white Australian males. My father continued to dispense penicillin.

From Hannan Street, I turned in to Boulder Road and finally Egan Street, first of the many streets I've lived in. Where I learned to ride a bike, played hopscotch with neighbours on the wide red nature strip, bought fruit and vegetables from the back of Mario the Greengrocer's truck, and saw Rusty our cocker spaniel die under the wheels of a car. Where each weekday, I walked down the block on my way to school; where each Sunday I walked up the block to Wesley Church. Not so much a tapestry as a rag rug of memories.

I slowed the car to a crawl. On my right, 50 metres ahead, stood the hotel where I'd booked a room, on the site of my former home; on the left was the Tattersall's Club, a two-storey building with a tin verandah extending visor-like over the footpath, unchanged after all these decades. I felt my tightly held emotions fall apart. My limbs turned to jelly. If I'd been standing, I might have sunk to the ground. I swear I caught a glimpse of my young self, brown leather satchel strapped to her back, through my tears.

'Mum, are you okay?' My daughter patted my arm, her face creased with concern.

'It's the same.' I pointed at the club, and reached for a tissue to wipe my eyes.

A historical marker of the town I'd known. By extension, evidence that I had belonged here – a feeling I'd rarely experienced anywhere since. After my family left Kalgoorlie, an illness my mother's family referred to as 'melancholy' but which was likely depression had engulfed my mother, complicating life. Later, my husband and I shifted from one city to another and then another. When our children were young, I never seemed to fit in with the other school mothers, although I suspect this feeling is as common among mothers as head lice among their children. Now my children were leaving home and I feared becoming irrelevant. But here was Tattersall's, proof that I had belonged. Maybe, just maybe, I could experience that feeling in this town again.

On the opposite side of the street, at least four houses had been demolished to make way for the hotel. In place of our front fence, a line of trees stood like sentinels between the footpath and the hotel car park. A few miserable palm trees had infiltrated the mix in a failed attempt to present the tired brick building as an oasis in the middle of this frontier town. My beloved jacarandas were gone.

Four-wheel-drive vehicles, orange safety flags hoisted at the back, overran the hotel car park, like an introduced mechanical species. Yet another sign of the big-business mining town Kalgoorlie had become. The Super Pit required the men – and the majority were men – to live locally, but some workers from other mines were fly-in-fly-out. They worked hard and in many cases drank hard, and returned to their families on their days off. The male-to-female ratio of the town, I was told, was four to one. If so inclined, a single woman could find a man who would treat her as if she were more precious than the gold he mined.

Before my departure from Sydney, my father asked if I would stay in this hotel. I knew he wanted me to; he had also grown up in the house where the hotel now stood. Perhaps he too viewed the hotel site as a repository of happy memories. Perhaps he viewed our shared memories as a precious connecting thread, now that I'd grown up and gone my separate way.

Whatever his reasons, I knew I wanted to stay there too. In my mind, the hotel had assumed the transformative powers of a Narnian closet. Passing through the doors would be like stepping back in time. I would encounter versions of my younger self. See what motivated her, what she saw, what she heard. Find clues as to why she asked that question in the Kalgoorlie Hospital car park.

I parked my car in one of the few remaining spots in the hotel car park and fetched our bags from the boot. Inside, I asked if it was possible for us to have a room at the Boulder Road end of the hotel, where our house had stood. The receptionist said it was. Upstairs, I saw that our twin beds stood above the site of Barry's backyard. I squinted to blur my focus and there she was – a slip of a girl astride a 44-gallon drum, holding the reins and digging her heels in. I gave myself a shake and the girl dissolved. Louise was looking out of the window. Her eyes were wide, her forehead slightly furrowed. She looked shocked. I wasn't surprised. The flat, dry vista before her must have looked completely foreign compared with the lush green rainforest she'd known up in the Byron Shire. And Kalgoorlie's fibro houses were a far cry from the concrete mansions in our affluent Sydney suburb. We left our bags and returned downstairs. According to my father, a eucalyptus tree planted by my mother six decades earlier had survived the demolition and I wanted to see if it was still standing.

Outside, I saw that, in fact, two trees endured from my childhood. I walked over to the one I remembered best, nearest the side fence, the tree my brothers and I had often tried to climb. No matter how hard we scrabbled at the smooth white bark, the branches always remained beyond our reach. Despite a thickened trunk and ugly stumps where lower branches had been lopped to allow for a driveway of commercial proportions, the tree was still recognisably the one my mother had planted. I climbed the kerb at the tree's base, and stepped onto a dead palm frond. My daughter watched me try to wrap my arms around the massive girth of the trunk. My embrace reached less than halfway. I smiled at my daughter. She smiled uncertainly, perhaps anticipating more tears. The branches were even further beyond reach than when I was small. I breathed in the eucalyptus scent, pressed my cheek to the bark and closed my eyes. I could picture my mother, the vivid blue and emerald swirls of her 'tent' dress falling about her body as she pointed a hose at a small patch of lawn. I opened my eyes. Above me, the leaves rustled in the light wind. My relationship to my past, I was beginning to understand, was complicated: in some ways I wanted it unchanged, in others rewritten.

That afternoon, Louise and I set off for the British Arms Museum at the top end of Hannan Street, where I was sure I would find records of Kurrawang. On the way, we passed a group of Wongi people – fringe dwellers or fringies as Greg would later refer to them – milling outside the Centrelink

Office. They reminded me of the people I'd seen opposite Wesley Church as a child – shabbily dressed, barefooted and disorderly. As a child, I didn't know the Wongi people had a different culture. I didn't really understand that they spoke a different language. Or that their ancestors had lived in Australia for thousands of years before the arrival of white people. I felt like a foreigner in my home town. A strange, new feeling.

Inside the museum, the first exhibition we encountered was of old photographs, including one of my former home being manoeuvred from the back of a truck onto the empty block at 55 Egan Street. Before leaving Sydney, I had dug out a photo of the house from a cardboard carton I found among my mother's possessions. The sprawling bungalow of my memory looked far shabbier than I recalled and had shrunk, according to the rules of childhood revisited, to the size of a modest four-bedroom cottage. The only features true to memory were the tall asbestos fence and the jacaranda trees, their lacy lime foliage giving little hint of the trumpet-shaped blossoms that in spring empurpled the pavement.

The museum photo was different. With the verandahs not yet added, the house looked naked and vulnerable. To the left, the dark walls and steep-pitched roof of Barry's house were already in place; behind, the solid square shape and dark bricks of the foundry looked oddly forbidding.

The house's genealogy was family legend, my father the keeper. Custom designed for a doctor, with two surgical offices up front, the house was transported in the early 1900s from Southern Cross, 60 miles to the west, to Kalgoorlie. One of the first things my grandmother did when she moved in with my grandfather and their baby son, my father, was to disassemble the air cooler. It consisted of two sheets of chicken wire strung between the top and bottom of the side verandah. The cavity between the sheets of wire was filled with coal. Water from hoses trickled down through the coal, cooling the air as it flowed through – an inefficient and dirty system that blocked the sunlight. My grandmother said she would rather the heat.

Behind a recreated miners' cottage in the back of the museum stood a detached washhouse, complete with a copper and concrete tubs. I stared at the building as if through a hole rent in time. And what I saw was my mother in a cotton housedress, apron around her waist, her black curls soaked in sweat as she tonged washing from the machine and fed it through the hand wringer. The washhouse was dark and dingy and moist with steam, the smell of smoke and soap in the air. My mother piled the wrung-out washing into a trolley basket and wheeled it out to hang on the Hills Hoist. Her warning as she trudged back inside: 'Don't swing on the clothes line.' After her Depression-era childhood and nursing in the Kimberley, marriage and a move to Kalgoorlie must have seemed like salvation, even if it involved caring for a young family in what are now museum-worthy conditions.

Before my trip, I went through my mother's photo album from her Kimberley days. I'd viewed the photos many times but had never lifted them from their sticky corners. This time I did. In captions on the reverse sides, my mother referred to the Aboriginal subjects as 'house-girls' and 'dusky matrons', and expressed indignation at a friend's joke: with her olive skin and dark hair, my mother looked like she shared a blood relationship with the Aboriginal people she nursed. I remember now her enthusiasm about the story of the possible African ancestor. Did her attitude towards people of colour change over time? Or was a relationship with an unknown African fine in a way that a relationship with Aboriginal people was not? Aboriginal people were, in some ways at least, more knowable, which meant it was impossible to dwell purely on the exoticness of the 'other'.

Thinking of this, I remember how very different – and in many ways more difficult – my mother's life was compared to mine. I stuff my dirty clothes in a machine, add soap, shut the door, dial up a wash and return an hour later to bright whites and bleed-free colours. In much the same way, with a few keyboard clicks, we can access past lessons and accumulated wisdom to inform our attitudes. But every generation has its hidden captions.

Upstairs in the museum, Louise and I came across a display depicting the Mount Margaret Mission, which is located some 224 miles northeast of Kalgoorlie. Established by Rodolphe Samuel Schenk, the Mission operated from 1921 to 1975. Shenk aimed 'to develop a self-sustaining community where he could minister without interference or distraction'. Although the use of Aboriginal languages was apparently discouraged, the Mission provided 'an alternative for children of mixed descent who were otherwise likely to be removed to the more distant Moore River', which had a harsh reputation.

I peered into the next cabinet, expecting to find a Kurrawang display. Instead, I found mining tools, rocks and other relics of bygone days. No photos, no letters, no documents – not one jot of information to guide me through the Mission's arcane past, even though it was closer to Kalgoorlie than the Mount Margaret Mission. The absence of any record for an institution that had existed for over two decades struck me again. Surely we should know what happened, I thought. And surely we should honour those who'd passed through its gates.

After leaving the museum, we passed Paddy Hannan's Tree, two blocks from where my house had stood. It's not the original tree, but it marks the original site of Paddy Hannan's find. No child grows up in Kalgoorlie without a rudimentary knowledge of the town's golden history, and I was no exception. Teachers in my all-white, top-streamed classes at Kalgoorlie Central had hard-wired into me the story of the three Irish prospectors, Hannan and his offsiders Thomas Flanagan and Dan O'Shea, who had found gold here in 1893. Hannan's claim sparked a gold rush. Hundreds and then thousands of prospectors converged on the region. In an area with less annual rainfall than a man could spit, the usual process of panning, whereby flowing water is used to separate heavier gold deposits from sediment, wasn't an option, so the men hauled in dryblowers. They shovelled dirt into a wooden box at the top and the heavier gold specks fell through a series of metal sieves, to a tray. Dust from all the dryblowers formed a choking red cloud, visible for miles.

At breakfast the next morning, I chose a table which was roughly where my family's kitchen table had stood. Louise chattered about her new school and we both ate scrambled eggs. Men in orange hi-vis vests ate at the other tables. Sitting there, I could picture myself as a child as clearly as if that child was seated at the hotel table beside me, picking at her baked beans. As if we existed together simultaneously. It was like being inside one of those books with transparent plastic pages, each page adding a different layer of the body – the blood vessels on one page, the muscles on another, the organs on another, the bones on another. When all the pages sit one on top of another, they complete the picture. With the hotel restaurant, those layers were of time. Those books also reminded me of the town itself. It had physical layers above and below ground, the presence of one necessary to make sense of the other. The town had layers of people – the Wongi, white settler descendants, and other more recent immigrants, who came from Greece, Italy, China, Yugoslavia. And now there were further layers: miners and non-miners. As for Australia ... we might call ourselves a democracy, we might talk egalitarianism and equal opportunity, but our population is as layered as any. Our history too. The difference being we've worked hard to make the layers opaque. Those Mission kids? When I was a child, no one gave me cause to believe they were anything other than orphans.

Kurrawang Mission

The plan was to collect Greg from Tony's house after breakfast and head to Kurrawang. Louise opted out, needing to catch up on required reading for her new school. I set off in my rental car. The winter sun had a sting in it, so I parked under a shady tree outside Tony's house and walked over to a separate carport, where a group of Aboriginal men, including Greg, were tinkering under the bonnet of a car.

Greg introduced me to a man, also a member of the Stolen Generations, who had grown up in Mount Margaret Mission. I missed his name. Greg went in to change his shirt. I turned to the man.

'So you grew up in a mission?'

The man nodded. Said something in a voice so soft I would later wonder if he was conditioned young to not being heard. He spoke fast. His vowels were fluid and the consonants other than 'w', 'p', 'b', 'r' and 'l' were indistinct to my ear, one word seeming to slide into the next. As a child, I would have called his accent 'Aboriginal', a term I now recognise as reductive, akin to referring to German as European. The man's first language was most likely one of the Western Desert languages, of which there were at least 17. He might equally have had trouble understanding me.

The other man, to my left, looked my age, heavyset and fierce-looking with a thick, bushy beard. I asked if he was Tony. He nodded and extended his hand. We both looked at the grease stains and laughed.

'Maybe I won't shake hands,' I said.

Tony withdrew his hand. I felt a twinge of regret: it had taken so long to find Tony and I was letting a bit of grease come between us.

'Remember me?' I said. 'We knew each other as kids.'

Tony gave me a quick look and shook his head.

'Nope. Can't remember you.' He spoke clearly and precisely, his accent more anglicised than Greg's. Perhaps from entering the Mission at a younger age, when he was six.

I shared my memory of the water tank. Tony pressed his lips together, shook his head and smiled apologetically. I felt mildly disappointed but unsurprised. After all, I had remembered only his name and one mundane image. An image I had transformed into a monument of my childhood.

Greg returned and we set off for Kurrawang.

'Wasn't your truck-driving job supposed to last three months?' I asked.

Greg sucked in a breath.

'Health problems,' he said slowly. 'I got the flu and then on top of that I got another attack of that heart problem I've had before. Atrial fibrillation, they call it. Had to go back to the city.'

Great, I thought. *I'm driving a time bomb around the countryside.* His family had already suffered the loss of Greg's wife. I didn't want to be the one responsible for them losing Greg. Selfish, perhaps, but this project wasn't supposed to inflict misery.

Some distance from Kalgoorlie, Greg told me to turn right into Sharpe Drive, named after the Mission's founders. A few hundred metres later, we crossed the Perth–Kalgoorlie pipeline, brainchild of CY O'Connor, who'd been depicted as a hero when I was at school in Kalgoorlie. O'Connor's popularity had taken a nosedive in recent years – Mundaring Weir, built to supply the pipeline, had resulted in the flooding of Aboriginal sacred sites, and underground water in the Kalgoorlie region had proved more plentiful than O'Connor had estimated.

After the pipeline, we crested a long narrow rise, where the train track used to run. Ahead was Kurrawang. We drove in. Try as I might, I failed to recognise any of the buildings, although we hadn't ventured this far when we'd collected Bronwyn for our Esperance holiday. At a corner, Greg told me to turn right and park in front of a small house, which had once been the boys' dormitory. Like my childhood home, like Tony's current house, it had fibro walls, corrugated iron roofing and closed-in verandahs. The walls were bright orange, perhaps to disguise the effects of windblown red dust. The house was roughly the size of the one my family of five had lived in, maybe smaller. According to Greg, who had to rely on memory, somewhere between 25 and 40 boys had lived there.

We got out of the car. Steeped in the scent of eucalyptus, the air was hot and dry, so thick it felt like cotton wool on my skin. The washed-out blue sky stood in stark contrast to the rusty red dirt. Dirt that blows in your eyes, clogs your pores, deposits under your fingernails. Dirt that marks you for life.

The buildings might not have looked familiar but the

atmosphere gave me the same prickly feeling of unease I'd had when we'd come for Bronwyn. The place looked deserted. I felt as if we were standing in a museum of past lives. In the silence I strained to hear the voices of the Kurrawangians from the early 1900s, voices slurred by the 'purge' and 'swankey' they downed to obliterate the hard reality of their lives. I strained to hear the children of the 50s, 60s and early 70s, Bronwyn, Tony and Greg among them, speaking contraband Wongi words – the Ugle children's Noongar language quickly lost on Wongi land. It would not have surprised me to turn and see young Aboriginal children peering out from behind trees. And I thought if I listened hard enough, I'd hear the sound of grown women keening for their stolen children from behind perimeter fences, and the swish of a cane as it arced through the air, the thwack as it hit skin. The hairs tingled on the back of my neck and my skin felt especially porous. Kurrawang was as good a place as any to believe in ghosts.

Greg relaxed, dropping some of his habitual wariness around me, and he strolled around as if his surroundings were as comfortable as an old shirt. It was easy to imagine a younger Greg tearing past as he pushed a wheelbarrow bearing one of the smaller boys, determined to win the race. Greg wandered back to me. Explained the layout inside the dormitory: three bunk beds in a room, two boys in each bed, head to foot. Sometimes there would be one big boy on the top bunk and two smaller on the bottom.

'When one of the little fellas wet the bed, the other would wake up and there'd be fights.'

Greg pointed out a patch of empty land to the right of

the boys' dormitory, the site of the former girls' dormitory. It had been erased, in a way the girls' memories likely couldn't be.

'Can I take photos?' I said.

'Yes.' Greg grinned. 'If anyone comes, I'll say, "My Mission".'

His voice held a note of pride, similar to the tone I heard in my own voice as I showed my daughter around Kalgoorlie. She might see a dustbowl, but I saw layers of time, thousands of different moments that had shaped the person I'd become. Perhaps it was the same for Greg. I probably could have asked him, but the question/answer format already accounted for more of our interactions than felt comfortable. And perhaps I sensed an aversion to direct questioning from Greg himself. Later, when I encountered *Mullumbimby*, by Melissa Lucashenko, an Australian writer of Goorie and European heritage, I would learn that many Aboriginal people disliked direct questions: 'Learn by watching and listening, using your *mil* and *binung*, was the centuries-old habit, and not by asking bloody silly questions all the time'.

Greg stood quietly while I pulled out my phone and snapped away.

'Did you celebrate birthdays?'

I thought of the ice cream cakes my brothers and I blew candles out on each year, of the sense of belonging birthdays gave me, of the year my mother threw my brother and me a shared party complete with balloons, party hats, brightly wrapped presents, pin-the-tail-on-the-donkey and, best of all, a magician who helped me produce a sponge cake from a seemingly empty tin.

'We got a cake in our dorm after dinner.' In an 'and-that-was-that' voice.

'You weren't allowed to speak with your sisters on your birthday?'

'No.' Anger.

'Were there presents?'

'No.' Greg paused. When he spoke again, his tone was brighter. 'But we got presents at Christmas. And good tucker. Bacon for breakfast, with eggs and toast. They lashed out then.'

He pointed behind me.

'The old building on the opposite side of the road? It was the workshop, where the generator was. We used to take turns at getting up in the morning to help start it. We checked the oil and put water in the engine and then one of the missionaries got it going. Every night they turned the generator off at nine.' He chuckled. 'My word, it was dark. Used to scare the living daylights out of me.'

This was the most animated I'd seen Greg; the first time, really, that he'd volunteered information.

'What about a toothbrush and toothpaste?'

I remembered our nightly tooth-brushing ritual, and the fluoride tablets my mother doled out and the visits to the dentist for check-ups. After one visit, when my younger brother had to be bribed with a toy to sit still for a filling, my mother rewarded me with a toy sewing kit for being a good girl and having no dental caries.

'They never give us that at first,' he said, referring to the toothbrush and paste. He creased his forehead. 'I think that come in when Robert and Doreen Smith married and become house parents. That was in the new dormitory. It would've been first year high school. Three years after I got there.'

Greg wanted to show me something. We got back in the car and drove a couple of hundred metres down an old dirt track. Either side, eucalypt trees with skeletal trunks and limbs looked indistinguishable from one another.

'Here,' Greg said. 'The old native reserve. This is where the campies stayed – families with kids in the Mission and old people. I used to come down here with the other boys and visit.'

He looked around. Shook his head.

'That corrugated iron over there?' He pointed at a few sheets in the red dirt. 'It's from the old humpies.' Anger rippled off him like heat off bitumen. 'The community should have preserved it. It's part of the past. People should know.'

I nodded, pleased that Greg too wanted to preserve Kurrawang's history. I made a U-turn and drove back to the Mission. Greg directed me to a row of houses, around the corner from the former boys' dormitory. A friend lived there who might know where to find Bronwyn.

Greg checked each house carefully as we drove by at a crawl.

'That one.'

I pulled over. A couple of men stood on the front porch, one sat on the front steps and others stood around in the fenced-in yard. Greg went in to ask if he could bring me in for a yarn.

A few minutes later, he returned to the car and asked me to follow him. He led me to the man on the front steps, who was thin and looked old, with his wizened features, but might have been only in his sixties, aged prematurely from illness and a life of hardship. Voices drifted out from the dimly lit interior. Parked in the driveway was a big white 4WD, engine idling, music blaring. In the front seats, two young men dipped their heads to the beat.

The man stood. Greg introduced us and we shook hands. As with the man at Tony's house, I missed his name. I hesitated to ask Greg to repeat it. With a feeling of chagrin, I remembered the old practice of Aboriginal aliases.

The man was Wongi, darker-skinned than Greg. He avoided looking at me for the most part, a sign of respect between an Aboriginal man and a woman he didn't know, and I strained to understand him.

Greg stood to the side, silent and watchful. Eventually he stepped in.

'You know where Bronwyn Newland is?' He gestured towards me with his head. 'She wants to speak to her.'

I nodded. Smiled.

'She somewhere around. Not here.' The man shrugged. This time I understood what he was saying. He added, his tone helpful, 'Two of her kids are here.'

Bronwyn's children were here? Then surely she couldn't be far away. My pulse quickened with part-excitement, part-anxiety at the thought of seeing Bronwyn after all these years. Would she recognise me? How would she have changed? How harshly had life treated her?

The man called into the house, a rapid stream of Wongi. A girl in her mid-teens emerged, letting the screen door slam. The man glanced at me, turned to the girl.

'She know your mum.'

The girl nodded. I pictured her mother's face, swimming towards me through the Great Southern Ocean and through time. I searched her daughter's face for similar features: her eyes, the curve of her cheeks.

The man called out again and one of the young men sauntered over from the driveway. Tall, lean and slightly older-looking than the girl, he had about him an air of bravado. The man told him we wanted to find his mother.

The boy gave me an appraising look. He turned to Greg.

'I can tell you where she is. She live in the bush.'

I thought of the home I'd left in Sydney. The marble expanse of kitchen bench. The bathrooms. The sweeping ocean views. Our lives had diverged dramatically since we'd played in the school yard.

Bronwyn's son told us to take the Kambalda Road, drive a couple of miles to the big 'bells' on the right shoulder, and turn left into the bush. We'd find the camp. Greg thanked him, and we headed off.

Greg asked if I wanted to continue on to Coolgardie to visit Mr Sercombe, the missionary who had overseen the Mission for part of Greg's time.

I did. Much as I wanted to meet up with Bronwyn, I also wanted to hear how Mr Sercombe, who I knew to be English, had come to be at the Mission. I wanted to hear what he thought now about the children's treatment, particularly the practices of separating siblings and not allowing their parents access. I wanted to hear of any regrets.

I told myself I didn't want to pass up the opportunity to meet the man who could answer these questions. But was that really true? Was I really trying to postpone the moment I met Bronwyn? Perhaps she would deny the friendship I'd remembered and treasured all these years. When I first spoke to Greg, I hadn't wanted to know if my memory of Bronwyn was false; now I wasn't ready to face the possibility that I'd simply imagined our friendship.

I felt myself relax and breathe out as we left Kurrawang. It was one of the few places I'd been where the veil between past and present seemed as fine as dust. Or as thin as a layer of skin. I was beginning to understand that landscape is never neutral. It has memory. Just as human-instigated events leave their imprint and transform a landscape, the Super Pit being an extreme example, so too can a landscape imprint on and transform people. It could drive a man to 'purge' and 'swankey'. It could drive a man to cruelty. My childhood vision of happy young orphans and benevolent missionaries was in tatters. In comparison, my life had been one long magic cake pulled from a tin.

Greg later told me that the Mission shop, where people from the reserve could buy groceries, had burned down shortly before the missionaries vacated Kurrawang, destroying all the records. Many of the former residents considered the fire an act of arson. It would have been helpful to know the precise number of children who had been placed at the Mission. After Greg's parents were arrested, an aunt offered to care for the children. Native Welfare refused, saying she already had enough children – 11 – in the house. Yet Welfare had happily placed more children than that in one small house at the Mission. With white strangers. And Greg and his siblings were permanently placed; no second chances or attempts at rehabilitation for Aboriginal parents.

Months later, at my beachside desk in Sydney, miles from Kalgoorlie, I thought about Greg's anger at seeing the abandoned sheets of corrugated iron at the reserve. After losing his family, his home, his country, his language and his culture as a child, it made sense to me that he wanted to preserve the only place he subsequently knew as home. I reached for my phone to check with Greg. He reminded me that the reserve was created as part of the *Aborigines Act 1905*.

'Aboriginals were placed there,' he said. 'It was a gathering point where families could be close to their children in the Mission. The voluntary ones. Dances were held in the vicinity. It became a historic point and a cultural point. A significant site. But after the Mission closed, the area was disrespected. The people that bulldozed it never come from there.'

So my suppositions were wrong, a reminder of how difficult it is to understand the workings of another mind. A reminder too of the dynamic, not static, nature of Aboriginal culture. The reserve might have been created by the government as a form of control, but the people who had lived there had adapted and claimed the site as their own.

The mood between Greg and me lifted, like old skin sloughing off, as we left Kurrawang and crossed the pipeline.

'Used to be one of me favourite playing spots,' he said. 'When we got home from school, old Mr McGeorge, one of the missionaries, would give us biscuits for afternoon tea. They were worthwhile waiting for. We'd go in our room. We'd get changed into our play clothes and we'd know he was standing with his walking stick and hat in the door of the kitchen and we'd get our biscuit, our two biscuits, those pillows with the raisins inside, and then we'd run up here. We used to wait for the trains and wave at the passengers. Once we got bullets from the campies. We stuck them on top of the pipeline and smashed them with rocks.'

'Was it noisy?'

'My word, yeah. Sounded like a gun going off. There was nothing to do at the Mission, see. We had to make our fun. One time, on Guy Fawkes night, we got all this wood in the trucks, backed the trucks in and unloaded the wood. Then we stacked it up and put old Guy Fawkes on top. Later that night we lit everything up. Crackers and everything went off. We pinched some fireworks and lit 'em inside bottles and cans.' He continued on in a deadpan voice, 'And we did the right thing and threw crackers at each other. Went off with a big bang, they did.' He paused, laughed. I thought of our own Guy Fawkes nights in the bush with church friends. A flickering campfire. Roman candles soaring into the night sky, trailing sparks like shooting stars. Catherine wheels spinning. Children laughing the way Greg was now. He stopped. 'Lucky no one ever got hurt.'

The Waddy

Coolgardie had always felt like a ghost town to me, and the ghosts were brown. If there were buildings another colour, I didn't see them. The wide streets – potentially able to accommodate angled parking as well as three lanes of traffic on both sides – were mostly empty. A familiar feeling of melancholy settled blanket-like over me, stifling and uncomfortable. Greg directed me to Mr Sercombe's house, which was on a corner. A small lawn flourished out the front, the bright green startling against the ubiquitous red and brown and the washed-out green of the native eucalypts. In the back yard, a Hills Hoist spread its bare metal arms. Difficult to fathom why an Englishman had traded verdant green fields for this dry and dusty backwater.

The house looked closed-up and empty. We approached the front sliding glass door, knocked loudly and waited. I tried to peek in through the curtain. Greg knocked again. Again no answer. We returned to the car and set off in search of Bronwyn.

As we headed along the Great Eastern Highway towards Kalgoorlie, the silence between us felt companionable. I didn't rush to fill it, simply enjoying the warmth of the sun streaming in through the windows and the engine's soothing hum.

I thought of Greg telling me that several of Bronwyn's children had done jail time. I wondered if his sons had had similar troubles. Had his family really avoided the intergenerational consequences – the drinking, the violence, the incarceration – of past wrongs that still devastated so many of Western Australia's Aboriginal families? It seemed as good a time as any to probe. I cleared my throat to break the silence.

'Did your boys ever have run-ins with the police?'

'As a matter of fact, yeah,' Greg's reply shot back. 'One of my boys bought this pushbike and one day, he decided to ride it to work. He wasn't wearing a helmet and he got pulled over. The cops asked him for ID.'

Greg's son had shown his licence. The police then asked who owned the bike. Greg's son said he did. The police asked to see the receipt.

'He said he didn't have it on him. Why would he be carrying around a receipt?'

The police had asked Greg's son if he had stolen the bike. He said he'd paid for it with money he'd earned and saved. They asked if he had a police record. He said he didn't.

'When my son got home, he came to me, upset. They let him go without charging him, but they said, "Shouldn't you have a record by now?"'

Greg looked for a reaction. I shook my head. Wondered what it would be like to always be running into the brick wall of negative expectations. Almost immediately I found myself wondering if Greg had ever had trouble with the police. And then I wondered if my low expectations were of him – I hadn't forgotten my brother's mention of a newspaper article – or of the police.

'Have *you* ever been in trouble?'

Greg was quiet for a few seconds.

'Yes.' He sighed. 'About four or five years ago.'

'What happened?'

Greg told me a nephew of his had wanted to go out with a girl, but for some reason, the girl's brother objected. The boys got in a fight and the nephew won. The girl's extended family got involved. Greg warned them to stay out of it or expect a fight.

Greg paused, mid-story. I looked over to find him watching me. I nodded encouragement and looked back at the road, still deserted apart from the occasional passing car. Greg continued with his story.

Since that day in the blue bubble car, I've visited the house where Greg was living at the time. Picture Greg on an old, rug-covered sofa in front of a TV in a lounge room. Shades down to keep the glare off the screen. See Greg's back stiffen at the sound of shouting in the street. Watch him rise from the sofa, cross the room and lift a corner of the blind. See him frown as he spots a mob of Aboriginal men, around 15 in all, young and not-so-young, armed with knives and machetes, sun glinting on the metal.

Greg opens the front door. Goes out. Stands on the half-dead grass that he can never stand to waste water on. Nothing but blank-faced bungalows and empty cars to bear witness. The mob falls back about a hundred metres.

'You mad old bastard,' someone yells.

The biggest man in the mob steps forward.

'What's a smart-arse like you doing, bringing a big mob round to fight me?' Greg says.

He holds his hands behind his back, palms open. Hears footsteps behind him, one of his family. Feels the smooth, club-shaped weight of his waddy being pressed into his curled fingers. The wood is heavy enough to take down a male kangaroo. The waddy was a gift from an old Wongi woman out of gratitude for Greg's help. She told him it was no ordinary weapon; she had laced it with spirits. In his hands, the spirits would come alive and connect to him. Anyone else who held the waddy would experience the spirits' anger. The mob leader steps closer.

'What are you Ugles getting involved in this argument with my nephew for?' he says.

'Who the hell do you think you are?' Greg asks. Quick as a flash, he whips the waddy out from behind his back and hits the man square in the kneecaps. The man staggers. The rest of the mob surges forward, and the fight is on.

The next day, Greg, in front of his TV again, hears the sound of cars screeching to a halt out front. Car doors bang and heavy footsteps thud on the front path. Someone hammers on the door, a closed-fist sound. Greg opens the door, counts 11 or 12 policemen on the pathway, all in the hated blue uniform, the first one holding a piece of paper in front of him, like a shield. The others carry clear plastic bags. All wear plastic gloves. On the street behind them, four police cars stand at various angles to the kerb, hungry beasts of prey, ready to pounce.

'Greg Ugle?'

'Whaddya want?'

'Someone filed a complaint, mate. Said you threw spears in the street. We got a search warrant.'

The police push past, brushing Greg aside. Greg's grandchildren scream, run behind their mother. The police split up, bulky blue shapes filling each room, spilling out into the corridor.

'I've found some weapons.' A shout from the living room.

Greg follows the other policemen in. Light from the television illuminates the scene. Halfway up the opposite wall, as if caught mid-flight, several spears are fixed to the wall. Greg crosses his arms, rocks back on his feet.

'I don't see any weapons; all I see is artifacts,' he says.

The police ignore him. Take down and bag the spears. Continue their search. In the kitchen, they open doors, slam them shut, pull drawers so hard they nearly escape their tracks.

'What's this?' A policeman brandishes a long knife with a sharp blade.

'A hunting knife, mate. For skinning kangaroos.'

'We're taking it in.' The policeman drops it into a bag.

A yell comes from the backyard. Out they all troop.

'What about this, mate?' A policeman wields an iron bar.

'Dunno,' Greg says. 'Looks like an iron bar to me.'

'Don't get smart with me,' the policeman says. He bags the bar.

The only other weapon found is the waddy. Greg warns the police not to touch it because of its special powers. A young female sergeant holds a bag open and scoops the waddy in. She makes sure not to touch it.

But back at the station, a policeman apparently touches the waddy.

In the car, Greg paused. Made a sucking sound through his teeth, as if to say, *what can you do?*

'This strange thing happened,' he said. Apparently the policeman had been found guilty of a crime, lost his job and his wife, and went to jail. I glanced over. Greg gave me a knowing look. He clearly believed the policeman's careless touch had sealed his fate. I had my doubts, but I knew if it had been me, I wouldn't have touched the waddy. According to Greg, the incident was reported in the newspapers. Probably the article my brother had read, I thought. No wonder he'd been concerned. If I had read the article, I might have had second thoughts, and Greg and I might never have met.

After checking a transcript of our conversation for accuracy, Greg added some details of the altercation. Next to the last sentence of the previous paragraph he wrote, 'We would have met.'

He was right. He wanted his story known; I wanted to know the story. If the Molokai incident had never happened, something else would have eventually motivated my search for my former friends.

I also knew that I needed the relationship, the potential friendship, more than he did. It's taken me hours at this desk of mine to figure out the simple truth of why. I don't believe it's possible to hurt another person without hurting oneself, an invisible hurt, a tear in the soul that allows the essence of one's humanity to leak out, like bleeding from a cut. Awareness of the loss might come infrequently or only in the dead of night or when staring at the bottom of a beer glass. But it almost always comes. A collective group can't hurt another collective group either without hurting itself. And I belong to a collective group that has hurt. The past wounded me as well as Greg. And even though the hurt was not in the same league, not even close, for me to achieve a personal reconciliation with the former Mission kids, the healing had to be two ways. One aspect of healing for me meant Greg extending friendship. But the more important aspect of personal reconciliation was still what I could do for Greg and Bronwyn and their families. In my opinion, saying 'sorry' without some form of reparation was close to meaningless. But as to what form that reparation would take, I didn't know. Not then.

Finding Bronwyn

The slime dumps reared up in the distance, ominous grey bluffs massed on the far edge of town, dominating the flat landscape. We approached Kambalda Road.

'Turn here,' Greg said. 'They said Bronwyn's camp's out this way.'

As a child, I'd often camped with my family. While Mum whipped tea up at dusk, often camp pie, my brothers and I helped Dad pitch the tent. Gas flames hissed from the Primus and metal clanged on metal as we hammered tent pegs into the resisting ground. We unrolled sleeping bags, unfolded camp chairs and raised and lowered tent flaps. Our skin reeked of the sharp chemical smell of insect repellant and we were soon clothed in red dirt.

Spring was my favourite time to camp. Acres and acres of everlastings burst into flower, almost overnight, a delicate dusting of pink, yellow and white over the hard red earth. The flowers taught me that the cliché about beauty and the beholder is only part of the truth. The rest is that beauty can be enhanced and made more potent by harsh surroundings. I'd loved camping – my parents, my brothers and me, isolated from the world, protected by a ragged army of trees. By day the camping area was a playground with unlimited possibilities. Branches, ground and dirt assumed any role we liked. At night, a place of shadowy secrets beneath a sky lit up by pinpoints of light, like the helmet torches of thousands of celestial miners. But for us camping was a choice.

Mining trucks thundered along towards Kambalda, a nickel-mining town that came into being during my childhood. The 'bells' Bronwyn's son told us to look for turned out to be drums for cyanide, used in gold extraction in days gone by.

I took in the size of the drums, several metres high and as wide as a small room. I remembered my father's story of evicting a man from his drum-home. I had considered the eviction harsh – where would the man live? The drum in front of me gave substance to the reality of the cyanide and suggested a different perspective: my father might have saved the man from poison-induced organ damage.

A flash of white in the bush caught my eye. I slowed the car and turned onto a track with, as Greg noted, fresh tyre marks. A couple of old caravans, a few cars (old bombs as we would have called them as children) and a humpy of corrugated iron, tarpaulin and branches came into sight. Several wisps of ash-grey smoke spiralled into the bleached blue sky. I parked under a tree and waited in the car, while Greg went to explain me and my purpose. The place felt isolated, about as far from my desk as I could travel in Australia. Despite the sweltering heat, I kept the windows wound up.

Fifty metres away, Greg hung back from a woman, his body language carefully non-aggressive, and I remembered that despite the history Greg shared with Bronwyn, he was a Noongar man on Wongi land. A small brown-skinned boy whizzed past on a bicycle. He threw me a curious glance. I smiled and waved.

Greg started back towards the car. I wondered if my visit was a hard sell, or if Bronwyn was even here. I wound down the window.

'It's her. She says she'll talk.'

I followed his meandering course through the trees to a clearing. Three parked cars defined a rough triangle of land. At two points of the triangle, fires smouldered, giving off the smell of eucalyptus. An old double-bed mattress, covered with worn blankets, lay on the ground next to one of the cars. A woman taller than me lugged camp chairs, setting one alongside the other.

The woman turned and looked my way and ah … almost four decades since I'd last seen you, there you were, Bronwyn. Wearing a polo shirt, loose olive-brown track pants of some synthetic fabric, socks and sandshoes and rings and chains, bright gold against your dark skin. Relief enveloped my palpitating heart at finding you looking as if life had not got the best of you, despite living in poor and difficult circumstances.

In the curves of your cheeks, I saw echoes of the girl I had loved. In your brown eyes, the lively intelligence and quick wit of the school friend I had looked up to. You gave me a piercing glance. Turned away.

'Remember me? Amanda Webster?' I said.

I smiled to hide my anxiety, but you probably weren't

fooled. The wind soughed in the trees. In the distance, traffic rumbled along the road Greg and I had left behind. Unsmilingly, you looked into my eyes, looked away. Moved a chair a few centimetres to the left. Dragged on your cigarette. You took your sweet time, made me wait. But not as long as I'd waited to find you.

'Mandy. You called me Mandy. You came with us to Esperance one Christmas. Stayed at our holiday house. Remember?' I said.

I wanted to say, *remember the sound of two little girls giggling under Galloping Gertie? Remember the smell of the lavender in the flower bed behind the house? The taste of those orange nasturtium flowers by the pathway to the front door?* I wanted to say that all these years I'd preserved memories of you as carefully as if they were wrapped in tissue and stored in a cedar chest, a sprinkle of naphthalene to keep the moths at bay. But I didn't. In case you didn't remember.

What came next is etched into my memory as a pivotal moment of my adult life. I've been carrying your memory for so long, you see, and meeting up with you again would impact my priorities. You gave me another look, longer this time. Nodded. Your face broke into a broad grin, and you said, 'I remember, Mandy. I remember.' You pointed at the chairs. Invited me to sit. I did.

Greg positioned himself away from us, away from the women's business, on an upturned milk crate. On the mattress, another woman picked at the pale underside of her bare foot with a needle. She wore a loose cotton dress, a woollen beanie pulled low over her forehead. To her right sat your daughter, the girl I'd met at Kurrawang; to her left another girl, her expression vacant, also your daughter. She was on depot drugs, you would later tell me, long-acting antipsychotic injections, which I know are given where compliance is a problem. Given to your daughter for a psychosis induced by recreational drugs, although, if you ask me, in this situation recreation seems like the wrong word. Two puppies tussled over a bone. Nobody paid them any attention, least of all you.

You told me your daughter's children were made state wards until the age of 18, which, when you think about it, makes them the third generation at least to be removed in your family. The laws regarding removal might have changed, but in many ways nothing has changed for some Aboriginal people, has it? The children's English grandmother was given custody, you said. And that Skype enables your daughter to keep a relationship of sorts alive with her children. I can imagine locking away the pain caused by that arrangement deep in a compartment of your heart, and throwing away the key.

The two cans of Emu Bitter in drink holders in the armrest of your camp chair escaped my notice until you pointed them out. But believe me, Bronwyn, if I had to live in a bush camp, I'd be tempted to start the day with a beer. Claiming the beer to be your brother's, you denied that you drank. I nodded, wanting to believe you. Wanting desperately to believe that life had been kinder to you than it must have been to those people my childhood self saw opposite the church. You tossed the end of your cigarette into the nearest fire. Extracted another from a packet on the armrest. Searched a leather pouch for a lighter. After lighting the cigarette, you returned the lighter and packet to the pouch, which you wedged between yourself and the canvas of the chair. Your movements looked nervous to me. Had I caught you off-guard? Were you worried about how I saw you? Or were you buying yourself time to get a read on me?

A bearded man, open shirt revealing a swollen belly, appeared from behind me. I turned to see where he had come from and saw another car parked between trees, an older man on the ground nearby. The man before me wobbled. His eyes looked unfocused and bleary. Your brother Arthur, you said.

I offered him a bright smile. He staggered a little. Giggled, and told me he was drunk. It was 11.30 in the morning. Later, you told me he lost his children to Welfare. Later still you would tell me he lost them because he and his wife had fought a lot. Difficult to stop, isn't it, that vicious cycle of loss and alcohol, once it gains momentum? Often ends the way it did for Arthur a couple of years later. In a hospital bed, wired to machines, his eyes yellow, yours stinging from the smell of antiseptic, his belly swollen, yours with an unfixable ache, him taking his last breaths. You know what I mean.

You brought up the subject of the book I was writing. Said you liked to read. So I'm hoping you're reading this chapter, because it's for you and for me, for us. I want you to know what you meant to me, how much I wanted to reunite. How much I wanted to replace my fictional version of your life with the truth. This chapter stands as a record of our reunion. A measure of our friendship.

Before I forget, let me say how much I regret wearing a pearl necklace that day. Do you remember it? Later a writer friend would say of my accessory choice, 'Who did you think you were? The Queen?' The truth is, apart from the odd moment such as in the car on the way to your camp, I was battling to establish any sort of rapport with Greg. He'd agreed to this trip to Kalgoorlie and had done his best to help me. And we'd shared a few laughs. But there was an invisible barrier between us, and I swear he was intent on maintaining that barrier. Heaven only knows, he has reason enough. I was white and belonged on the other side. I could look through, when he allowed, but never belong. Without giving it much thought, I'd fallen back on the age-old practice of dolling oneself up, adding the pearls to my ensemble of shirt and trousers. ('What a poser', we might have said as girls.) But sitting on a camp chair in the bush, I felt more Lady Muck than queen and wished I'd left the damned pearls in Sydney. Arthur asked you for a cigarette. You gave him one. He lit it. Took a few drags. Looked from me to Greg. 'She your wife?' he said. He tilted his head towards me. Greg glanced my way. Do you remember how he hesitated, as if he didn't know how to explain me? I smiled. Said we were friends. Greg nodded. Repeated the word *friends*. Really, I felt like Greg's probationary friend.

Friends can be difficult to come by in this world. I guess that's one reason I came looking for you. Sentimental, perhaps, but a special understanding comes with old friendships, don't you think? Old friends have some idea, at least, of the early influences to shape each other's lives, although as it turns out, I had fewer ideas about those in your life than I thought. But we share a common language, populated by words like 'poppet head' and 'fringe dwellers', more particular to the goldfields than many other parts of

Australia. Our bodies understand the environment in similar ways – the feel of dry searing heat on bare skin, the smell of sulphur in the air, the sight of slime dumps on the horizon, the moan of the wind in dry eucalypt leaves. Most importantly, we share memories of each other untainted by adult complications, perhaps the truest form of friendship possible, based solely on an intuitive understanding of the other person's heart. I didn't know it when I saw you in the bush camp, but you would be the only person to not question my motives in writing this book.

If you are indeed reading this book, Bronwyn, you'll know by now I thought you were an orphan. I pictured you sharing midnight feasts with the other girls. I imagined life at Kurrawang as one long, fun-filled camp, like the Fresh Air League in Esperance, where I stayed for a week or two one year. (How amazing to know that the League was established by Kalgoorlie citizens only seven years after Paddy Hannan discovered gold there, for the purpose of giving any 'pallid little sufferer' from the Goldfields the benefit of invigorating sea air!)

The story you told me in the bush camp would have been beyond my comprehension as a child. The way your father took you and your siblings from your mother when you were living in Kalgoorlie because she was drinking, and moved you to Cue, north of Perth. The way Native Welfare removed you from your father after your mother complained, but instead of returning you to your mother, placed you in different hostels for a while and then in Kurrawang. You and your four sisters and, later, Arthur. None of you knew it then, but you had been made state wards.

From what you told me, I now know that the Mission was nothing like the Fresh Air League. Not yet a teenager, you had to mother your younger sisters. You had to change their nappies and, early each day, you woke one sister, who wet the bed, to allow her a hot shower before the missionaries noticed and punished her with a cold shower, even in winter. You were a child-mother. And me? I was allowed to be a child, dressing my doll Valerie in her bridal clothes while I dreamt a white wedding for myself.

At one point, you stopped speaking. Frowned and seemed lost in thought. Then you glanced around. Pointed to some yellow flowers, brazen against the orangey-red dirt. Told me they reminded you of the time you ran away at 16 and walked into town. From there, for a couple of years, you travelled through the desert, up into the Northern Territory and down to Adelaide. Those were the years I was travelling by bus back and forth from the private girls' school I attended. Eventually you returned to Kalgoorlie. As most people from the Goldfields do. The lure of the past as strong as the lure of gold for the early prospectors.

After maturing early, you had a baby at 18, you said. Gave it to a relative. The matter-of-fact way you delivered this news shocked me a little, but who knows what pain lay beneath the surface of your casual words. You told me about falling in love with Ken Smith in 1975, and running away with him. And about the 27-year partnership that ensued, during which you bore another nine children. Quite a feat in the eyes of a mother of three, especially as you and Ken managed an Aboriginal community up north at the time, the prerequisite skills all self-taught. Enjoyable work, you said, but it ended badly. So you returned to Kalgoorlie.

Then life came tumbling down around your ears. The heartbreak of your four-year-old son dying under the wheels of a 4WD outside your house. How do you get up, get dressed, put one foot after another when you've sustained such a loss? And then to lose your partner two days later in a head-on collision: a good man, you said. No wonder depression set in. A story like yours goes a long way to explain those Emu Bitters, which I now know didn't belong to Arthur. And perhaps the threat of lung cancer years down the track seems irrelevant when you know how swiftly and suddenly life can end.

Oh Bronwyn, as a child, I had no idea what you were going through. Since then, in many ways the differences between our lives have increased. Other things we have in common. We both feel a mother's love for our children, for example. But much of your life is beyond my understanding. I can begin to guess at your grief at losing a child. But only begin. While grief is grief, I have the resources to do whatever I can to cushion my sadnesses.

Living in the bush suits you, you claimed, with more than a hint of defiance in your voice. The peace, the way nobody bothers you. It sounded as if you were making the most of your circumstances, a skill life has probably taught you. But it can't be easy without whitegoods, a soft bed and a hot shower.

When I asked about your housing options, you told me you and your children were evicted from a subsidised Homes West property for allegedly shouting and swearing at people in the street. 'They don't know me,' I remember you saying. You puffed on your cigarette. Frowned. Said the government people should visit you and sit on the ground to talk and find out what it's like. I agree. When you talk with and listen to a person, you begin to know their humanity.

Since the eviction, you've lived in the bush. And since we met in your camp, you've told me you owe Homes West a large sum in damages. It sounded like you were fresh out of options until you repaid that sum. Whatever the damage to the Homes West house and whatever the cause, it seems wrong to toss a mother and her children on to the streets. Your daughter, a similar age to mine, has dropped out of school, which must have been hard going while living in the bush.

While at your camp, your grandson, who looked younger than the boy on the bike, sidled up and wordlessly handed you a tin of spaghetti to open. You pulled the metal ring and tossed the lid behind you into a bush. This might sound judgmental, but I'd expected you'd show more care for the land. ('You white people and your stereotypes,' I can imagine you saying.) After spending more time than is probably warranted thinking about it, I've come to realise you had no rubbish collection service. While you could still have collected the rubbish yourself, I guess you had other priorities. Like how to put food on a non-existent table without a kitchen, without a fridge, without a stove. And with too many troubles on your plate. Not to forget that white people litter too. And the carbon print from my big toe alone probably exceeds yours altogether. Of course, the mines, owned and largely operated by white people, cause far more damage to the environment than all the litter in Kalgoorlie.

The beat of loud music reached your camp before the engine noise. This part of the story might well be too routine for you to remember. A white 4WD appeared – the one I'd seen at the Mission. It was your son, bringing hamburgers to his sisters. The juxtaposition looked strange to me – the evident poverty, the expensive car, the bush camp, the fast food. But I see now that in the absence of a kitchen, fast food comes into its own. And expensive cars, I would later discover, compensate poorly for some losses. When your son left, you suddenly looked at your watch. Sat up. Said, 'You gotta drive me to the jail now, Mandy. I gotta visit my kids.'

Just like that, as if you were asking me to drop you at the shopping centre. Matter-of-fact, like when you described the deaths of your son and your partner. As if you accepted these facts as your lot in life. And perhaps your ability to accept these facts is an invisible mark the Mission has left on you.

It took me a moment to find my voice and agree.

You asked me to return the next day. I again agreed. We embraced, and then I drove to the jail, with Greg in the passenger seat beside me and you in the back. But I was rattled, and when we arrived, I slowed, unsure where to park. Behind the barbed wire fence, people gathered around wooden tables. I'm sure you sensed my discomfort. From the back seat, you shouted commands. I started to pull over.

'Not there! The next driveway,' you said. I swerved back on to the road. 'She's trying to kill us!' you said, mock horror in your voice. Gallows humour from a woman who as a child lived in what was almost a jail – miles of red dirt and scraggly trees standing in for barbed wire. Finally, I parked to your satisfaction. You left, and I took Greg home and headed back to the hotel.

I wonder now how it was for you – the sudden appearance of a white woman in your bush camp, wearing pearls and toting a fancy handbag, spruiking friendship on the grounds of a decades-old connection. Wanting to turn that friendship to advantage by subjecting you to interviews.

I didn't even know how to name our relationship, yours and mine, a difficulty that should in itself have indicated caution. It seemed simplest at the time to settle for 'friend', although in truth at that point we were less than friends and more than subject and interviewer, and I had no way of predicting whether that would change. Still, your invitation to return pleased me. You were giving me a chance and it felt like a gift.

My reunion with Bronwyn made me suspect that in wanting to return to Kalgoorlie, I wanted more than to learn the truth, feel a sense of belonging and reconcile with the past and with my former school friends. I thought my need to return might also represent a belief that I had lost my way. Become too much the corporate wife, with my designer-label clothes, my fancy house and my pearls. I thought perhaps I was trying to retrace my steps, return to a crossroads where I had taken a wrong turn. Not that I knew what the right turn was, other than to do something more useful with my life. But I was wary of any remnant 'missionary' urges from my childhood. Nor did I want to give in to self-indulgent urges. In *Craft for a Dry Lake*, Kim Mahood writes of journalist and welfare worker Daisy Bates, 'She also began a tradition which has steadily gained momentum, that of white women aligning themselves with Aboriginal women as a means of freeing themselves from the conventions of their own society.' That wasn't going to be me. Not that there's necessarily anything wrong with rejecting the social norms of so-called 'civilised' white society.

I returned to Louise and asked how her day of reading had gone.

'Great,' she said. 'Except it was scary when I went out for lunch. I had to walk past a pub and there were men everywhere.'

A knot formed in my belly at the thought of men, a few drinks under their belts, leering at my gorgeous 15-year-old daughter. I had worried about leaving her alone, but another couple of weeks and she'd be gone, miles from me in another hemisphere. An adventure, her choice, and a privilege. Unlike Bronwyn's or Greg's mothers, I'd had years to teach Louise the things I thought she needed to know, and months to let the umbilical cord stretch and fray to the point where I was ready to let go, to trust her on her own. If it didn't work out, she could jump on a plane and return to the bosom of her family. For now, she was ready for a break from her reading and eager to see more of the town where I'd grown up.

We drove over the railway line at the top end of town and out along the Menzies road. It stretched ahead, an endless black gash in the red dirt. To our right, a tall stack belched grey smoke, laden with God-only-knew-what chemicals. This was the Gidji Roaster, which heats gold that is bound in various sulphide compounds to release gases.

A road train appeared on the horizon, speeding towards me, forcing me to ease back on the accelerator and move over to the shoulder.

'Aggro driver!' I said.

'Mum! Your speech has changed since we came over here.'

She was right: I had slipped into the vernacular of my youth; long-forgotten expressions I was now hearing at every turn, many of them abbreviations. I was saying 'arvo', not 'afternoon' and 'ta', not 'thank you'. The night before, I'd told my daughter it was time for tea, not dinner, and had asked if she wanted sweets rather than dessert.

My daughter surveyed the barren landscape.

'I can't believe you came from here.'

In some ways I couldn't either. I'd moved so many times over the years that home for me meant people, not geography; certainly not this cratered land. And yet although my vocabulary slips were partly unconscious, didn't I welcome their comforting familiarity; weren't they my verbal certificate of citizenship?

'Do you have any water?' asked Louise.

'No, sorry.'

'Just looking at this bush makes me thirsty.'

I'd thought we were headed towards Menzies, an old ghost town I remembered from those family picnics and camping trips, but as the miles passed I started to worry. This was not the place to break down. Especially without water.

I turned the car and together we drove back through the gloaming to our hotel room with warm beds and a shower, and a restaurant below. I thought of returning from that Esperance holiday all those years ago, leaving Bronwyn at the Mission to rejoin what I'd thought of as her happy life. And in the hotel shower, when the water ran cold before I could rinse the conditioner from my hair, I thought of Bronwyn in her bush camp and at Kurrawang, urging her sister into a hot shower before the missionaries found her wet, foul-smelling bed.

The Cyanide Code

On our last full day in Kalgoorlie, I drove myself around town. I noted traffic lights where signed intersections had existed; underground power lines where wooden poles had stood; a gold-leaf-covered cupola on the old post office roof, organised by a community committee; suburbs of smart brick houses and landscaped gardens where the bush had encroached. The town was a living museum of change to catalogue.

An old family friend I'd visited had told me the old post office had been converted to a court house. 'Now they'll have drunken Aboriginals on the street in the middle of town. What kind of impression will that make on visitors?' he'd said.

I had a sneaking suspicion I had no right to challenge him. Easy to judge, knowing I would return to my socio-economic bubble in Sydney. Not for me the hopeless, daily slap in the face of the town's failure, the country's failure, to shelter and feed the homeless Aboriginal people who congregated in St Barbara's Square, outside the supermarket, and on the outskirts of town, many of whom still suffered aftershocks from the tectonic shifts in culture since colonisation.

Time has given me another perspective. Ensconced at my desk, I think back to the grudging sympathy I felt for our family friend. But he too lives in his own bubble of privilege. Has no need of my sympathy. Has, in fact, become immune to any sense of responsibility for the homeless Aboriginal people in town, if he ever felt any. And they don't need my sympathy either. They need a whole lot more. They need those bubbles to burst and rain affluence on all.

On hearing of my subject matter, another woman I'd encountered had frowned. 'Why the Aborigines?' she said. 'There are so many other things to write about.' And a nurse I met who'd known my father listed the ward names from their era: General, Men's, Women's, Maternity, Children's, Surgical and Isolation. 'That's where the infectious cases were sent,' she explained of the last ward. She paused. Whispered, 'And the Aborigines.'

Daddy, are Aboriginals people? It seemed increasingly likely that my juvenile mind had not acted in isolation.

In the afternoon, I left my pearls in my hotel room and paid Bronwyn a second visit. She was dressed for the occasion in brown pants and a clean shirt and greeted me with a smile. She sat on a camp chair; I took an upturned milk crate. I asked after her sons in jail. She said they were fine, but didn't elaborate. Still caught in limbo between friend and interviewer, I didn't press the point.

The childhood memories we swapped rarely overlapped, as if we'd remembered alternate lines of a history book. The boy who'd been riding a bike the previous day wandered past, peeling a banana. He threw the peel on the ground and took a bite.

'Is that yummy?' I asked.

He looked at me without answering. I realised he might not speak English. I tended to forget, probably not the only white Australian to do so, that when Cook arrived in 1770, around 250 Aboriginal languages existed, most with several dialects. Of the 250, 160 have since become extinct, and a further 70 are under threat. That said, English is still a second language for many Aboriginal people in remote areas, such as Meekatharra, where the boy and his mother, the friend of Bronwyn's I'd met the day before, lived.

The woman came to the campfire nearest Bronwyn and me. She tugged her woollen beanie lower, picked up a handful of kindling from beside the fire and carefully arranged the sticks on the smouldering ashes. She blew into the ashes. Over the answering flames, she strung a blackened kettle on a wire.

When the kettle had boiled, the woman poured water over a tea bag in a tin mug. She took a biscuit from an open packet that lay on the roof of a nearby car, and sat next to me in the empty camp chair.

'Hello,' I said.

'Hello,' she whispered. She dunked the biscuit in the tea and took a bite.

Bronwyn gave me a sharp look.

'That's Nancy Donegan. Her husband died in police custody a couple of years ago.'

Nancy's story is on public record. In keeping with the tradition of not speaking the names of the dead so as not to recall or disturb the dead person's spirit, her husband is now known as Mr Ward. He was arrested for drink-driving at Laverton in 2008. After spending the night in the lock-up, he faced an unlawful cell-door hearing, conducted by a local Justice of the Peace. The JP failed to offer bail, later telling the Kalgoorlie Magistrates Court that Mr Ward did not request it. Mr Ward had no legal representation at the time.

Although an elder with extensive ties to the local community and not a flight risk, Mr Ward was locked in the rear, metal-lined prisoner's pod of a police van to be transported to the Kalgoorlie jail. Neither of the prison transport officers assigned to the job checked the pod's air conditioning. Nor did they stop during the four-hour journey to check on Mr Ward. The installed CCTV system was later shown to be malfunctioning. Mr Ward had no way to communicate with the officers. No way to tell them the air conditioning was not working.

Outside, the temperature climbed to over 40. In the back of the van, Mr Ward collapsed from heat stroke. On arrival in Kalgoorlie, the transport officers found him unconscious. He was unable to be revived. A WorkSafe prosecution found the transport officers partly responsible for his death. The officer in the passenger seat, considered more responsible, was fined $11 000.

The family received a $3.2 million payout from the Western Australian government, of which Mr Ward's widow Nancy Donegan received $1.4 million. Each of four children received $400 000 in trust accounts. All of the money, including Nancy's, was to be managed by the Public

Trustee, to protect her finances for the future, but simultaneously restricting her options. When I saw Nancy at the camp, she didn't appear to have any money.

The Aboriginal boy I'd seen the previous day delivering hamburgers to Bronwyn's children was Nancy's son. Suddenly the expensive white 4WD didn't seem so out of place. Sadly it fitted in all too well to their collective story.

Bronwyn pointed to the little boy, who was back on the bike and onto his second banana.

'He's Nancy's.'

Bronwyn looked off to her right and took a deep drag of her cigarette.

'Welfare took my kids for a while too.'

A sudden sense of the misery of their stories, a long dark shaft, seemingly endless, into the past.

'No! Did they?'

'Yeah. A few years back.'

Bronwyn said that after taking her children, in an echo of the past, Welfare placed them in a home in Norseman, near Kalgoorlie. Bronwyn went to the Welfare office and said she was going to 'get my kids back'. She drove to Norseman and parked outside the home. Her children apparently saw her and came running. Bronwyn took them without telling anyone.

This part of the story sounded scarcely plausible – not the removal of the children but the perfect timing of their presence outside the home when Bronwyn had arrived, the lack of subsequent pursuit by authorities. But the implausible, a different kind of implausible, had happened many times in Australia's history. It had happened to Bronwyn's mother.

'It's still happening to Indigenous people,' Bronwyn said. 'More than white people.'

The other woman nodded, and I did too.

'If police see a drunk Aboriginal woman in the park holding a baby, they take the baby.' Bronwyn ground her cigarette into the red dirt.

The moment opened up before me: would I speak my mind, say what I knew many other Australians would think – that it didn't seem entirely unreasonable to remove a baby from the arms of a drunk person?

'Can the woman get the baby back?' I didn't want to scuttle our fledgling friendship.

'They make them do a course first. Detox.'

We retreated into our thoughts. I had a fair bit of sympathy for the plight of the hypothetical woman in the park. The injustice wasn't difficult to figure out. Undoubtedly many white women with children hit the bottle when, for whatever reason, the pressures of motherhood overwhelm them; not just underprivileged white women but the chardonnay mothers of the wealthier suburbs. Whatever the socioeconomic circumstances, it's likely that many white mothers at some point hold an infant in one hand, a glass in the other. Most, however, have the luxury of doing so behind closed doors. If the Department of Community Services gets involved, there's usually a lengthy investigation before a child is removed.

I needed to return to the hotel, to my daughter. Bronwyn and I swapped phone numbers. She agreed to a photo. Her older daughter took my phone and Bronwyn chose a spot.

'Away from the cars,' she said. 'In front of this tree.'

We stood arm in arm in front of an acacia tree and posed for the camera. Then we looked at the photo: Bronwyn standing straight, shoulders back. Her dark wavy hair, released from a ponytail, fell to her shoulders. Behind us the blue sky and a golden burst of acacia blossoms. Beneath us the red dirt. And beneath it, the gold.

I picked Louise up and we headed out along Kanowna Road to the Kanowna Belle, a smaller pit mine. To the side, a viewing platform offered an elevated view, the mine's sides steeper and less terraced than the Super Pit.

But it was a sign at the lookout, the implicit threat it contained, that intrigued me: The Cyanide Code. A quick Google search revealed this to be a voluntary guideline for the gold mining industry, developed in an attempt to improve standards of waste disposal. The word 'improve' seeming to imply past failures and present shortcomings. The empty cyanide drums near the track to Bronwyn's camp seemed suddenly emblematic of other past and present failures.

After a Thai food dinner, Louise and I retired early. The following dawn, our last morning in Kalgoorlie, I woke and drew back the curtains. A black crow strutted across the roof of the building behind, condensation glistening on the red corrugated iron. A light breeze lifted the leaves of a peppermint tree and my mother's old gum tree. The Mount Charlotte poppet head formed a striking silhouette against a banded sky of white, yellow, pink and dove-grey.

I gripped the cold metal railing and watched the yellow band expand and intensify, until it looked as if the land were bathed with molten gold. The place was starting to reassert its hold on me.

The Aboriginal Protector

'You know Grandfather was an Aboriginal Protector, don't you?' My older brother Graham sounded cheerful. He leaned back in his chair.

I nearly choked on my eggs.

I was in Melbourne for a writing conference and had skipped a session to meet with Graham, his wife Terri, and his daughter Anna in a café. A typical family get-together: How's your health? Work? What are you doing for Christmas?

Terri, who sported a pink streak in her fashionably cut hair, had asked after my writing. I described my visits west and my meetings with Greg and Bronwyn. Graham was surprised I had remembered the names of my former friends from the Mission.

'I don't remember much about Aboriginal people from back then,' he said. 'I remember some of them used to camp on our front lawn and have beer parties. They squatted in the old Cobb and Co Coach building over the road from our house, too. And I used to ride past their camps on the slime dumps. They never bothered me.'

Less than two years separated Graham and me in age. In cahoots with each other as children, we formed secret societies with passwords and coded door knocks, and ganged up on our younger brother Geoffrey, once tricking him into drinking paint from a half-filled tin outside our playhouse. But I hadn't been privy to Graham's bicycle escapades over the slime dumps.

We'd ordered more coffees from the waitress. The mention of my recent visit to Kurrawang Mission kindled a spark of recognition in my brother's eyes.

'I stayed at the Mission one night.'

'You what?' It was as if he'd admitted to owning something I'd long coveted.

Graham nodded. Eyed me intently.

'With the Sercombe boy? Nigel?'

'Was that his name? Might have been another brother. Malcolm, I think. I remember they turned the electricity generator off at nine. It was very dark.'

Graham said he had played inside, not outside with the Aboriginal children. Mr Sercombe had driven them to school the following morning. And that was the extent of Graham's memory of his stay.

Then he dropped the news about Grandfather in my lap. I pushed my eggs aside, my appetite gone.

'Do you mean as in … ?'

'Yes.' He still sounded chirpy. 'During his time in Norseman. I think the title came with the position of hospital doctor.'

I could feel Anna and Terri watching me.

'How do you know?' And then, before he could answer, 'Are you sure?'

'Dad might have told me. Or Grandfather. When I was younger, we corresponded.'

Graham had ridden a few psychological slime dumps in his teenage years, such as his ongoing argument with our parents over hair length. Secretly, I'd sided with Graham. Publicly, I kept my mouth shut – I was having problems of my own with my mother, who planned on a life of nursing, religion, unshaved legs and teetotalism for me. Eventually Graham moved to Sydney for a year. He and Grandfather, always close, began corresponding. So it made sense that Grandfather might have told Graham about being a Local Aboriginal Protector.

Under Western Australia's *Aborigines Act 1905*, the Chief Protector could appoint 'fit and proper persons' to be local protectors. The local protectors were in charge of Aboriginal people in their area. One of the local protectors' tasks was to identify and report 'half-caste' Aboriginal children. Now it seemed my grandfather had been one of those 'fit and proper' persons.

Grandfather had arrived in Western Australia sometime in the mid 1920s, during Auber Octavius Neville's reign as Chief Protector. Deeply feared in Aboriginal communities, Neville advocated the 'breeding out' of Aboriginality. 'Half-caste' children who looked white and could potentially be integrated into white society were at the greatest risk of being removed from their families, often under the flimsiest of excuses. Of one girl, 'Dilly', Neville writes, 'I should think this fact that the girl, who is only quarter-caste, is found in an aboriginal camp should be sufficient cause to treat her as a neglected child.'

Graham settled the bill. The coffee machine wheezed. A waft of cooked egg lingered. I thought about my grandfather. If he was indeed a Local Aboriginal Protector, had he identified local, fair-skinned Aboriginal children for removal?

We gathered our belongings and filed out into the sunshine. I returned to the final session of the writing conference, and from there to the airport. During the hour-long flight, I thought of nothing but my brother's revelation and what, if it were true, my grandfather's title might mean to me. I found myself wondering if it boiled down to this: had I come from bad seed? Was my grandfather's way of thinking, the particular wiring of his brain and patterns of synapses, genetically coded and passed down to me through my father, the double helices of our DNA like a Christmas paper chain, linking generations?

It took me a while to come to my senses.

Although I came to accept the notion of 'bad seed' as a nonsense, I wondered what, if any, responsibility I bore for any hardship Aboriginal people suffered due to my grandfather's actions as Protector.

Former prime minister John Howard contends, 'I do not believe, as a matter of principle, that one generation can accept responsibility for the acts of an earlier gener-ation. I don't accept that as a matter of principle.'

I didn't agree, and my opinion related to my family's history in Australia.

First off the boat, in the 1820s, only 30-odd years after Captain Arthur Phillip established a British colony at Sydney Cove, was my great-great-great-grandfather Charles Pemberton. He was a rogue, 'sent down', or expelled, from the hallowed halls of England's Oxford Medical School, for being 'somewhat wild and addicted to drink'. Undeterred by disgrace or inadequate qualifications, he secured a position as the medical officer on a convict ship, bound for Australian shores with its unfortunate cargo.

His future wife Elizabeth Ann Glover set sail in 1832, arriving in Van Diemen's Land, as Tasmania was then known, aboard the *Princess Royal*, the first of the 'bride ships' commissioned to transport young, single women from England to Australia as prospective brides for the overwhelmingly male population. The women, Governor Arthur complained, were mostly 'depraved characters' from public institutions. He might well have included triple-great-grandmother Elizabeth in this category – she bought her freedom from a penitentiary by agreeing to ship out. No record exists of her particular crime, although if she, like me, were plagued by a dripping nose, she might well have stolen a linen handkerchief, a prevalent crime at the time, subject to harsh penalties for its villainous nature.

Elizabeth redeemed herself in Governor Arthur's eyes with her ability to 'brew, bake, clean house very well'. Elizabeth's brewing skills and Charles's addiction to drink evidently created a match made in heaven. The couple married, and Charles swapped his scalpel for a meat cleaver to become a pork butcher in the Victorian town of Geelong.

Other branches of the family fled England's urban slums over the next two decades, one great-grandmother expressing relief at having 'escaped the cold hand of charity in England'. Her daughter Alice married my great-grandfather Charles Webster, and subsequently gave birth to my grandfather.

My ancestors left England as drunkards, paupers and criminals. Doubtless they toiled long and hard to claw their way up the socioeconomic ladder, but the fact remains that they purchased stolen land with the products of that toil, and gained an education that was largely unavailable to Aboriginal people. The other indisputable fact is that their actions and privileges led directly to my position as doctor's daughter in the top-streamed class. Equally, the system that benefitted my ancestors and me placed the Ugle siblings and Bronwyn in the Mission and the class for the 'slow learners'. If I'm happy to enjoy the benefits, then it's probably only fair to share in the responsibility. I would be my ancestors' emissary in helping make amends. The trick, I knew, even at the time of my brother's revelation, would be to choose positive action over hair shirt.

Regardless of my family history, I thought I should accept a measure of responsibility as a privileged citizen of an affluent democracy. In the final analysis, it's not the why that matters but the fact that I have made this decision.

I also disagree with Howard on the subject of an apology. Saying 'sorry' can be a simple expression of general regret rather than an admission of personal guilt, as in, 'I'm sorry you lost your job.' Saying 'sorry' can be a reaching-out, not an abject grovelling; a recognition of the fundamental humanity of the other, not a condemnation of self; a wish for a two-way healing.

Of course, Greg and Bronwyn's concerns tended to be more immediate, among them how to pay the bills and secure land for their children. Still, I could offer my apology in the spirit of a personal reconciliation. But what about my grandfather, a man I had loved? Could a person reconcile with the dead?

The Hypothetical Grandchild

As a child, I loved visiting my grandparents in Esperance. The name of their small fibro house – Tinabulla – sounded Aboriginal to me. Only later did I learn its true provenance: my grandfather's corruption of 'a tin of bully beef', a dietary staple on the French battlefields during World War I.

Grandfather held court from his rocking chair. Dressed in trousers held up by suspenders, he presented a benign and congenial figure with his snowy white hair, bushy eyebrows, blue eyes and rounded cheeks. He rarely spoke ill of anyone. Never spoke ill of Aboriginal people. Every so often, he would put the conversation on hold. Strike a match, cup the end of his pipe in one hand, hold the flame to the tobacco with the other hand and emit a few emphatic puffs that smelled rich and peaty. When he tired of my younger brother and me, he would dismiss us and challenge my older brother to chess. Silence and an atmosphere of deep concentration would descend on the loungeroom. On a shelf nearby, an American clock, popular in the day and adorned with a statue of Mercury, the Roman god of financial gain, kept time.

Within a year or so of my family relocating from Kalgoorlie to Perth, my grandparents moved to a flat in a nearby suburb. They lived quietly, filling their days with books, Scrabble and tender love, until my grandmother developed Alzheimer's Disease, eventually requiring admission to a nursing home. Several years later, his physical and mental health failing, my grandfather joined his wife, the reunion, heartbreakingly, meaningless to her.

As his mind gradually succumbed to the vagaries of vascular disease, Grandfather's conversations became shorter but remained, always, amiable. Gangrene took hold, hospitalising him for much of his final year as surgeons amputated part of a foot, a few inches at a time. He died in hospital. By then, I had moved interstate. Too young to appreciate that funerals are for the living, I didn't attend. Grandfather was gone.

On my return to Sydney from the Melbourne conference, I set about reading the Chief Protector reports from the 1920s available online, in search of any reference to my grandfather. The reports contain every imaginable statistic – population size; blankets available for distribution; Aboriginal people suffering from diseases such as heart disease, tuberculosis and syphilis; mules, goats, and cows in each community; and Aboriginal girls in domestic servitude to become 'enceinte' (pregnant).

Nowhere did I find my grandfather's name.

But I sensed his presence behind the abbreviated medical statistics for Aboriginal people that he as the sole doctor in Norseman must have contributed: Conditions and health – fair; Epidemics – nil; Venereal – nil.

My husband rang from his surfing holiday. I passed on my brother's news.

'It's not your fault, honey,' he said. 'Don't beat yourself up.'

I wasn't. At least not consciously. The title of Local Protector was no hereditary peerage. But the news was confronting, even without proof of either the title or any wrongdoing by my grandfather. It made me wonder what biases, what residual colonial impulses I'd swallowed along with the chocolate brownies my grandmother baked. Impulses I needed to recognise to overcome them, which would be necessary if I wanted to effect a true reconciliation with Bronwyn and Greg and their families, or to contribute to the fight for equality for Aboriginal people.

I wondered, too, if I would have accepted the title of Aboriginal Protector if I had lived in the 1920s. If I would have signed papers to remove children from their families. How much easier it is to be on the side of justice when you have retrospective knowledge. Worth keeping in mind when considering one's stance and course of action with other problems that have come to light – the refugee crisis, for example, or climate change, issues on which future generations will judge people like me.

Grandfather left an unpublished memoir, *Writings of Allan Webster*. Previously I'd skimmed the pages; now I determined to read them more thoroughly.

Grandfather had divided *Writings* into three sections: 'Letters to a hypothetical grandchild'; 'Well-written fragments of the Great War'; and 'A Goldfields' doctor's experiences and stories of a more literary bent'. His usual tongue-in-cheek style.

I skimmed the letters telling the hypothetical grandchild, *my dear child,* what to expect if intent on medical school. The title of the second section, the 'well-written fragments', summoned memories of Grandfather's wry smile, but his war stories, like many Australian war stories, contain no mention of Aboriginal people.

Grandfather opens the third section from a third-person perspective, imbuing the writing with a sense of formality and distance that echoes the geographical and emotional relationship of his older to his younger self, the one who'd made the cross-country journey.

The youngest of seven children, Grandfather was born in Victoria in 1896. In his teens, he won a scholarship to a fancy school. But, due to lack of interest, his glory days were short-lived, and his academic career stalled by age 14. Grandfather left school and became a government clerk. When war broke out in 1914, he enlisted and served with the 10th Field Ambulance. His captain noted his aptitude and recommended military school in France for post-war rehabilitation, which enabled Grandfather to enrol in medical school on his return to Melbourne.

On graduation, his only job offer was Resident Medical Officer at the hospital in Norseman, a two-bit gold mining town, already in decline, in Western Australia. Grandfather hastily married his long-term and long-suffering fiancée, Gwendolyn Burnip, and they packed and boarded a train. The scene set, Grandfather changes the point of view to the singular first person to 'let Allan go on with his story'.

'We saw the desert, our first aboriginals, spinifex, lovely sunsets, camels (our train hit one, one night) and we arrived, pop-eyed, in Kalgoorlie.' A couple of days later, the newlyweds caught another train to Norseman, 200 kilometres south of Kalgoorlie: 'My heart, how young we were.'

If Kalgoorlie, with a population of around 30 000, had seemed another world to a city couple from the east coast, Norseman, with a population of around 100, and 'tin sheds everywhere, hardly a decent house in sight', must have seemed another planet. Behind the houses stretched a dry salt lake. Elsewhere was red dirt and the endless monotony of faded-green bush. The days were 'long and quiet', the silence broken only by the sound of barking dogs or of wooden beams thudding against gold-bearing ore at the distant State Battery. On Thursdays, the entire population would gather for the arrival of the mail train from Kalgoorlie. Thursday evenings, everyone stayed home to read their letters and respond in time for the outward-bound mail train in the morning, my grandfather often feeling his way to the Post Office through dark, unlit streets to deposit his letters.

My grandparents settled into the 'Hospital Residence', a galvanised iron and wood structure for which, my grandfather notes, the 'now-evicted tenants were robbed at 5/- a week'. The daughter of a well-to-do furrier, my grandmother must have wondered what she had gotten herself into.

Grandfather's *Writings* make it easy to picture her in the kitchen. I see her at the table, preparing dinner. Cutting and chopping, peeling and scraping, mixing and basting, her eyes stinging with smoke from the kerosene lamp, which burdens the already stifling air with its heat. Her carriage is erect, her bosom generous; she dresses modestly, and her long chestnut hair is coiled above the nape of her neck. Beneath her apron, her belly swells.

She ponders her situation: a bit of a come-down, her

friends in Melbourne might think; indeed, she herself has experienced moments of panic at the strangeness of it all. At those times, her heart has felt as if it leapt in her chest, like the kangaroos she goggles at each day in this dehydrated landscape, and her throat tightened and threatened to close, and she wondered how she would cope with a baby, so far from home. But her initial shock has ebbed and now she feels a rush of gratitude. She and her husband, a kind man with a gentle humour, always considerate, can shape a life of their choosing with their child, here on this inland island, surrounded by a sea of salt and red dirt.

Although their house is a ramshackle structure, the townspeople have provided a warm welcome and furniture, all the more charming for its inventiveness: a double stretcher for a bed and 'several kerosene cases, stained with potassium permanganate, and some chintz' for bookcases. The second-hand linoleum mostly conceals the holes where white ants have had their way, and the scattered goatskins feel warm and soft underfoot if she wakes at night in need of a glass of cool water from the canvas waterbag. Her husband took a scholarly pleasure in explaining that the water slowly leaked through the permeable canvas and evaporated, thereby consuming energy and cooling the water. In the washhouse out back, the carbide drum set in bricks with a fire beneath serves perfectly well as a copper to heat water for the washing. In a few weeks, nappies will give it a run for its money. Hanging from the ceiling, the Coolgardie safe of perforated metal allows air to circulate while keeping food from the reach of rodents and those sticky swarms of flies, still so foreign to her city sensibilities. When the baby arrives, she will need a crib – a crate perhaps, or an old suitcase. They will sort something out.

She sets the table and puts the finishing touches to tea. Tomorrow the weekly train from Kalgoorlie will deliver a fresh block of ice, wrapped in straw and sewn into a bag. The daily task of chipping a piece off still fills her with pioneering pride.

She hears the screen door creak open and bang shut. Her husband wanders into the kitchen.

'Hello, Gwennie,' he says.

He pecks her cheek and his glance falls to her belly. She flushes modestly. He walks over to the portable gramophone he bought with his first monthly cheque and loads his new record – *The Mikado*. Then he turns to my grandmother.

'There's a bush native just past the last house,' he says, adopting the town vernacular. 'The policeman took me to see him. The native's friends must have brought him. They've gone now. He's pretty crook. One of his lungs is absolutely solid with pneumonia. I gave him some syrup of garlic. Seems to work for all the abos' colds. There's nothing else I can do.'

'Poor man,' my grandmother says. 'Shouldn't he be in the hospital?' Not that the hospital amounted to much.

'He seems happy enough where he is and he'd hate it. His friends built him a shelter before they left.'

Later, my grandfather will draw a picture for my grandmother, a picture he will draw each time he tells the story to his yet-to-be-born children. In the picture, a semicircle of saplings shelters a man on a rough horsehair mattress in a central clearing. Beside the man stands a jar of water and a plate of food. In the opening of the semicircle, a small fire smoulders. My grandfather will explain, time and time again, how the saplings deflected the wind, and how the fire smouldered day and night, filling the clearing with warm, moist, eucalyptus-infused air. Even though the Aboriginal man was half-naked, he always seemed perfectly warm. My grandfather will tell how he never saw another Aboriginal person, but the fire never went out, and each day, fresh food and water appeared. My grandfather knew he could never have replicated those conditions within the basic confines of the local hospital.

In the smoky warmth of her kitchen, my grandmother clicks her tongue. She turns to the stove and ladles soup into a cup.

'At least take him this.'

My grandfather carries the cup of soup to the clearing and sets it on the ground. Every day, soup and syrup of garlic. After two weeks the man disappears.

'Must have got better,' my grandfather tells my grandmother that evening over tea at the kitchen table. 'No thanks to me, really. All I ever gave him was that syrup of garlic.' His eyes light up, as bright as the desert night sky. 'Must have been your soup.'

'How ignorant I was in those days and how ill-prepared by my training for the responsibilities that were mine,' Grandfather writes.

The responsibilities. Was Grandfather referring to his Aboriginal patients? His Aboriginal charges as Local Aboriginal Protector? Or was I overthinking a casually written sentence?

I waded through accounts of successes and failures until a story of a visit to Balladonia Station, to an Aboriginal man with a fractured femur. Grandfather's salary didn't permit a car. For home or station visits, he relied on the hospital secretary, who doubled as a taxi driver, or he rode 'in a cart or a dray, or hanging on the back of a motorbike' – the latter a mind-boggling image when I consider the staid and conservative pipe-smoking chess player of my memory. In this instance, Grandfather took the taxi. Once at Balladonia, after the 'kindly' folk fed him, he set to work.

> I put the old abo up in a Thomas Splint, gave him a shot of morphia, and loaded him on to a truck. He slept all the way to Norseman and was evacuated by rail to Kalgoorlie a couple of days later.

My grandfather's postscript? The Native Affairs Department took months to reimburse the £20 taxi fare, causing Grandfather to 'stoop', for the first and only time, to asking a politician to intervene.

I figured that Grandfather's use of the terms 'abo' and 'bush native', although disrespectful and dehumanising, was commonplace at the time and hardly indicative of evil intent. No mention was made anywhere of being the Local Aboriginal Protector. Perhaps because he never needed to invoke the title's powers and considered it irrelevant. Or perhaps because by the time Grandfather wrote his memoirs, the title seemed no more important than other titles he had since acquired, such as Flying Doctor and Medical Officer for the Roads Board, neither of which rate a mention in his *Writings*. Indeed, titles might have seemed of little consequence in the larger drama of his true passion – medicine.

For his services, Grandfather said he received a monthly pay cheque of £50. A salaried position at the local hospital meant he was a government employee, a position that might well have come with the title of Local Aboriginal Protector.

My father had little to offer regarding his father's history when I asked him, other than to confirm the pneumonia story. My father certainly had no knowledge of any Local Aboriginal Protector title and mistakenly thought Grandfather had been in private practice in Norseman.

I wrote to the State Records Office and received a reply. My grandfather was indeed a salaried government employee. The figure quoted was 300 pounds a year. The official confirmation increased the likelihood that I was indeed the granddaughter of a Local Aboriginal Protector.

The State Records Office also sent details from two archived letters. One, from the Norseman Hospital Committee to the Minister for Health in 1928, praised my grandfather as 'a very capable man whose skilful handling of some very difficult cases is making him popular ...'

The other letter, written in 1929 from the Inspector of Aborigines to Chief Protector AO Neville, responded to apparent allegations that my grandfather had sent Aboriginal people to Kalgoorlie rather than treat them himself in Norseman. The Inspector said he was satisfied that the medical conditions had required repatriation, irrespective of race, his conclusion bringing me relief nearly a century later. But the Inspector went on to comment on the lack of suitable accommodation for Aboriginal people at the hospital, 'neither a tent nor tarpaulin etc.' and my relief gave way to disquiet. I couldn't imagine the grandfather I'd known excluding anyone from hospital, although I could imagine him subjecting them to a carbolic scrub and perhaps barring visitors whose hygiene he considered not up to scratch. But this was the 1920s, when segregation was very much the rule in Australia: Aboriginal people were refused entry to public swimming pools, hotels, pubs and schools. They were not permitted to try on clothing in stores, and they had to sit at the back of the cinema – if they were even allowed in. If official policy excluded Aboriginal people from the hospital building because there was no separate ward for them, then Grandfather would have been a stickler for the rules.

In closing, the Inspector of Aborigines describes my grandfather as 'a young man, enthusiastic, splendid character, teetotal and humane. Can be trusted with natives.' A declaration I took to mean he thought Grandfather would treat Aboriginal people fairly, without exploitation.

Sister Girl

Many phone calls later, in February 2013, I secured a meeting for Greg and myself with Mr Sercombe. I collected Greg from his son's house in Perth. On the way to the airport for our second trip together to Kalgoorlie, I asked after his health.

'Not so good. They give me drugs to thin my blood again.'

'Because of the atrial fibrillation?'

I knew he'd had another episode of the fast, irregular heartbeats before Christmas. Untreated, the condition can cause a clot to form in one of the heart chambers. The clot could dislodge and travel to the brain, causing a stroke.

'Yes.' He sounded regretful. 'They pensioned me off.'

After an uneasy sleep punctuated by nightmares, I woke early the next day. I dressed and headed out for a walk. In Hannan Street, an Aboriginal man called out to me.

'Sister girl, sister girl.'

The man slumped on the pavement, his back against a storefront, legs stretched out in front of him. He tilted his head and cast me a sideways glance.

'Sister girl, I'm in from the desert.'

Despite his wheedling tone, he was somehow appealing – his face, though ravaged, was handsome with its broad cheekbones and I admired the crafty manipulation in his choice of address. Even without those benefits I would have stopped.

'You give me two dollars?' he said.

I thought of a friend who runs a coalition for the homeless in the US. She advises donations through charities only, for the multiplier effect on your dollar. But I didn't want to turn my back on a hungry man with money in my pocket. And first thing in the morning, it was probably food he wanted.

'You want something to eat?'

'Fish and chips, thank you, sister girl. And orange juice.'

'Where do I buy it?' At eight in the morning.

He pointed to a store in St Barbara's Square.

'And $5, sister girl.' He smiled to soften the blow of rapid inflation. 'For my children. For ice cream.'

I was buying into a moral dilemma and I knew it; the transaction is never simple. For the Wongi man, 'in from the bush', a full stomach. For me a share in the warmth radiating from those fish and chips. Fish and chips that cost money that, according to my US friend, might well have funded food for two Aboriginal people, three even, had I channelled it through a charity. And here I was undermining such charities, by providing positive encouragement for begging, in the form of an unhealthy breakfast, only to disappear back to my own life within days, leaving the Wongi man to fend for himself. It's an old argument, one people use to keep their hard-earned cash in their pocket.

But donating money through charity is no guarantee of relief to the less privileged. In many charities, layers of administration eat large percentages of donations. Perhaps, too, charities play a more important part in caring for the less privileged in the US, where, despite what my Molokai friend might say, the welfare system was not as good. In time, I would find an Aboriginal organisation – Wongutha Birni – run by Aboriginal people, to donate to, where my money could have a multiplier effect. But a different multiplier effect might have been in play that morning. The transaction, albeit brief, between a middle-class white woman from the suburbs and an economically deprived Wongi man from the bush might pay a less easily calculable dividend.

By the time the food was ready, the man had joined a loud, unruly group of Wongi people in the central rotunda of the square. I approached, holding out the white styrofoam container like a truce flag, which would seem to imply that I was approaching the enemy. I wasn't. But to them it might have seemed as if their enemy was approaching them, and I wanted to forestall any antagonism. The nearest woman grabbed the container. The man seemed to have forgotten his request for money. He seemed to have forgotten me. Relieved, I left. Giving food was one thing. But money? I didn't want to enable any paint-sniffing or alcohol habits, although I knew that in presupposing such habits I was making massive assumptions. I also knew that in buying food, I was freeing up Centrelink money for other, possibly unhealthy, expenditures. But who was I to criticise anyone over making unhealthy choices with their money? When I was younger and stressed by estrangement from my family (a story for another time), I knew all about prioritising 'comfort' rather than making healthy choices with my limited resources, and even then I knew my parents would step in if my situation became dire.

For me the question of giving money wasn't merely academic. I was fortunate to be financially secure, whereas the Aboriginal people I was interviewing lived constantly on the brink of poverty. While the decision to pay for their stories had already been made, I was yet to confront the issue of our vastly different resources, obvious because I could afford plane fares from Sydney and hotel bills. I'd already observed a more communal approach to money among the Aboriginal people I'd met than among my non-Aboriginal friends and family. When I first paid Greg, for example, he immediately settled a relative's unpaid account for his electricity to be reconnected. Inevitably, someone would ask me for help.

Considering the communal approach to money brings to mind the way bonds are often much stronger in Aboriginal families than in white Australian families. I think about Greg's story, of the aunt who had offered to care for him and his nine siblings after his mother attempted suicide and his father was jailed, even though she already had children of her own. How strange and tragic, then, that the children were convicted of being neglected and sent to live in dormitories in a mission.

My interaction with the man in from the desert left an impression on me for another reason. At some level, I knew it was all connected: the Mission, the prevalence of illness, the alcohol and drug problems, the violence, the bush camp, the hunger, the poverty. In my heart, I knew it all linked back to colonisation. As I wandered back to the hotel to meet Greg for our visit to Mr Sercombe, my hands still greasy and smelling of fish and chips, I just wasn't sure how.

Living by Faith

When I offered the rental car keys to Greg, he shook his head and said firmly enough to discourage me from arguing, 'You drive.' The man was a mystery. He liked cars, liked to tinker with them, and had described the male as dominant in heterosexual partnerships in his community. He'd also had little good to say about white people and still seemed suspicious of my motives, yet here he was passing on the chance to take the wheel from me. Why, I wasn't sure, but where I saw driving as a form of control, perhaps he saw overtones of *Driving Miss Daisy*. I also wondered if his refusal was his way of making clear the nature of our relationship, of underscoring our economic differences by emphasising that I was the one with the money for a rental car, the one in control. Not for a moment did I stop to consider why I, supposedly a feminist, wanted him to drive. In appealing to his masculinity, was I hoping to soften the man up? Was I overwhelmed by the prospect of yet another interview with a stranger? Or was I indulging in a misguided attempt to compensate for our socioeconomic differences? In any socially complex situation, it's as difficult to assess one's own motives as another's.

No matter what caused us both to act the way we did, we both knew any suggestion of my being in control to be an illusion. Greg's refusal to drive was in itself a form of control. And not the only one. He was the one with the story, not me. I could only ever be a voice. Or an echo. And while he knew I wasn't afraid to ask questions, he also knew I was unsure of my standing with him.

Greg planned to leave after introducing me to Mr Sercombe, so he would be free to express his opinions, uninhibited by Greg's presence (this was Greg's idea). Remembering Greg's references to Mr Sercombe as family, I was keen to see how they related to each other. For the first few miles, I bombarded Greg with questions about Kurrawang. After a while he seemed to tire of my interrogation.

'You know you can refuse to answer my questions, don't you?' I said.

'I can tell you now I'm not going to answer many questions about my missus.' He sounded determined, almost angry, and stared straight ahead.

'I understand.' I hesitated, unsure of what to say. He'd said 'many' but I knew I would never ask anything about his wife, rather than risk upsetting him with the wrong question. The man had suffered – was still suffering – enough. 'I'm sorry she died.'

We lapsed into our usual awkward silence until we pulled into Coolgardie, which was as forlorn-looking as ever.

Mr Sercombe's house was taking the full blast of the western sun on a sweltering day. I knocked on the curtained glass door. An elderly man slid it open. He was tall and lean, his short grey hair thin and parted low on one side, and had about him an air of elegance. His face was somehow familiar, like a half-remembered dream. He greeted Greg.

'Hello, Mr Sercombe,' I said. 'I'm Amanda … '

'It's obvious who you are,' he said, not unkindly, as he glanced at Greg.

Mr Sercombe seemed happy for me to address him formally, and I formed the impression that authority sat well with him. He stepped aside and invited us in to a small lounge area, open to the adjoining kitchen. He introduced a grey-haired woman in a simple striped dress, belted at the waist, as his wife Dorothy. I stepped towards her and started to explain my brother's friendship with Malcolm. She stopped me, explaining that she was Mr Sercombe's second wife, not Malcolm's mother. Both she and Mr Sercombe had lost their spouses in the past five years, she said, and had found each other in their loneliness. As I listened, I was aware of Greg talking to Mr. Sercombe. They spoke in cordial tones and Mr Sercombe seemed pleased to see Greg but, physical differences aside, I would never have mistaken them for father and son. The formality between them bore no resemblance to a familial bond.

Greg left and Mr Sercombe took a phone call.

'He's sick,' Dorothy whispered. 'He's got oesophageal carcinoma. It was diagnosed at the end of 2011. He was eighty-two at the time. They gave him four months to live, but eighteen months later he's still alive.' She paused and looked me in the eye. 'It shows the power of prayer.'

Dorothy offered me a cup of tea and put the kettle on. I took a seat at the small, Formica kitchen table. Nothing looked new, but the place was neat as a pin. A wood-burning stove stood alongside its gas compatriot. A chipped dresser housed a mismatched collection of china, salt and pepper shakers, and knick-knacks. A crocheted rug was draped over the back of a plain sofa in the lounge room and family photographs created a colourful mosaic on the walls.

Dorothy set the tea on the table and took a seat. I accepted a piece of the cake she offered, the same pale, shop-bought fruitcake I remembered from my childhood. Citing gluten intolerance, she took none herself. We chatted, and I sipped my weak, milky tea, which, combined with the heat, brought me out in a sweat. When Mr Sercombe had finished his call, he took a seat at the table. Dorothy left the table but remained nearby in the kitchen to fuss over a saucepan on the stove and, I guessed, to keep an ear open to the conversation. From time to time, she prompted Mr Sercombe. He spoke slowly and carefully, his expression serious, his hands, for the most part, resting on the table.

Mr Sercombe had been in his forties, married with six children and living in Teignmouth, in the English county of Devon, in the early 60s, when Mr Sharpe, Superintendent of Kurrawang Mission, had visited their local Brethren Gospel Chapel. Mr Sharpe had shown slides of elderly Aboriginal men, apparently uncared for, lying on the ground, and asked if anyone was willing to travel to Australia to carry out God's work. The missionary's words touched Mr Sercombe's heart.

'I said, "Lord, I'll go, I'm willing to go." A shiver went down my spine and I knew God heard.'

Two obstacles prevented Mr Sercombe heeding the call: his wife Alicia had heard no such call, and he had recently been appointed managing director of a business. Although he kept in contact with Mr Sharpe, Mr Sercombe began to think nothing would come of his vision. One day, five years later, his wife fell ill. Concerned, he rang her at lunchtime and she told him her ill health was a physical manifestation of a spiritual insight: they should go to Australia.

They sent their children off to pray over the decision, and when everyone agreed, sold the house, packed and left for the other side of the world, much as my ancestors had done over a century earlier.

Initially, Mr Sercombe worked for Mr Sharpe, doing whatever was asked of him. Each week he did the 'town run', collecting food supplies including five sheep, slaughtered and skinned, from the abattoir. Back at the Mission, it fell to him to butcher the sheep, 'the thing I hated the most'. He was also put to work in the garden.

'I was hoeing cabbages worth a few cents when I was used to the agricultural business, dealing with thousands of pounds.'

Mr Sercombe's arrival must have been an answer to Mr Sharpe's prayers: six months later he retired to Esperance. From there, he continued to oversee financial affairs and retained overall control of the Mission's operation. Mr Sercombe became Manager-elect under the Department of Native Affairs, not Superintendent as I had previously thought. Unlike my grandfather, Mr Sercombe had never held the title of Aboriginal Protector. Although he had cared for members of the Stolen Generations, he was not responsible for their removal from their families.

I asked if he had been a salaried government employee.

'No,' Mr Sercombe said. 'I lived by faith.' Nearly five

decades after his arrival in Australia, his English accent was still evident in his quiet, modest voice.

When he first arrived, he said, he paid board, whatever he could afford from the sale of his house. Since leaving Kurrawang, decades ago, he'd set up a ministry and continued to live by faith. Whenever something was needed – a house for him, houses for local Aboriginal people, a building for a church – prayers were offered up and apparently answered.

Living by faith sounded like an alien concept to me. It struck me as an enormous commitment. It took me a while to realise that some of the money Mr Sercombe lived on after leaving Kurrawang would have come from 'freewill offerings' during the church services he conducted in Coolgardie, or from tithed money. Government funding and donations were a source of income for the Mission. Mr Sercombe said the government contributed for each child. Unsure of the exact amount, he estimated $9 per child. In addition, local Brethren and other people donated money and clothing.

'Did people donate money specifically to fund the missionaries?'

'I can't answer that. I don't know. That was Mr Sharpe's side of things.'

Mr Sercombe seemed defensive, hurt even, as he explained the voluntary nature of his work, aware, no doubt, of the bad reputation many of the missions had acquired in recent times. He gave numerous examples of the good work done; for example, back in the 60s, new dormitories built using voluntary labour, mainly by fellow Christian Brethren from Melbourne. Poor public opinion, he added in a diplomatic tone, might be due to lack of awareness of the volunteers' sacrifices.

Judging by their modest house in a town that had seen far better days, and the simple routines of the Sercombes' lives, the size of the donations the Kurrawang missionaries received was minuscule compared with the tide allegedly flowing the way of some of the Exclusive Brethren on Australia's east coast and the television-happy American evangelists.

Mr Sercombe took time to consider his answers to my questions, and, having sought his agreement, I took notes as he spoke. Although I hadn't yet mentioned it, I intended to offer him the opportunity to review transcripts of our conversation, and anticipated changes. I liked the man, but he gave the impression of wanting to manage the Mission's image. I doubted very much that he would admit to any wrongdoing by either him or the other missionaries, although I already knew that it had taken place in the form of separation of siblings, restriction of parental access, and severe physical punishments.

I felt some reluctance at asking difficult questions of a dying man. I pushed on, however, thinking that his imminent death might encourage openness on his part.

By now, I was dripping with sweat. The air conditioner stood silent, a form of economy, I suspected. Even owning an air conditioner must have seemed a luxury to Mr Sercombe after the restrictions of a petrol-fuelled generator at the Mission. One of many hardships, as I was about to learn.

'The couple who lived in the boys' dormitory left and I was unable to find a replacement. Not everyone is willing to work voluntarily unless they are called to the work. So I looked after the boys.'

On a typical day he rose at 6 a.m. to supervise the boys as they dressed for school, made their beds and tidied up. Everything needed to be kept neat, he said, because the department could spring a visit at any time. Besides, he added hastily, cleanliness was important for hygiene.

At 8.30, the boys lined up for the school bus.

'My children lined up with them. I inspected them all. The Aboriginal children had to look as neat as mine.'

With the children gone for the day, Mr Sercombe opened the Mission store so the people from the reserve could buy their supplies.

'Then at ten-thirty I'd go and have elevenses with my wife.'

After 'elevenses' he carried out office work with the help of another missionary until lunchtime. Two Wongi women from the reserve helped with the laundry, ironing and mending.

'In return their sons were accommodated in the boys' home at no cost to them. After lunch I would start preparing the vegetables for the boys' dinner. I cooked for them.'

'You cooked for all the boys?'

'Yes. One or two of the boys used to help with the cutting up and so on. Greg was a good boy. He did the rosters for me. Some boys did the washing up and others cut the sandwiches for school the next day.'

On their return from school, the boys changed into play clothes, tidied away their school clothes and ate afternoon tea, usually biscuits (Mr McGeorge's raisin cushions). Dinner, as Mr Sercombe referred to it, was at 5.30 p.m. Whereas in the past the boys had eaten with the girls, in their dormitory, albeit at separate tables, now they ate in the recently completed and larger boys' dormitory, with Mr Sercombe and his family.

At bedtime, Mrs Sercombe read stories to the young ones, as did Mr McGeorge. I had no memory of Greg telling me this and realised only later that both these innovations took place after Greg had left.

Mr Sercombe confirmed that he switched the generators off at 9 p.m. for reasons of 'sheer economy'. Afterwards, he drove down to the reserve to check on the old men, perhaps the same old men in the photos Mr Sharpe had shown in England, who had drawn Mr Sercombe to Kurrawang in the first place. The men slept on mattresses on the ground in front of a fire. Mr Sercombe would position the metal heads of the unused beds behind them to act as fire guards.

He would return to his house at around 10 p.m. for a cup of tea with his wife.

'Then I went down to sleep in the boys' dormitory.'

'You left your wife and children to look after the boys?' This, too, must have been after Greg's departure.

'I couldn't leave them there alone.'

'Wow. A long day!'

'Yes. When I left the Mission and went to Perth for four months, I wondered why I wanted to sleep all the time.'

Up to that point, I had hesitated to mention the Stolen Generations children. The problem was, the more I talked to Mr Sercombe, the more I liked him. He seemed like a

Christian in the very best way, unlike the hell-and-brimstone variety I'd grown up with, and apart from our initial conversation, Greg had spoken well of him. But I was interviewing him to obtain a 'balanced view', in Greg's words, of the Mission and wanted to hear his take on the issue, so I decided to press on with my questions.

'There were two Stolen Generations families at the Mission, weren't there?'

'Oh, I think there were more than that.'

He named a man who came in from the Trans line, which was how the Indian Pacific railway was known, with a baby, reminding me not to use the man's name as he was dead. The man's wife had been drinking – had she endured removal from her family as a child? The statistics from the *Bringing Them Home* report bear repeating: between one in three and one in 10 Aboriginal children were removed from their families. Whatever the genesis of the wife's problems, the man had to give up the baby.

'I remember the two of us walking down the road, crying.' Tears sprang to Mr Sercombe's eyes now – the first sign of real distress I'd seen in this reserved and stoical man.

He went on to say he'd formed the opinion, at the time, that the parents and children should have been brought in together and placed in a house with a carer.

'But that would have required housing and we didn't have it.'

The solution he'd envisaged was in line with my childhood view of the missionaries. Was Mr Sercombe recasting past events in a more favourable light? Nothing in his demeanour suggested prevarication, and his voice was earnest. Does a dying religious man clear his conscience as he prepares to meet his maker? Or does he concern himself with the opinions of other mortals? I wasn't sure.

Dorothy was bustling around in the kitchen, and invited me to stay for lunch. I declined, not wanting to impose. Aware that time was running out, I mentioned that Greg had told me that Mr McGeorge had hit the boys with his walking stick. Mr Sercombe looked surprised. He spoke of another missionary who was 'slap happy'.

'He was young and childless. He didn't stay very long.'

Mr McGeorge, on the other hand, was 'only having a bit of fun'. As far as Mr. Sercombe was aware, no abuse had ever taken place. Later, Mr Sercombe would add to the transcript of our conversation, 'He [McGeorge] was a very kind old gentleman.'

I couldn't discount the possibility. Nor could I discount the possibility of the occasional overly hard whack with the stick. Kindness and corporal punishment were not mutually exclusive in those days. Mr Sercombe himself admitted that it had surprised him, on arriving in Australia, to find how readily teachers resorted to the cane. If he'd used it himself, he wasn't saying.

I asked Mr Sercombe about CAPS – the Christian Aboriginal Parent Directed School in Coolgardie. On the phone, Mr Sercombe had mentioned his position as a board member. He seemed to imply his position reflected the respect the local Aboriginal community had for him. Now, he told me he'd been the sole remaining white person from the original board. Only later would it occur to me that the Brethren Church had installed the board, not the Aboriginal community.

Finally, I broached the most difficult subject I wanted to raise that day: the practice of separating male and female siblings, a practice initiated by William Sharpe and perpetuated by Mr Sercombe. I spoke of Greg's anger. Mr Sercombe hesitated. Looked regretful.

'I can understand that. I would feel the same way if it had happened to my children. I didn't think about it back then.'

And that was it. No further comment.

Neither of us mentioned the policy of assimilation, which I knew about from Russell McGregor's writing. Put simply, it was a policy of bringing Aboriginal people into white Australian society. In the 1950s, the Commonwealth Minister for the Territories Paul Hasluck was an outspoken advocate. He believed that Aboriginal culture had broken down, leaving individuals 'stranded'. The need to 'protect' Aboriginal people had given way to the need to 'assimilate' them. One can interpret William Sharpe's rule of separating the genders as paranoia about potential 'immorality'. But the same argument can't be applied to quarantining older siblings from younger, as happened at Kurrawang, a policy in line with the aims of assimilation. Likewise separating children from their parents, distancing them from Aboriginal culture.

William Sharpe instituted the rules; Mr Sercombe was a man who followed orders. Still guilty, but a lesser charge? At the time of the interview, I liked to think so, although I knew the Aboriginal people who'd grown up at the Mission would probably disagree.

Still, few absolute truths exist in this story, just the memories of the characters, myself included, and how we acted.

What I did know is that while Mr Sercombe, misguided or not, devoted his life to caring for Aboriginal people, most of his non-Indigenous contemporaries lived white, insular lives. They couldn't be guilty of repressive behaviour towards Aboriginal people: they simply weren't there.

Mr Sercombe would make only one significant change to the transcript. He would revise his initial answer to my query regarding his dealings with the Department of Native Welfare, which was hardly critical in nature, to 'there could have been better understanding'. Other than that, he would correct the odd fact and replace an awkward word with a more sophisticated one, editing I readily accepted. The one exception was his substitution of the word 'home' wherever I had written 'dormitory'. He'd used 'dormitory' during our interview. Besides, Greg never referred to the buildings as home.

Dorothy was setting out plates and I was preparing to call Greg to collect me when he arrived. Dorothy reissued the invitation to lunch. I looked at Greg. He was as difficult to read as always. I thought he might enjoy a meal with this man who had figured so prominently in his adolescent years. A father figure who certainly wasn't treating Greg like a son now. I accepted Dorothy's invitation.

Mr Sercombe got up from the table and sat with Greg in the lounge. I offered to help. Dorothy asked me to set the table. She opened a kitchen drawer and lifted a dish-cloth from the cutlery.

'I cover it at night,' she said. 'Sometimes we get mice.'

She leaned over the stove, lifting a lid to check on the

meat, poking the potatoes to see if they were cooked, then draining the water from the pan into the sink. She was afraid there would be insufficient food and I felt bad for accepting. She said we'd make do, prompting an image from my childhood Sunday School classes in Wesley Church of Jesus multiplying the loaves and the fishes. Dorothy had no such miraculous means at her disposal. She mashed the potatoes, added water and mashed again, then added more water until the potatoes formed a sloppy grey mess in the pan. Mr Sercombe liked mashed potato, she said. I thought of his oesophageal cancer and realised mashed potato was probably one of the few foods he could easily swallow, the sloppier the better.

Dorothy served the meal – stew, beans, carrot and the mash – and we sat at the table, Mr Sercombe opposite me, Greg to my right. Mr Sercombe indicated he would say grace and held both hands out for Dorothy and me to take. Greg took Dorothy's other hand and then glanced uncertainly at me. I extended my hand and he took it and we bowed our heads. When Mr Sercombe had blessed the food, I contributed a low 'Amen'.

It was a companionable meal. Mr Sercombe washed small mouthfuls of food down with ginger beer, the only thing that helped, he said, and Dorothy filled any silences with her cheerful chatter. Greg and I ate. After the main course came pudding.

When we stepped outside, Greg, after having happily driven off while I talked with Mr Sercombe, handed me the keys.

Small Discriminations

For dinner, I had reserved a table at a restaurant midway between Kalgoorlie and Boulder with a reputation for a good steak – one of Greg's favourite foods. The room was large enough to accommodate a number of people, many of whom were miners. At a bar at one end, men sluiced dust from their throats with beer. Nearby, a wall-mounted television spewed news. Various combinations of black and white chairs around the tables seemed unintentionally symbolic of a racially divided town. Greg sat in a black chair; I took a white.

We ordered eye fillets, black peppercorn sauce, chipped potatoes and steamed vegetables. And water. Greg had told me he didn't drink, and although I longed for a glass of chilled wine, I abstained. Combined with tiredness and excitement, it would have made me tipsy, and Greg's good opinion mattered. Conversation got off to a slow start, not for want of effort. Unable to establish common ground, we quickly fell into our question-and-answer routine. It made for an awkward dynamic, as if I were casting myself in the inherently superior role of inquisitor. Greg could have asked questions of me but didn't. At the time, I put his reticence down to lack of interest in the boring white woman (novel thought!), only later learning that direct questions are not the Aboriginal way. 'We beat around the bush,' Greg would say, confirming the exhortation in Melissa Lucashenko's book.

I said I wanted to catch up with Bronwyn. Greg told me she had bought a cheap bus with native title money and was living in it with her family. He'd seen her 'up north' during the Christmas holidays. I was on my own when it came to Bronwyn, he said. Her life had been hard. Greg had his own challenges and didn't want to buy into hers.

'But she looks after her family,' he said, referring to her clan. 'In the bus. She looks after them.'

He was right. Despite losing her life partner, despite being evicted from public housing, despite problems with her children, despite poverty, despite circumstances I knew nothing of, Bronwyn took responsibility for her extended family more than most people I knew, myself included. She was a lesson in the coexistence of resilience and fragility. She was a lesson in the danger of typecasting.

I told Greg I wanted to go kangaroo hunting, not stopping to consider the appropriateness of my request. A hunt, horrifying as the prospect was in some ways, would be my 'omnivore's challenge'. Further, I fancied myself as a home-grown anthropologist, ready to pull on her boots, breach the pristine covers of her notebook and charge into the field in her quest for knowledge. After all, the book I'd long known I was writing – a strange hybrid of memoir and investigative immersion – justified such an expedition, right?

I couldn't bring myself to admit the complicated truth. Ever since our first meeting, when Greg mentioned hunting with Tony, I had subconsciously equated an invitation to join them with acceptance as a friend. Strange, I know, but hunting was important to Greg, and my mind, caught off-kilter between past and present, made that leap. Besides, hunting represented a return to the landscape, to a rekindled love affair with it.

Greg appeared to take my request at face value. Said he would see if he could arrange something with Geoffrey Stokes, the Aboriginal man with the same name as my brother, who ran a bush tucker tour business. Unintended or not, Greg's proposal to hand me over to a tour guide put me fair and square back in my outsider's place.

Alarming, really, how easy it is to blunder into racist territory. It's like dog shit. One minute you're walking along, happy as Larry, and the next you've stepped in it. You might not even know. You just walk right on, trailing a dirty mark and a stink. Whether I like it or not, you the reader might already have traced my tracks through these pages. After a few quiet moments enjoying our steaks, I told Greg I thought I remembered him telling me about a white ancestor. I asked him to confirm he had 'white' blood, as if 'white' and 'black' blood were two separate entities, titrated to varying ratios in human test tubes.

This then has been one of the most salutary lessons for me. I had read about what it means to be Aboriginal, that it had to do with family origins, with identifying as an Aboriginal person, with being accepted by an Aboriginal community and with identifying with country, a definition that still falls short. I knew too that sadly Aboriginal identity is often largely defined by white authorities. I was aware of the controversy and subsequent lawsuit over Andrew Bolt's inflammatory article, 'It's so hip to be black'. Yet here I was reducing Aboriginality to a mathematical equation, dangerously close to the bad old days when language such as half-caste, quarter-caste, and octoroon prevailed.

Greg seemed unperturbed by my blunder. Or he kept his perturbation to himself. Or perhaps after growing up in a mission and facing racism almost every day since, he was to some extent inured to its sting.

'I'm a fullblood Aborigine.'

And that's the other thing I was learning: some terms may be used by minorities about themselves, but not by those outside the group. I looked at Greg. I thought I must have misremembered his ancestry.

'So you don't have any white ancestors?' The big white cow continuing her rampage through the china shop.

'Well, yes I do. A white man raped my great-great-grandmother and she had a child. My great-grandmother. There's another white man from back then too.'

'You have white ancestors but you say you have no white blood?' I could feel myself frown, perplexed.

It didn't occur to me that Greg might not want to claim a rapist as a blood relative, and I'm impressed now at the restraint of his answer in the face of my well-intentioned blunder.

'I'm in denial.' He grinned.

With Greg's revelation in mind, I would later revisit a poem I'd seen in an anthology edited by Margaret Bull, my former headmistress, the woman who'd written her thesis on

Kurrawang's children. In 'The Wonggi's Lament', John Carins, a white English immigrant, gold prospector and sometime poet, assumes – boldly! – the voice of a Wongi man. After a few verses in which he laments the coming of white man in search of gold and the loss of Aboriginal land, he writes, deploying a lamentable verb in the process,

Our sons now ape the white man's ways,
Our daughters are things of shame
Ground into the dust by the combo's lust
Since ever the white man came.

The Wongi, in their 'slum camps of evil fame', doubtless did lament 'combos'. The term referred to white men, many married to white women, who 'forced themselves' (the phrase used in the anthology footnote) on Aboriginal women and girls. Small wonder Greg refused to lay claim to such a man as a blood relative.

Equally concerned about combos, for reasons related to 'preserving' the white race and breeding out Aboriginality, were government administrators. As with other areas of Aboriginal affairs, Western Australia's Chief Protector AO Neville, in conjunction with the Northern Territory's Cecil E Cook, led the charge. Neville found himself forced to abandon his initial squeamishness about miscegenation for the greater good of his desired white Australia: marriages between 'half-caste' women and white men were to be encouraged to promote gradual 'whitening' of the blood of future generations. Marriages between white women and Aboriginal men, on the other hand, were off the table, as were marriages between any 'fullblood' Aboriginal people and whites. Left to themselves – quite literally by being rounded up on reserves – the 'fullbloods' would eventually die out. Problem solved.

Or so Neville thought. The presence of Asian men in Western Australia's pearling industry presented an obstacle to Neville's purification plan. A paper published by Dr Katherine Ellinghaus of Monash University in 2003 on interracial marriages in Australia quotes travelling inspector and Aboriginal Protector James Isdell's evidence to the Roth Royal Commission: 'We are talking about a White Australia, and we are cultivating a piebald one.' (The 1904–05 Roth Royal Commission itself was tasked with reporting on the administration of the Aborigines Department, aspects of Aboriginal employment, the native police system, treatment of Aboriginal prisoners, distribution of relief and the general condition of the Aboriginal and 'half-caste' population.) Early legislation making non-marital sex between white men and Aboriginal women taboo gave way to clauses targeting marriage between Aboriginal women and Asian and Pacific Islander men, the two other groups of men likely to spoil Neville's dream of a white Australia.

The term 'part-Aboriginal' is still widely employed. Yet 'part-Aboriginal' is only a short step from the abhorred 'half-caste'. The word 'part' suggests a person is less than whole, fragmented, belonging to no man's land. Am I part-Australian with my South African, Scottish and English heritage?

Future conversations would reveal that the definition of Aboriginality was almost as perplexing to Greg as to me.

He seemed very aware of varying shades of skin colour. His final criterion turned out to be the broad, flat nose characteristic of many people of Aboriginal descent, the nose he has himself. Referring to people he saw on television, he said, 'We look at the nose and if it's flat, we say, "They're one of us."'

Greg and I hoed into our thick, juicy steaks. Between mouthfuls, I asked if he could expand on his encounters with prejudice.

'Happens all the time,' he said. 'This morning when I got to breakfast at the hotel, two servers come up to me. When you arrived later, only one server come up to you. I'm a Blackfella, see. They're expecting trouble.'

I nodded.

'We like the small discriminations,' Greg said. 'They remind us of who we are: Aboriginals.'

In my experience, people who are hyperaware of not wanting to discriminate or who are determined to prove they're not racist, perhaps because they know they come from a background of racism, are more likely to discriminate in this way. That was certainly the case for me during a trip on the *Zephyr*, the daily Amtrak service between Chicago and San Francisco. On day two, after a late breakfast, my husband Kevin and I made our way to the observation car. Only two seats lay vacant, an African-American man to the right of them, a white man to the left. Every other seat was taken. My thoughts accumulated, like peak hour traffic at an intersection: *If I sit next to the white man, I might look racist. If I sit next to the black man, I might look like I'm trying to prove I'm not racist.* I reached the seats and hesitated. My heart accelerated and seemed about to launch itself from my chest.

It was January 2010 and I'd put my research on hold for this holiday. The first evening and night on the train had passed without a hitch. I loved the dreamlike state induced by the constant motion; the apprehension, however delusional, that my tourist experience was as authentic as the unfamiliar foods such as grits, warm 'biscuits' (or scones as Australians know them), and chipotle black bean burgers; and the chance encounters with other travellers, most of whom were American, and all of whom until now had been white. But this seat choice confounded me.

The African-American man must have sensed our presence because he turned and smiled, the corners of his eyes crinkling. He was lean and fit-looking, dressed in jeans and a sweater, older than me. His wife, skin as fair as mine, blonde hair cropped, turned and smiled too. The man told me we were welcome to the seat.

My thoughts ground to a halt. I stood there and gaped, aware only of the African-American man and the white man and those two empty seats. I'd encountered African-American people on buses many times, and had never thought twice about taking the first empty seat. But this was somehow different: because he was the only African-American passenger (it was a different matter with the staff), my choice would be more obvious. At the same time, I knew I was being ridiculous. And I knew my stalled thoughts had something to do with my relationship to the past. The empty seats were equidistant from me, no help at all. My husband, unaware of my complicated internal drama, was no help either. Ever the gentleman, he stood back and waited for me to make up my mind.

The *Zephyr* swayed. I grabbed the back of a seat to steady myself. There was no steadying my thoughts, and my overheated heart threatened to stop in its tracks. Was the man aware of my turmoil? I decided to sit next to him to prevent causing offence, and then at the last minute, for no good reason, I changed my mind and parked my sorry and vacillating self next to the white man. My husband sat next to me.

Kevin is more extroverted than me and can charm most people. There's more: he grew up in an all-white neighbourhood. Back then on the *Zephyr*, before I embarked on this book (and before Kevin paid attention), he saw Australia's past racial injustices as a general issue, unrelated to him on a personal level. The minute he took his seat, he and the African-American man, whose name was Richard, started to chat. I wanted to slide into Kevin's slipstream and join the conversation, but engine noise made hearing difficult, and my seat was angled away. I sat back. Waited for my heart to slow. Ever the conscientious tourist, I tried to memorise every last inch of the scenery, which lives up to Amtrak's extravagant claims, the mountains and valleys a zigzag of extremes, buried in snow.

By late afternoon, the *Zephyr* had pulled into a designated rest station. Kevin and I made our way to the door. The conductor helped us onto to the platform. Warned us to take care on the ice.

The crystalline air caught in my throat, and when I

exhaled, vaporous puffballs bloomed before my face. Several people lit up cigarettes. To escape their smoke and the cold, we wandered into the tiny shop to browse glass cabinets of cheap turquoise jewelry, wire racks of postcards and stands of potato crisps. As we left the store, we ran into Richard and his wife Krista. If Richard had noticed my earlier awkwardness, he gave no sign. He lifted the camera slung around his neck.

'Let me take your photo.'

Kevin and I huddled close and smiled. After exchanging a few words with our new friends, we returned to the platform and stamped our feet in the snow to keep warm until the conductor's whistle summoned us back into the steel-womb safety of the *Zephyr*.

I did feel safe in the encapsulated world of the *Zephyr*: the carriages lined up neatly end-to-end, wheels solidly in place on the tracks; the invisible presence of the engine driver at the controls; signals keeping road-borne threats at bay; and the porter in his navy-blue uniform maintaining a nocturnal vigil, while I lay beneath regulation-issue blankets.

But that night, as I pressed my nose to the cabin window and peered out into the soupy darkness, despite feeling physically secure, my earlier feeling of discomfort persisted. I thought of the girl who played powdered-milk-tin volleyball, oblivious to her playmates' skin colour. I thought of the girl who had snuggled up to Bronwyn on a mattress in the back of a car. I thought that somewhere along the way, I'd left behind that girl to become a woman who panicked when faced with the choice of sitting next to a black or a white man, and I didn't want to be that woman. Only now, several years later, do I see the repeated pattern of the little girl hightailing it down the side path and keeping her distance from Aboriginal people in the street, and I wonder even more about the influences acting on that young girl. And only now do I see that the *Zephyr* incident wasn't all about me and how I felt. It was really about the effect my behaviour had on the man with black skin.

It's 7 a.m. the day after our black-and-white-seated dinner, and I'm crossing Hannan Street when I notice a police car by the side of the road. Two policemen are pulling on plastic gloves, blue like their uniform. An elderly Wongi man slumps against the Exchange Hotel. A clownish smear of fluorescent orange paint coats his lips. Orange paint gleams on the dark skin of his hands. He moves slightly, reveals orange smears on the seat of his pants and down the back of his legs. A fleeting memory comes to me of my mother's Kimberley photos of Aboriginal men in ceremonial ochre. An aching sadness for the Wongi man fills me.

He's likely come in from the desert, one of a number of Aboriginal people from the area to do so. Perhaps he's come to town in search of food, courtesy of that familiar story of non-Indigenous activities, mining in particular, encroaching further and further onto his hunting grounds. His first language is unlikely to be English. Having come from a remote area, he could well be illiterate, his job prospects virtually non-existent. I know, too, that the cultural need to travel to one of the alarmingly frequent family funerals could interfere with welfare payments that are in any case difficult to survive on. In a similar situation, I might fall prey to paint's hallucinogenic promises.

The policemen amble up to him. One says, 'What's going on, mate?' By now, I've passed the Wongi man and I'm lingering in front of the offices of the *Kalgoorlie Miner* newspaper. The policemen say they've received complaints; it's time to move on. They're taking *their* time, perhaps inhibited by their audience. Nearby, next to a verandah post, loiter two white men. They bandy around the word 'intoxicated'. Can't have an intoxicated Wongi man disturbing the patrons, for crying out loud! But the drunken white men who, months earlier, had leered at my 15-year-old daughter from inside the pub? A different story.

Greg had a coda to add to the pub story. In the 90s, he said, pubs in Kalgoorlie had security men on their doors. Their dogs were trained to bark at a tug of their leashes whenever an Aboriginal person walked past. Consequently, Aboriginal people stayed out of the pubs. If, however, Aboriginal people stopped by the bottle shops, the publicans were only too happy to unload their booze.

Richard's photographs from the *Zephyr* landed in my inbox a couple of weeks after our return to Sydney. He invited us to meet up if we returned to the United States, especially if it involved 'slow moving transport in the Midwest'.

The seat incident continued to trouble me. My indecision initially struck me as not exactly racist – in my eyes, Richard was neither superior nor inferior – but as something uncomfortably close: an over-investment in the most superficial of indicators – skin colour – as predicating racial difference. But really, what is racism if not basing a decision on perceived racial difference?

Not Just the Money

'Sister girl, sister girl.'

Today he was in a different spot, opposite the supermarket, a younger man by his side. I stopped and reminded the older man of our previous conversation. He claimed to remember. This time he wanted a pie and orange juice, his friend a sandwich and a Coca-Cola.

'And a tomato sauce.' The older man called out as I started across the road.

When I returned with the food, they thanked me. The older man bypassed the $2 request from our earlier encounter and went straight for $5.

'For ice cream. For my children.' His ingratiating look was practised enough to suggest it had worked before. I wasn't the only face of charity in town.

I hesitated and then handed over the money.

After several meetings, enough time remained for me to visit Bronwyn before dark. I drove out to Ninga Mia, an Aboriginal community just out of town, where she now lived. A young man gave me directions to Bronwyn's bus, several hundred metres down a track, under the trees.

It was more obstacle course than track, the roughest I'd ever driven. Clouds of powdery red dust billowed around the car. Precipitous hillocks in the middle of the track threatened to take out the undercarriage and I had to dodge potholes big enough to swallow a tyre. Not once did I contemplate abandoning the car and going by foot: I wanted my getaway car on hand. As I drew closer to the bus, I saw several parked cars. Closer still I recognised Bronwyn's youngest daughter in the nearest car; outside, a group of Aboriginal men; in the air the angry thump of ear-splitting music. I wound a window down and called out to the girl, who had an arm in a sling.

'You're Bronwyn's daughter, aren't you?'

'What?' she yelled.

'Bronwyn?' I yelled back.

The girl pointed towards the bus, a little further into the bush. The men shot me hostile looks and yelled. I had no idea what they were saying. A couple of them banged the roof of the parked car, a boom box on wheels.

'Get outta here.' A man's voice rose above the noise.

Fair enough, I thought. I'd ventured, uninvited, onto their turf. Still, my lily-livered heart blanched as I drove slowly towards the bus and parked behind another couple of parked cars, each with a few occupants. A group of Aboriginal people were gathered beside the bus, its angle obscuring my view of those near the door. A small child peered out the back window. Two puppies ran between the cars, barking – the ones I'd seen at the previous camp.

A woman came towards me. I said I was looking for Bronwyn. She told me to wait where I was, so I did. After a few minutes another woman yelled out to me and waved me towards the group.

'She's there,' she said. 'In the striped top.'

Bronwyn, in brown and white stripes, was cross-legged on a rug near the bus door, smoking. She held cards, as did the other women near her. She looked at me, said nothing. I made my way through the group. As I approached she took $5 from another woman and slipped it into her wallet.

I squatted next to her, and we hugged. She introduced me to the others as her best friend from school, a bit of a stretch but I wore the compliment with ridiculous pride. She told me she didn't live there. Seemed embarrassed by her surroundings. I told her I'd tried without success to ring. She said her old phones had stopped working, showed me her new one. A number of the people were drinking, to relieve, as I'd come to understand, the tedium of no job prospects, the discomfort of no proper accommodation and the pain from an intimate acquaintance with loss that stretched back through generations. Even so, the atmosphere felt threatening. I told Bronwyn I couldn't stay. We arranged to meet the following day at Monty's.

In retrospect, even more threatening than the atmosphere were the misconceptions or – let's get it straight – the prejudices that made me feel threatened in the first place. Would I have been so quick to leave a group of well-dressed white people drinking on a picnic in the bush? My behaviour was no better than the hotel servers who'd rushed up to Greg. And in this instance, blaming it on my childhood was a stretch. But having recognised my error, I must move on. Self-flagellation would serve no useful purpose to anyone, least of all Bronwyn and her friends. The best thing for me to do is to resolve to do better next time.

At Monty's the next day, 30 minutes ticked by as I sipped a decaf cappuccino and waited. Bronwyn still hadn't shown up. Either she'd forgotten, or she didn't want to see me or had no transport. In a strange sort of way I had come to know where I stood with Greg: we shared a mutual respect and he tolerated me while keeping his distance. At least that's how it seemed. With Bronwyn it was different. I didn't yet trust our friendship. She might have felt the same way because our time together had been brief.

A white bus pulled up near the museum entrance, further up Hannan Street. I thought it might be Bronwyn. It wasn't. I decided to give her another five minutes. And then five more. Another white bus cruised down Hannan Street. It turned right and pulled up alongside the café. Aboriginal people sat in rows inside the bus. Around me, the waitresses stood together, eyes trained on the bus, bodies slightly tensed.

Bronwyn came in, wearing the same striped top, her hair in a tousled braid. While she sipped a Coke, I polished off the remainder of my toasted cheese sandwich. Several of the bus's occupants climbed out onto the pavement. Raised voices drifted inside.

I asked after Bronwyn's family. She told me all four of her sons were currently in jail.

'In Kalgoorlie?'

She shook her head. 'Perth.'

They'd apparently committed misdemeanours in jail and were sent to a more secure facility. Bronwyn worried about them, too far from their people.

Every so often, someone from her bus would wander into the café and Bronwyn would yell at them in one of the languages used by the Wongi people or Wongutha nation, and they would leave. Clearly, she led the group.

I asked after Arthur, the brother I'd met at the bush camp.

'He's in jail.'

'What for?'

'Drunk driving. Silly bugger. I told him he should've parked under a tree.'

A funeral was taking place the next day, northeast of Kalgoorlie. Bronwyn planned to drive the family in her bus. They needed a new back window to keep the dust out. Bronwyn had no money. This was it, in a beat-around-the-bush form – the request I'd been expecting. I thought again of my American friend: 'Don't give to individuals.' I understood the buying power of money, its use to lobby governments for change. I knew all about that damned multiplying effect. But where was the charity to buy my friend a new window? Under the table, I counted out $400 and handed it over. I hoped I was doing the right thing.

We stood to leave. Hugged each other. Bronwyn whispered into my ear.

'Goodbye, sister.'

For the Record

Greg and I exited the security area at Perth Airport. I wanted to ask if I could record a short interview with him. I'd not done this before, and because he still seemed wary of me, I was apprehensive about his response. To be fair, what I interpreted as wariness might well have been something else – reticence around a married woman, for example, or his own assumptions about what the relationship between interviewer and interviewee should look like. Before I could change my mind, I blurted out the question:

'Can I interview you on tape? To make sure I've captured the way you speak?'

'Sure,' Greg said. 'I'll just get my luggage.'

He headed to the carousel while I bought coffees and found seats. I pulled out my tape recorder, a small pencil-shaped object, and switched it on.

'Do you prefer to be called "Aboriginal" or "Indigenous"?'

'"Aboriginal." Anyone who is born here could be regarded as Indigenous.'

I asked a few questions about the Mission. Greg sounded awkward, too aware of the tape recorder. After a few minutes, I turned it off.

'So what do you think of the white woman asking all

the questions?' I smiled and kept my voice light, wanting to relax him to the point where he might open up more.

'Well, the Aboriginal people in Kalgoorlie are talking about you.' His smile was knowing, teasing even.

'What are they saying?'

'They're saying she might be all right. But they're not sure yet.'

It was the closest he'd come to expressing his opinion of me.

I asked his plans for the coming months. He said he wanted to fix up a secondhand four-wheel-drive.

'Go walkabout,' he said. 'I like my own company. I like to think.'

I thought of the bush and the red dirt, the campfires and the night skies, the animals and birds, and the potential conversations with this thoughtful man who shared my passion and whose connection to the land was doubtless even stronger than mine, and I felt a longing for his friendship and to share the trip.

Greg seemed in no hurry to leave, and for once the mood between us felt relaxed and comfortable, as if a seed of trust had germinated. Again, I felt an urge to venture into unexplored territory – unexplored until now because Greg had seemed uncomfortable with the subject.

'In your online Stolen Generations testimony, you mentioned that some Aboriginal girls were raped at the Mission.'

Greg nodded. His facial muscles tensed.

'By Aboriginal boys?'

He nodded again. Cautious. In the crowded, noisy

terminal, it suddenly felt as if we were the only people there.

'Are you sure?'

'I saw it.'

'You *saw* it?'

'Some of the older boys asked a couple of the girls to meet them in the shed behind the boys' dorm. Two of the boys come and got a couple of us younger boys. They made us watch while they raped the girls.' Greg looked troubled, sad.

'Did anyone report the rapes?'

'No. Not as far as I know.'

'Are they all still alive?'

'I think the women are. They've had difficult lives. One of them went bush, to the desert. The men are all dead.' Greg shifted uncomfortably in his seat. His tone suggested he was of the opinion the men had received their just desserts.

More details would come in dribs and drabs over the next couple of months. Greg would describe the boys as 'smart alecs', in their early teens. Two of them were largely responsible for the bullying he had endured in his early years at the Mission, which explained the fear Greg had expressed about the Wongi boys, and the sense I'd had that there was more to the bullying than Greg had let on. Now he told me that the rapes took place at night. The older boys forced the two younger boys to keep a look out for the missionaries. Upset by what he saw happening, Greg 'tried to stop things'. The older boys threatened to kill the younger boys if they disclosed their secret. Greg thought the missionaries must have known of the rapes from the blood stains on the girls' dresses. He said he no longer felt guilt. It had happened a long time ago, and the rapists had died young, in their early twenties: alcohol-related deaths.

'They was brutally belted. The whole thing, it was part of what we as boys went through. I don't know what you'd call it.'

A result of intergenerational trauma is what Judy Atkinson, Professor of Indigenous Australian Studies at Southern Cross University, might call it. In *Trauma Trails,* she writes that contrary to some strands of feminist analysis, in Indigenous families, rape can be considered both a violence and a symptom. To begin to understand rape as a symptom, one must look back to Aboriginal culture before colonisation.

Aboriginal people lived in extended family groups within larger language groups. As with any group of people, violence was part of life. It was dealt with through time-consuming and arduous ceremonial processes, of which connection to country was an important part.

Enter Captain Cook (or Lieutenant as he was at the time) and, later, Captain Arthur Phillip and his band of white settlers. They raped Indigenous people and inflicted other violences. They stole land, displacing the original inhabitants, who were often forced to move to land inhabited by other Aboriginal groups, which led to more conflict. They banned languages, ceremonies and traditional lore and imposed Western law. They introduced disease, alcohol and Western food. Together these influences 'fractured and dismantled' gender and age relationships. In the absence of normal ceremonial practices, healing and resolution never took place. Succeeding generations inherited the dysfunctional effects of trauma. Other Indigenous populations, notably in Canada and the US, have suffered similar, well-documented fates.

In the early twentieth century, medical doctor and ethnographer WE Roth said he'd found 'no instance of what would now be called child abuse by white society … ' among the Queensland Aboriginal people he'd worked with. Judy Atkinson reports that many of these people had already suffered severe trauma. She goes on to posit that the intergenerational effects of the trauma had yet to overwhelm traditional child-rearing practices.

So what had changed by the time four older Wongi boys forced the two younger boys to witness two gang rapes in Kurrawang? Using Atkinson's reasoning, the answer is obvious: the trauma had reached a tipping point in Aboriginal communities due to child removals, continued racism, a high rate of imprisonment, the dependency effects of welfare, aggressive government interventions and the use of drugs and alcohol as coping mechanisms.

Having reached a tipping point, the trauma led to child abuse. Any child who observes or suffers violence or abuse can learn to inflict the same, a recognised phenomenon in both non-Indigenous and Indigenous populations worldwide.

We must therefore understand the crimes the Kurrawang rapists committed in the context of white settler history. The rapists doubtless came from traumatised communities. What community in the region had not suffered repeated trauma since colonisation? The rapists likely witnessed or suffered trauma themselves. They might also have suffered beatings at Kurrawang. It's possible they were sexually abused. We now know such abuse was common in missions such as Retta Dixon in the Northern Territory. With adults spread thinly at Kurrawang, a situation Mr Sercombe had acknowledged, a bad apple could easily have taken advantage of their charges.

The children were virtually prisoners. They rarely or never saw their parents. Apart from school and the occasional outing with white friends, they remained on the mission. They couldn't have been more vulnerable. Although I have been unable to uncover any evidence of sexual abuse on the part of any of the Kurrawang missionaries, most of the potential witnesses are dead, which in itself speaks volumes about the Mission and its legacy.

That day at Perth Airport, Greg named neither the girls nor the boys involved, and I didn't press him. He would tell me more if and when he was ready. Much as I wanted justice for the women in the form of acknowledging the crime, I was wary of conducting a kangaroo court on the page by naming men who were no longer alive to defend themselves.

What I did do was tell Greg that in being forced to watch the rapes, he had suffered abuse. 'Did you tell anyone when you were assessed for compensation as a member of the Stolen Generations?' I asked, not that any amount of money could ever compensate for a childhood that had been stolen in more ways than one.

'No,' Greg said. 'I didn't know it was abuse. Even if I had, I wouldn't have said anything. If you admitted abuse, you had to do mandatory counselling, and I didn't want to do that.'

Within Talking Distance of Town

'You know Grandfather was an Aboriginal Protector, don't you?' my elder brother Graham had said. Was it true? I couldn't let the question rest. Almost as pressing was the question of why I was so obsessed with someone else's actions, even if we were related. Someone now dead.

The town hall housed the *Kalgoorlie Miner* archive. Hours ticked by while I squinted at microfiche back copies, searching for confirmation of Grandfather's title of Local Aboriginal Protector during his time in Norseman. The archivist conducted his own mini-search and informed me of Grandfather's position as medical officer of the Kalgoorlie Roads Board after his move to Kalgoorlie in 1929.

I unearthed an article written in 1950 by a local politician to the Minister for Native Affairs. It referred to the illness the Sharpes had mentioned, an epidemic among Aboriginal people, apparently resulting in them 'clogging' hospital beds. The politician suggested a mission with its own hospital. Finally, I had found the original motivation for Kurrawang: fear of catching disease from Aboriginal people, rather than concern for their welfare.

Interest piqued, I followed a trail of letters in subsequent editions. The trail led me to a letter to the editor from a member of the Kalgoorlie Roads Board, which contained verbatim a report my grandfather had presented to the board. My grandfather had said:

> In view of the recent statement by Dr. C. B. Cook, of the Commonwealth Department of Health, that the aboriginal population of Australia may be regarded as a reservoir of infection which could endanger the health of the community, it is pertinent to draw attention to the fact that such a state of affairs has recently occurred in our district. Some scores of natives, entirely ignorant and neglectful of the most elementary rules of hygiene, camped for a time within talking distance of the town. A severe outbreak of respiratory disease broke out among them, with some deaths. By good fortune the severity of this outbreak was not experienced by the white population. The danger of gastro-intestinal disease was possibly more real with the filthy state of their humpies in the scrub, the absence of sanitary precautions, and the constant stream of natives coming to town to cadge food with their backs covered with flies. Again we were fortunate to escape serious trouble. It is, however, considered to be within the scope of this board to urge the Government to take such steps as will prevent a recurrence of such risks to public health in future.

To say Grandfather's report was a shock would be like calling the Super Pit a pothole. Almost impossible to reconcile the man who prepared such a report with the genial chair-rocker I knew as a child. Or the slightly addled but always polite and often funny old man I knew as an adult. In addition, my previous assumption that my grandfather would never have excluded Aboriginal patients from Norseman Hospital, unless officially required to, was looking shaky. I wanted to reach for a scalpel and excise his every last gene from my body. To put it mildly, I had temporarily misplaced my internal compass.

According to the letter writer, my grandfather recommended banning Aboriginal people from within a 10-mile radius of Kalgoorlie and Boulder. At 10 miles, Kurrawang was too close.

I'm in Mullumbimby, where we're privileged to own a *second* property (while across the country Bronwyn is unable to rent, let alone own, one), at my beloved wooden desk, a relic from my childhood. The desk's cubbyholes brim with pens, staplers, antihistamine packs, old letters and diaries, china dogs and a hoard of other treasures containing secrets from the past. I select a cowrie shell covered with Aboriginal-style dot painting that had belonged to my mother. I hold the shell to my ear and listen for the sound of waves. I try to imagine the person who painted the shell. And fail. Just as I fail to imagine the man my grandfather was back then.

When I've shared the gist of my grandfather's report with friends, many have been quick to spring to his defence. 'You have to consider it in the context of the era,' they say. And sure, it's easy enough to imagine Kalgoorlie's patriarchs mulling over grandfather's report. On one side of the tracks they might say to their little ladies, 'Did you see the doctor's report? He's hit the nail on the head about the abos. And by the way I'll need a pressed shirt for tonight.' On the other side of the tracks it might be, 'Pass me a tinnie will you, love? Didya cop what the doctor said? Good riddance to bad rubbish, if you ask me.'

But what exactly are my friends saying? That a reservoir of racism existed at the time, like the reservoir of respiratory virus my grandfather feared, and therefore to succumb was almost inevitable and not one's fault? Difficult then to explain people like activist Mary Bennett, who was alive in the same era as my grandfather and was an advocate for Aboriginal families. Had she acquired some form of moral immunity, and if so, how?

If racism was a virus, it came in different strains. In a letter to the editor, in which he agrees with Grandfather's proposed ban, a resident of Lamington, the most affluent Kalgoorlie suburb at the time, pretends to do so with the best interests of 'the Aboriginal' in mind. The resident concludes that there are worse problems in town: 'He may be filthy in our eyes, yet in the bush he always makes a fresh camp to have temporary cleanliness. In his natural state he is as clean as any other animal in its natural state. However, when he meets the whites and the drink etc., he slips back rapidly and then becomes filthy.' Responsibility for recent health issues, the Lamington resident believed, lay with the municipal rubbish tip. 'The aborigines could not be half as filthy, have half as many flies or carry half as many germs [without it].'

Impossible, now, to dismiss the question my younger self asked of my father in the hospital car park as one child's random question. If the past is the foundation for the stories of our lives, helping us to locate ourselves in a moral universe, then I was spinning in outer space. My past, my family's past and my town's past were all turning out to be quite the lie. I wasn't sure what the implications were for the future.

A week after my grandfather's food-cadging histrionics appeared in print, the newspaper published an address by Mr Sharpe to his congregation. He referred to 'the present plight of natives', and condemned my grandfather's suggestion, saying, 'Given the proper facilities and guidance … the native could prove himself capable of becoming a useful member of the community.' *Capable of becoming a useful member; as clean as any other animal*: Aboriginal people were either lesser or lacked humanity in the eyes of Sharpe and the Lamington resident. And of course, in wanting to set up a mission, Mr Sharpe had his own agenda: he wanted to care for 'sick' souls as well as sick bodies, and the younger you got access to those souls, the greater the chance of success.

During his address, Mr Sharpe showed coloured lantern slides, including one of a map representing Aboriginal populations in the various Australian states. Mathematics ultimately worked against Western Australia's Aboriginal people. With over a third of the total Australian Aboriginal population (26 000 of 76 000) within the state's boundaries, clashes between Aboriginal people and settler Australians were inevitable. Likewise, problems within the Aboriginal population were bound to be magnified compared with other states. A situation ripe for men like my grandfather, essentially decent men with limited understanding and foresight, to come up with ill-conceived solutions for what they saw as an Aboriginal threat to more civilised white society. If those ill-conceived solutions have been recorded in some universal balance sheet, I like to hope that the many occasions my grandfather provided free treatment to Aboriginal people have kept him in credit. Certainly, no evidence has turned up of any wrongdoing on my grandfather's part in his two-year role as Local Aboriginal Protector. But if Grandfather's balance sheet isn't in credit, then shouldn't I inherit his debt along with the education and economic advantage that came because of his privilege?

What my grandmother thought of my grandfather's recommendation I'll never know. My father and an aunt both remember their mother giving food to Aboriginal people when they came 'cadging' at the laneway gate. My aunt remembers a table and chairs kept in the backyard for the purpose. As for my grandfather's comment regarding flies on Aboriginal people's backs, my father laughed when I read it to him. He said, 'I think we all had our backs covered in flies.'

Making a Little Child's Life Complete

A black-and-white photo of Beverley Joy Noble, whose name I encountered early in my search for my former school friends, appeared in the 18 March 1954 edition of the *Western Mail*, with an article written by Estelle Sharpe, 16-year-old daughter of Kurrawang's superintendent Mr Sharpe. Beverley Joy's mother Bowee was the woman found in a Kalgoorlie gutter, dead three days.

The photo reveals only Beverley Joy's head and gingham-clad shoulders. A white bonnet, like a nurse might have worn, looks out of place atop her dark curls; she has large, clear eyes and chubby cheeks, and she's smiling.

Estelle explains that Beverley Joy's family is itinerant, wandering from place to place, eating bush food such as goanna, rabbit and 'bardies' or witchetty grubs (thick white wood-eating moth larvae, a couple of inches long), instead of nice food 'like your dear Mummy gives you every day'.

Beverley's family visited the Mission several times. The missionaries gradually convinced Beverley's father Gidum of all the advantages they could offer his children: proper food, clean clothes, a bed and eventually school; 'everything that make [sic] a little child's life complete'. Gidum and Bowee relinquished their children, Owatta (five) and Gadilgah (seven), as their names really were, to the missionaries, who renamed them Beverley Joy and Ron. 'That day,' Estelle writes, 'was one of the greatest in Beverley's life.'

She describes five-year-old Beverley Joy as being three feet two-and-a-half inches tall, and 'generally bubbling over with life'. She wore dirty rags and the soles of her bare feet were 'hard and cracked with walking on the hot ground in search of food'. Although upset at the separation from her parents, Beverley 'could not speak for joy' when the missionaries presented her with clean clothes after a good scrub. 'The new wonders in life ... soon wiped away any tears that may have fallen.' When Beverley Joy sat at the table for tea, 'her eyes grew big with astonishment and she nudged her brother alongside and said, "*Nungana*, Ronnie! *Myee bullgana*!" which means "Look, Ronnie! There is plenty of food!"' Pyjamas, a clean bed, and a tiny sleeping doll topped off the day's excitement, prompting Estelle to wonder at Beverley's dreams that night.

Fast forward to Christmas and even greater joy in the form of another dolly. The 'climax', however, awaited just around the corner: Beverley would go to school. 'As small as she was she realised the possibilities that lay behind that word ...' Then came the golden opportunity in a town where gold is all: Beverley was chosen to present flowers to Queen Elizabeth, during her visit to the goldfields as part of her 1954 Coronation world tour. Happiness apparently shone out of Beverley's big brown eyes. March 26 would be, Estelle concludes, 'a really wonderful and great day for this little girl who six months ago was living in the bush'.

For me, Estelle's letter was a lesson in blinkered optimism and the arrogance of taking liberties in interpreting another's thoughts, something I'd been guilty of myself, especially with Greg. Still, I found myself wondering, as I had when I first encountered Bowee's story, if, given her ineligibility for child endowment (a government subsidy given to parents for each child, requiring the family have a fixed address) and the circumstances at the time, the children did indeed stand a better chance in their new life. Sure, Estelle exaggerated in her description, and her testimony doubtless embellishes the truth (Beverley Joy's speechlessness on being scrubbed and presented with clean clothes probably owed more to her lack of English than her joy, and even if she could speak English, she probably would have taken more than a few hours to adopt Gadilgah's new name, Ronnie). Estelle also minimised the pain the children would have felt at being separated from their parents, their language, their culture and their country. But the bottom line was that they were fed and clothed and had a roof over their heads. They were safe. Or so it seemed.

By contrast, in several years' time, Beverley Joy and Ronnie's younger brothers would die from infectious diseases while in their parents' care. Estelle's prediction that school might well give Beverley Joy and Ron their best chance for a reasonable future was also feasible. It wasn't fair, but it was the way it was. Or so I thought. However, I wondered why the missionaries didn't let the family live on the reserve rather than removing the children from their parents.

Zealous in their beliefs, the Brethren believe in the Creation story. They practise full-immersion water baptism, and discourage the inclusion of Father Christmas and the Easter Bunny at Christmas and Easter. They are meant to reject the notion of earthly riches, and prefer to gather in modest buildings. Many tithe 10 per cent of their income. Some churches require women to cover their heads to receive communion; most do not permit women to become pastors or teach from the pulpit.

In practical terms, the missionaries needed formal guardianship in order to receive child endowment to fund the children's care. But there seems to be no good reason why the rest of the family could not have stayed in the nearby reserve, close to their children. There's certainly no evidence that the parents ever refused such an offer. I can only conclude that the missionaries wanted guardianship over the children's souls, too, and that goal was more easily achieved by separating the children from their parents.

Activist Mary Bennett, the family's advocate, writes of Beverley Joy and Ronnie's residence in Kurrawang, 'It does make one wonder what these friendly responsive little mites could achieve if only they were allowed to maintain their kinship and humanity, the sense of touch, the sense of a vigorous community seeking good for all.'

Despite Bennett's misgivings, the material aspects of Beverley Joy's life did improve, although who knew what she made of her prospective presentation to the Queen, the lead-up to which was thoroughly covered in the press. According to newspaper reports, daily curtsey practice ensured that when the Boulder mayor and town clerk visited Kurrawang, they found Beverley Joy to be of 'good demeanour and deportment'. Boulder councillors donated white cloth for Marjorie Sharpe to sew a dress fit for a princess for Beverley.

The Queen arrived in Western Australia during a polio epidemic, necessitating special precautions to protect her health. Only outdoor functions were allowed and, according to reports in the *Australian Women's Weekly,* no one could approach within six feet of the Queen. Her food, including peeled grapes, was specially prepared. The staff aboard the Queen's ship, the *SS Gothic*, provided her salads, 'washed and prepared in a very slightly antiseptic solution that was quite tasteless'.

A photograph in the Tasmanian *Mercury* records the 'really wonderful and great' presentation day. Accidents of birth determined who would present and who would receive. Beverley Joy, in a wedding-cake dress with a flamboyantly flared skirt, tried to present her bouquet, but the Queen refused and, in accordance with the polio protocol in place for everyone, gestured a white, elbow-gloved arm towards a stool that had been placed in front of her for the flowers. Beverley Joy, the *Women's Weekly* reports, 'soon got the idea'.

In effect, Estelle Sharpe wrote the outback version of the Cinderella story. Greg had told me he knew Beverley Joy. I remembered him telling me she'd gone to the desert. He'd sounded unsure, evasive even, and his tone prompted me to suspect a flaw in the fairytale.

Balay Wadjela

In a Perth food court, Greg's voice came from behind me: 'I'll have three chickens with feathers on.'

Not a single visit to my home town in four decades and now I couldn't stay away – this was my third trip to Western Australia in under a year.

I cringed. Felt myself flush. Tucked my phone in my bag. No psychology degree needed to understand a joke at my expense. Several times now, I'd petitioned Greg to take me kangaroo hunting, an idea I still didn't realise was ill-considered.

I turned and found Greg looking pleased with himself. Behind him was Ben, one of Greg's adult sons, whom I'd previously met at the airport, and Cheryl-Lee, Ben's wife. I stood to greet them. Ben hugged me. He looked like a slimmer, younger version of Greg: tall, with an athletic build and a short black goatee. Unlike his father, he smiled easily and often, his default setting. I wondered if he took after his mother in temperament or if life had leached the joy from Greg. Cheryl-Lee, a pretty woman with her hair in a short, wavy bob, had a reserved air, perhaps because she was unsure of my motives. Greg offered his hand.

'Don't I get a hug?' I said, teasingly.

Greg grinned and hugged me.

'Adrian's on his way,' he said, referring to his older brother. Greg had warned me that Adrian was 'scary'. I wasn't quite sure what that meant.

Ben and Cheryl-Lee went to buy coffee; I resumed my seat and Greg sat opposite. A kangaroo hunt was on for the weekend, he said: Geoffrey Stokes, the man my father had delivered the same day my younger brother was born, would take us. I wondered why Greg didn't just take me himself, but said nothing. Ben returned without Cheryl-Lee, and sat next to Greg.

I asked Ben's permission to take notes. He agreed. Stroking his goatee, he told me he was born in Coonana, a remote Aboriginal community east of Kalgoorlie. He learned to speak in English and Wongi, as he put it. After a few years, the family moved to Kalgoorlie and then Perth. I asked if he'd experienced racism at the schools he'd attended. He said he'd encountered it most on the football field.

'When we played an all-white private boys' school, I used to get called "a fucking black c".'

'He was a *moordjich* footballer.' Greg's eyes glinted. Really good, he explained. Better than talented. 'The black thorn in their sides. We used to give the other team's parents hell.'

Around us, a cleaner pushed a mop and people with takeaway cups dawdled by.

'Ben, you're a Noongar man yet you grew up on Wongi land. How do you identify?'

'That's a hard question to answer.' Ben sounded hesitant. 'I grew up Wongi. Mum and Dad taught us Wongi ways. It wasn't their fault.' He spoke of the laws permitting his father's removal, the time spent in Kurrawang, and, as with Greg, his voice took on a more rehearsed tone. 'I grew up Wongi but my cultural lines are Noongar,' his voice firm now. Then, in a quieter voice, 'It's hard.'

'Do you speak Noongar?'

'No.' More hesitation. Followed by a note of defiance, 'But I'm a proud Noongar man.'

Ben said he was 22 before he knew his father was a member of the Stolen Generations. 'We never sat down and talked about it or nothing but I found out. I knew he lived in the Mission but I thought it was a boarding school. I used to wonder why I never saw photos of Dad when he was young and I used to wonder where his parents were.'

'What do you feel about what happened to your father?'

Ben opened his mouth and then closed it. Clenched his hands together. Blinked rapidly. He brushed Greg's thigh with one hand, a tender gesture, received passively by Greg, who I'd yet to see show anyone much physical affection. People drifted past us, lugging trays and coaxing toddlers.

'It makes me sad. And angry. The government shouldn't have done that. It was wrong. But we were taught at home that Aboriginal means "first". I'm proud of who I am. The Mission, it's not part of who we are.'

'I taught my kids *balay wadjela*.' Greg shot me a hard look. 'It means "Watch out for the white man." I teach the same thing to my grannies.' By which I knew he meant 'grandchildren'.

The gap between us seemed to me to widen to the size of a football field, or the Australian continent or the ocean between Australia and England. The background noise seemed louder than ever – voices rising and falling around us, like waves at the beach, chairs scraping, coffee beans being ground. I felt suddenly tired and out of breath, as if I'd been climbing a steep incline. As if I was watching something I'd chased disappear from view. The Ugle men watched me quietly. I thought I glimpsed compassion in their eyes, an understanding that I was yearning for something that could never be mine: a sense of closeness, if not belonging, to the Aboriginal people who I had grown up with in Kalgoorlie, and recognition as being different to the run-of-the-mill white person, which of course I wasn't. As I was slowly realising, I was very much a product of a particular time and place. Those issues aside, my previous sense of Greg's wariness might not have been so wide of the mark after all. I was forever doomed to be a white person, someone to watch out for, and as such, any sort of meaningful personal reconciliation, a reconciliation with positive outcomes for both sides, seemed unlikely.

Pulling his phone from his pocket, Greg wondered aloud where Adrian was. Ben turned that easy smile on me. I wanted to explore his identity a little further.

'What does red dirt mean to you?' I said. People who had grown up around Kalgoorlie tended to have an almost visceral connection to the red dirt.

'Red dirt means home.'

'Because the soil's different in Noongar country, isn't it?' I looked at Greg.

'Oh yes.' He sounded definite. 'It's grey soil.'

'So which is home for you?'

'Red dirt,' Greg said, without missing a beat. 'You can smell it.'

Ben looked off to his left and laughed.

'Uncle Adrian's hiding behind a pole. He's looking at us.'

I looked off to the side and saw nothing but pillars and pale-skinned shoppers. I turned back to our table; if Adrian wanted to check me out, let him.

A few minutes later, Adrian appeared. His long grey beard, buzz-cut hair and stocky, ex-boxer's build imparted a fierceness to him; even without Greg's warning, I might have found him scary. Adrian sat next to Ben, so that all three men were lined up opposite me. I felt like an interrogator, which might have been their intention, at least subconsciously.

'Do you mind if I record our interview?' I asked, after introductions.

'You can use that,' Adrian said in no uncertain terms and pointed to my notebook.

I left my tape recorder in my bag.

'Feel free to ask me questions, too,' I said.

'All right. Tell me what you're up to.' And there it was: *balay wadjela*.

I launched into my elevator pitch. But the elevator ride was long, as if between platforms in a subway system, and this time I could hear the rehearsed tone in my own voice. When I finished, Adrian looked at me.

'I had a stroke and my attention span's like this,' he said matter-of-factly, holding his index finger and thumb an inch apart.

'Sorry.'

'Who else are you talking to?' Interested, not aggressive.

'Whoever I can find. Mostly your family.' I thought

of Beverley Joy Noble and asked if either Greg or Adrian knew her current whereabouts.

'Joy Noble?' Greg sounded like he'd gouged the words from stone. 'She's dead.'

I whipped around to face Greg. Stared at him, confused. Hadn't he previously told me Beverley Joy was in the desert?

'Does she have any surviving family?'

'She had a younger sister at the Mission,' Greg said. 'Catherine Noble. Lives in Coolgardie.'

I scratched a note, mostly to buy myself time to recover my composure, and then turned to Adrian.

'Are you angry about having grown up in the Mission?' I asked.

'I'm angry at our own people for not coming for us.' A scathing tone. And then, wonderingly, 'They didn't know where we were.' His anger at his parents and the fact that they had no way of finding their children existed in parallel like the train tracks in and out of Kurrawang.

'So what was Kurrawang like for you?'

'It was the best thing that ever happened to us, don't you think?' Adrian gave Greg a questioning look. I blinked in astonishment. Looked at Greg. He said nothing, face neutral, arms crossed, mouth firmly closed. 'If we hadn't of gone to Kurrawang, I reckon we would be dead now. It taught us so much stuff about living. It taught me everything I know now.' Adrian paused and reconsidered, then said, 'I really taught myself.'

'What did the missionaries teach you?'

'To be tight with *boya*.'

The three men laughed.

'Boya?'

'Money.' More laughter.

Again, Greg's expression gave nothing away. He was letting Adrian speak for himself. Adrian said his memories of the Mission were mostly bad. Once, he swore at Mr Smith, the missionary in charge of the boys' dormitory.

'He hit me across the left ear. It went through me eardrum.'

The next day, Mr Smith sent Adrian to Mr Sercombe, who told Adrian to remove his shirt for a beating.

'It was a big stick.' Adrian spread his arms wide to demonstrate the length, and approximated the diameter by curving thumb and index finger and pressing their tips together.

'We was in the Mission store,' Adrian said. 'Mr Sercombe had room to move around. But I was a tough one. I wouldn't cry. I did this.' Adrian screwed up his face and crossed his arms tightly in front of his chest, muscles bulging with effort.

'How many times did he hit you?' Mr Sercombe hadn't mentioned using the cane.

'Until I dropped. At least ten. He was on a mission – oh, Kurrawang Mission.' Adrian's tone was light, as if any effects of the beating were only skin deep, and chuckled at his joke.

I couldn't bring myself to join in. I remembered thinking Mr Sercombe was less guilty than Mr Sharpe.

'Why did you swear at Mr Smith?'

'Don't remember.' A pause and then a deadpan look. 'Smithy must've said something wrong.'

'What was the swear word?'

'Dunno. Think I said "bloody". But it woke me up and I never swore again.'

I asked Adrian if he knew about the rape Greg had mentioned.

'You told her about that?' Adrian swung round towards Greg.

Greg nodded.

'Shame on those boys,' Adrian said, still looking at Greg, all seriousness now.

'One of them girls was Joy Noble.' The words seemed to fall from Greg's mouth of their own volition.

The food court noise faded into the background, and time seemed to slow. In my mind's eye, I saw a chubby-faced girl in a white bonnet smiling at the prospect of presenting flowers to a white queen. I remembered wondering if life would be better for her in the Mission than on the streets with her parents. But it seemed she'd swapped one trauma for another. And according to Judy Atkinson, trauma inflicted by humans was worse.

'Shame on them,' Adrian repeated. Frowning, he shook his head.

'Do you remember what happened to Beverley Joy or the rapists?' I asked.

'No. We said nothing.' Shame and regret weighted Adrian's words, and I suddenly realised he had been the other young boy, forced to watch the rape with Greg.

Ben was silent, his eyes saucers. I scribbled more notes. Decided against questioning Greg further in front of his son.

'Do you remember your father visiting you at the Mission?' I asked Adrian.

'I blinked.' An unwavering gaze, full of challenge. Like he was daring me to pity him, daring me to think he cared. But, really, I had no clue.

'You mean the visit was short?'

'Yes. All the blame goes on him. The night it happened, he was the one fighting. Not Mum.' He looked at Greg. 'I run around the house four times that night. Remember? To get away from the police when they come to get us.'

'I was under the bed with Diane.' Greg shook his head.

'I was going to make him pay.' A reflective tone with a hint of regret. 'But when I got out of the Mission, he was a cripple.'

'Did you ever run away?' I asked Adrian.

'No. I was the number one son. After I got that hiding I wouldn't do anything wrong. We used to help find the runaways.'

He and Greg looked at each other and laughed. I watched on, struggling to keep up with their quicksilver banter.

'Yeah,' Greg said. 'We were the trackers. Big time. Running through the bush.' More self-mocking laughter that seemed to resonate with meaning, laughter that only they could share. 'We were the bloodhounds.'

'What did you have when you left the Mission?'

'They gave you nothing when you left. You got a goodbye.' He looked at Greg. 'We are the last survivors, our mob.'

Talk shifted to the trip Greg and I were taking to Kalgoorlie. Adrian looked uninterested.

'Do you like going bush?' I asked him.

'I'm urbanised.' Again the mocking tone as he deftly upended my stereotype, although I didn't understand what he'd done until later. 'Why would you spend hundreds of dollars on a bed and then go and sleep on the ground? And why would you go hunting when you can buy food?' He gave me a goading look. 'Or steal it?' he said, tipping another stereotype into my lap.

Ben's wife Cheryl-Lee appeared, bearing hot chips and gravy. She, Ben and Greg ate at one end of the table. I asked Adrian if I could buy him some lunch.

'No.' He looked me up and down. 'But you look like you could use a feed.'

'I'm fine.' I could feel a flush rising. He was toying with me, the do-gooder white woman who knew she couldn't bite at the Aboriginal man's jibes. I retreated into my notebook.

'How's your daughter?' Greg asked Adrian. 'The one over east. When's she coming home?'

'She's not coming back. Not since she got awarded a trophy,' Adrian said, scorn razoring his words.

The three men laughed their private laughter and I wanted, desperately, to crack their fraternal circle.

'What did she get the trophy for?' I asked.

'She married a white man. He's the trophy.' Another unwavering, challenging gaze, tone slightly belligerent.

'I want my grannies to marry Noongar people,' Greg said. 'To keep the culture alive.'

He explained that he and Adrian were regarded as tribal elders. I registered my surprise. I hadn't thought of Greg that way. Noel Pearson and Pat Dodson, yes, but Mission kids from my old school? The crystals in my kaleidoscopic view of the past rearranged themselves into yet another pattern.

'I don't like being called that,' Adrian said. 'I don't feel like I've earned it.' He paused. 'Maybe it's because I didn't say anything about the rape.'

I tried to tell him that the rape wasn't his fault. I wish I had told him that in being forced to watch, he too had been the victim of sexual assault. But I'm slow on my feet in a conversation, so I didn't. Adrian just gave me a blank stare, as if nothing I said would have any relevance.

Adrian and Ben needed to leave. I thanked Adrian. He started to walk away but stopped to talk to Greg. I grabbed my bag and hurried after him. I wanted to shake his hand, to acknowledge that the interview had gone well, and as a sign of respect.

The two men finished talking. I extended my hand. Adrian fixed me with his gaze. His hands stayed at his sides. I could feel the others watching.

'Oh no.' My outstretched hand felt large and clumsy, and still I persisted. 'You're going to leave me hanging?' I assumed a light-hearted tone, in keeping, I thought, with the sarcastic humour Adrian had adopted during our interview, but I could feel my white, white skin flush. 'You're not going to shake hands?'

'No,' he said. 'It's not traditional.'

I withdrew my hand.

'I'm sorry,' I said.

Adrian left and while Greg spoke to Ben and Cheryl-Lee, I stood to the side and reflected on how a little more knowledge of customs would have proved more useful than a truckload of good intentions. I felt exhausted from the effort of negotiating the undercurrents swirling beneath our conversation. In one way or another, we'd all confronted our younger selves. Me with my stereotypes; Adrian and Greg with their references to bloodhounds. I wondered if their self-mocking laughter was a form of *balay wadjela*, a way of keeping a distance between their adult selves and the young Mission boys inhabiting white-man stereotypes of Aboriginal people and carrying out white man's work. In many ways, all the Aboriginal children from the Mission left with more baggage than they thought, but Adrian and Greg had gone a long way with the unpacking.

To my surprise, Adrian returned the transcripts I'd sent later without any corrections. I asked Greg if Adrian was really okay with the 'trophy' quotation.

'Yeah, he is,' Greg said. 'His kids said, "Dad, you can't say that." He told them it was his story and he'd say what he wanted.'

Adrian's attitude to his parents reminded me of Greg's. In fact, it was Adrian who took Greg to the Autumn Centre, a retirement home for destitute Aboriginal people in Perth, to visit their father John Jackamarra, after Greg left the Mission. Adrian asked his father if he recognised the young man. Smiling, the old man said, *Bon-nor-rn*, the name Greg's mother chose at Mogumber Mission, where he was born. Before the nurses told his mother to pick an English name. Before she chose Gregory, after Gregory Peck.

Greg had stared at his father, seeking recognition, but saw only a crumpled-up old man in a wheelchair, a burned-out shell like the occasional car wreck in the bush around Kalgoorlie. Not someone he wanted as a father.

Adrian also took Greg to see his mother, the only time

Greg saw her, in the East Perth Cemetery, where she lived. Her clothes were ragged, her hair matted. Dirt crusted under her nails and she smelled of sour alcohol and body odour. There among the tombstones, the phrase the white boys had used sprang to his mind, *You stink. And you never came for us,* the other phrase playing over and over. His mother looked like a vagrant, an alcoholic. He kept his distance. Refused to talk to her. Wouldn't wrap his arm around her shrunken frame or kiss her weathered cheeks.

But from then on, he always insisted that, although they lived apart, his parents remained in a de facto relationship. 'He knew where she lived,' he would say, in what sounded to me like a desperate need to believe that the central core of his parents' love survived what was essentially the heart-imploding abduction of 10 children. A loss with no rituals to shape or contain its particular grief.

In 1981, John Jackamarra died. A year later, as if her partner's death broke the last thread tethering her to life, Elizabeth Ugle died. Greg attended both his parents' funerals. Dry-eyed, he watched as each coffin was lowered into the grey soil at Karrakatta Cemetery, in Perth. Later, he would be unable to identify their graves.

Greg told me that the missionaries and the other Aboriginal residents of the Mission seemed more like family to him. When any of them died, he grieved openly. By his late fifties, he had attended too many funerals. Of the 140 or so Aboriginal people who had lived at Kurrawang during the 50s, 60s and early 70s, only 15 were still alive. Had they all survived, the oldest would be around 65. Alcohol was a common cause of death, either through illness, violence or accidents. Greg himself didn't drink. Memories of his father's violence remained and he still connected the destruction of his family to his parents' drinking.

In the shopping centre food court, Greg said goodbye to Ben and Cheryl-Lee and rejoined me.

'Want to talk to Robbie in Mandurah?' He sounded enthused, rather than angry over the handshake incident as I had expected.

Feeling humiliated and drained, and hungry and thirsty to boot, I mostly wanted to crawl into a hole with some food, but yes, I wanted to talk to Greg's youngest brother, Robbie. I hadn't known him as a child, but I was keen to learn as much as I could of what life was like at Kurrawang, and Robbie, the youngest Ugle to be placed in the Mission, would have different memories to his brothers' and sisters' … and fewer of his parents.

'When?'

'Now.'

Mandurah was 70 kilometres away, not exactly the next suburb. It took me a few minutes to locate my rental car. I pointed it out and after giving Greg the keys, walked to the nearby McDonald's for a hamburger. When I returned to the car, Greg had assumed his usual position in the passenger's seat.

Happy Home

Mandurah had been on steroids in the decades since my last visit. The almost comatose seaside village had hypertrophied to a sprawling city, the second largest in the state, with new subdivisions swelling like bulging muscles alongside arterial roads. We wound through a maze of eucalypt-lined streets, past a school to a cul-de-sac. We parked and walked up a short driveway to a brick house, sitting higher than the street, a square of lawn out front. On the porch, a couple of sleek-looking cats stretched out on chairs.

Greg rang the doorbell. Robbie and his wife Ruth were out at the shops, but a young man Greg introduced as Ruth's son, who looked to be in his twenties, invited us in. I said, 'Hello', and kept my hand glued to my side. Once bitten ... Smiling, the young man extended his hand. I shook it. A couple of teenagers likewise shook hands. Greg chatted with them about school, work and family matters while I stood awkwardly to the side. In the background, a television blared.

A car door slammed, and Robbie and Ruth appeared, laden with shopping bags. Ruth's thick-lashed eyes fixed on me. She invited me through to the kitchen. She and

Robbie set the shopping down on an island bench, and Ruth offered me a cup of tea, which I accepted. Ruth put the kettle on. She tucked her waist-length dark hair behind her ears. Her gold hoop earrings glinted in the light. I watched her movements, dazzled. Ruth offered us a seat.

Greg and I lifted upturned chairs from the table, set them in place on the sparklingly clean floor and sat down. In front of a second, smaller television with the volume low, two sleeping toddlers were curled up on child-sized foam mattresses. Ruth passed out mugs of tea and returned to unpacking and putting away the groceries. Robbie took a chair opposite me. He was shorter and slimmer than Greg, compact and muscular, with a gentle, almost tentative manner. He leaned forward, braced a hand on a knee and jiggled his leg, running the fingers of his other hand through a white goatee. Everything about him evoked a nervous court witness called to the stand, and Greg had warned me Robbie was likely to weep. I decided then and there not to tape the interview or take notes. Instead, I'd rely on my memory and make notes that night. Robbie could correct my draft.

I started by asking Robbie for any memories of life before the Mission. He had none. Not a single memory of his parents. And of his early Mission years?

'It was so long ago.' He spoke quietly and hesitantly.

Robbie's memories of Kurrawang kick in when the missionaries Robert and Doreen Smith became his carers. He was living in the house set aside for younger children, away from the older children, unaware of his brothers' and sisters' existence.

'I thought the Smiths were my parents.' He briefly

lifted his gaze to meet mine. 'We called them Mum and Dad. I didn't know they weren't my real parents until a kid at school told me I was Black.'

'You didn't know you were Aboriginal?'

'No. I thought I was just like the Smiths.'

Greg sat statue-still. In the kitchen, Ruth ran water in the sink, focused and watchful. On the television, cartoon characters played out dramas of their own in front of the sleeping children.

'When did you find out about your brothers and sisters?'

'When I was a teenager.' Robbie took a deep breath. 'After most of them had left.'

The air felt thick, as if saturated with unwept tears. No one stirred. Then a cat stalked into the room. All eyes fixed on it. Relieved, I commented on the number of cats. Robbie hastened to explain that they were all micro-chipped and neutered. In his voice I thought I detected traces of the young child he'd been, fearing a beating for a crime he hadn't committed. I confessed to owning four dogs and two cats, all of dubious micro-chipping status. Robbie still looked tense. The cat slunk away.

To ease the atmosphere, I questioned Greg about the missionaries' cars. Robbie sat up straighter. He and Greg batted car names between them: a white Ford escort sedan, a purple Holden Commodore, an Austin tray top to transport the girls, a Bedford tray top for the boys.

'All of them got a new car every year.' Greg sounded critical. Then his tone grew thoughtful. 'They must have leased them.'

Or living on faith had worked well.

After Mr Sercombe's departure from Kurrawang, the

number of boys dwindled, as public awareness grew and government policy gradually shifted. Robbie and some of the other boys were moved to a government-funded Mission house in Boulder called Pukulari.

'There were ten of us,' Robbie said. 'The Smiths were in charge. We still called them Mummy and Daddy.' His voice imitated a child's for the parental diminutives, and he laughed, a hard, bitter sound. 'Every night I used to scrape Mrs Smith's feet with a thing like a spoon.'

Ruth, who had been listening from the kitchen sink, rounded the bench, *exploding* from behind it.

'She used to sit up there like Queen Bee with all her slaves.' She sounded indignant and her eyes flashed.

Robbie nodded. 'While she watched *Bellbird*.'

A wordless exchange passed between Robbie and Ruth and she took up the story.

'One boy lay on his stomach so she could use his back as a foot rest. Someone else rubbed her back. Someone else cleaned her fingernails.'

'I had to scrape her …' Robbie hesitated, looking at Ruth again, and I got the impression he drew on her strength, 'her calluses. With one of those special razor things with a handle. She had a big, fat foot too. If you didn't do what she wanted, she whacked you.'

Ruth said they had visited the Smiths once to ask for an apology for their treatment of the boys. 'She denied the pampering,' she said. 'Didn't say sorry. Said she wouldn't say anything else. She was scared we'd use it against her.'

On the floor, the two little children slept on, snuggled close together, limbs akimbo, faces smooth and peaceful, surrounded by family.

Greg, who had been sitting quietly, spoke up. 'The one good thing with Robbie in Pukulari was I could visit him. That's how he found out about us.'

Greg and Robbie started to reminisce with each other. Ruth returned to the kitchen, tidying things away, washing dishes or cleaning the bench; I'm unsure. I remember only an impression of deliberate busyness.

'Thanks for the tea,' I said. She nodded. She told me she and Robbie met in Kalgoorlie when she was 20.

'I grew up in Norseman Mission,' she said. 'We understood each other. I found a bank book among his possessions, one of those school bank books you put money in each week. Remember them?'

Robbie and Greg stopped talking. I nodded.

'Sure.' I vaguely recalled unknotting coins from a handkerchief to present to someone behind a trestle table in the school hall, who stamped my (blue?) bank book.

'I wanted to know if there was anything in the account, so I asked him.'

'I didn't know,' Robbie said. 'Didn't know anything about it. It was just with my stuff when I left Pukulari.'

'Everyone in high school got a cheque for $3 each week from the government,' Ruth said. 'Remember?'

I shook my head. 'Perhaps that was after my time.'

'It was an incentive to stay in school. I took Robert into the Commonwealth Bank and they said there had been money in the account but it had all been withdrawn a couple of years earlier. There was only one signature on the account – one of the missionaries'.'

'Do you know which one?'

'No.'

I turned to Robbie. 'Did you ever see the cheques?'

'No. I never saw them.'

I nodded. Grey light slid in through the south-facing windows, beyond which stood a caravan – home to Ruth's brother. The sleeping children still hadn't stirred.

Ruth walked over to a cupboard. She took out a small bundle of paper, which she brought over and placed in front of me.

'These are the only photos we have of Robert from before he was eighteen.'

I spread out the collection: 10 Aboriginal boys, a couple of white teenage girls, and two white adult women packed into an old white Holden with no roof; a group of younger boys and girls with a joey; a group of boys in their Sunday best – striped or Fair Isle sweaters or cardigans, neatly combed hair, parted to the side.

I picked up a photo of a white couple, flanked by five adolescent Aboriginal boys in long trousers, jackets and ties.

'This from the Pukulari days?'

'Yes.' Ruth pointed at one of the boys. 'That's Robert. And the Smiths.'

Robbie stood to the far right in the photo, facing the Smiths, not the camera. His expression was alert, as if awaiting instruction. Doreen Smith, a large, no-nonsense-looking woman, smiled blandly at the camera through thick glasses. Behind her, Robert Smith's smile was enigmatic. He was slim and looked self-contained, his posture unbending.

Greg moved closer and sifted through the pile. He singled out a photo and held it up for my inspection. 'That's Adrian,' he said, pointing to his older brother in the back row. Then he pointed to four other boys in the back row, taller than Adrian. 'They're the boys that did the rape.'

Together we stared at the photo, at the young black faces, no more than 16 or 17, no hint in their expressions that they were about to or had already committed a horrible crime. Or that they had probably suffered severe trauma themselves as young children. Then Ruth gathered the photos and put them away.

I asked Robbie if he'd seen much of his parents after he left the Mission. He shook his head and started to speak but his eyes moistened and tears spilled down his face. Shoulders shaking, he bent his head and shielded his face with one hand, as if he could hardly bear to observe the void in his life; his other arm he pressed across his chest, in front of his heart.

'Get me some tissues, Ruth.' His embarrassment leaking through gruffness as porous as a sieve.

No one spoke. Ruth passed him a handful of tissues. He lifted his head and dabbed his eyes.

'I saw Dad once or twice.'

'And your mother?'

He shook his head.

Again, no one spoke. Tears streamed down Robbie's face.

'Did you receive compensation, Robbie?' I asked. 'Did it help?'

'Money doesn't last.' Robbie dabbed his eyes. 'What happened to us lasts forever.'

In the claim he submitted for compensation as a member of the Stolen Generations, Robbie writes of Robert Smith strapping the Pukulari boys over the palm if they hung the washing out incorrectly. He writes of Mr Smith whipping their shirtless backs and bare legs with a hose. And of Mrs Smith flooring him with a punch.

Pukulari, I later learned, is Wongi for 'happy home' or 'happy rejoicing'.

After leaving Pukulari, Robbie carried his few possessions, obsolete bank book among them, to Greg's house in Boulder, where Greg lived with his wife, his brother Tony, and two brothers Robbie had no recollection of having previously met: Alfie, the oldest, and Adrian. Robbie wanted to stay there, but Greg arranged for Robbie to stay in a hostel. Decades later, in a letter to me, Robbie writes:

> I didn't want to leave so much that I was angry and feeling like no one needed me. He [Greg] put me back in an environment with rules, doors locked, curfews, and with other boys from the Mission whom I knew, and again I felt alone and lost and nowhere else to go.

Robbie had felt unable to share the painful memory with Greg. Greg, when I shared Robbie's letter, with Robbie's permission, was shocked and mortified. Said his house was already bursting at the seams, and Robbie was a hotheaded young man with a liking for V8s. Greg barely knew how to be a brother, let alone a husband to his wife and a surrogate father for his youngest brother. He did the best he could for Robbie in finding him the hostel. But Robbie wanted the family he'd only recently come to know.

Robbie did also say good things came of his three years at the hostel. He learned the importance of finding work and how to manage money, and the hostel managers never hit the boys. And then in Ruth he found the family he craved. Now, on feeling 'heard' by Greg and reaching some understanding of how overwhelmed Greg had been, he felt some measure of peace. The work of healing and forgiveness was theirs alone.

After leaving Robbie and Ruth, Greg and I zipped back towards the city in my flash yellow rental car. I was exhausted and for a few miles cocooned myself in my thoughts. To break the increasingly heavy silence, I asked Greg to describe the job he thought he might get, along the Trans line, cutting sandalwood. He said his first task would be to repair some machinery that had lain idle and to organise the workforce. The men would need a few days in Kalgoorlie to take first aid courses, to comply with occupational health and safety requirements.

'On the subject of health, how's yours?' I glanced over at him.

'Keep your eyes on the road!' he growled.

I stole another glance at his rigid shoulders, the stony set of his face. He stared ahead at the freeway, a mining-boom road unfamiliar to me. I reminded him I was a doctor and asked medical questions almost as a reflex.

'Went in one ear and out the other,' he said in a softer tone (of having been told I was a doctor).

He told me he'd gone for a check-up. The doctor had asked his expectations of treatment. Wanted to formulate a medical plan.

'Not going back there again.' His voice hard-edged once more.

'So you've decided to live with the risk?'

'Yes. I don't want to sit around the house, Amanda. I don't want to become a nobody.'

To a certain extent I understood his decision. This was a man who had covered many miles as a truck driver, who had always earned a living and who loved to go bush. To have that denied him would be to have the life he'd claimed bookended by loss. Besides, he's a betting man, likes a flutter at the races or an afternoon at the TAB with his brother or friends. Sets himself a limit. Takes a calculated risk.

But in this risk analysis, his calculations were incorrect. He wasn't a nobody. Not to his family. Not to the community he served as an elder. Not to me. I felt as if I should have pushed him. Instead, not wanting to lay myself open to another rebuff, I concentrated on driving, on the way the car handled so well, sensitive to my touch even at the higher speeds the Kwinana Freeway permitted.

My mind turned to Adrian. I steeled myself for a reprimand and asked Greg why Adrian had refused to shake hands. Greg said it was different for everyone. Older Aboriginal people were more likely to cling to tradition. And touching could have different meanings. After a death, people gathered in a sorrowing circle. When someone joined the circle, they shook hands with the bereaved or laid a hand on their heads. I nodded. Pressed my lips together. Thought of Henry and Grace, Adrian's children, killed on their way to collect their older sister from work when a stolen car involved in a police chase had ploughed into their car. Adrian hadn't mentioned them in our interview and I'd not wanted to stir up his grief.

'I hope you're happy with what I've been writing,' I said, after a short silence.

'If I don't like what you're writing, I'll just walk away from the project.' Greg paused and continued to stare straight ahead, not meeting my eyes. Breathing deeply. 'I won't say a word. I'll just walk away.'

It felt like we were back to square one.

That evening, I dined with my brother Geoffrey and his wife Connie. After dinner, Geoffrey took me into their spare room. From a bookshelf, he picked up a long cardboard poster container and an old sweets tin of accumulated 'treasures'. He carried them out to the living room and we sat side by side on the sofa. Geoffrey opened the tin and lifted the contents out one by one: army reserve badges, loose photos, a map of New York from a trip 20 years previously, and a do-rag from the same trip.

My brother had been visiting my husband and me in the Upper West Side apartment we lived in at the time; my husband's work had taken us to New York. One day my brother ventured out alone. A couple of elderly Black men approached him. Asked if he would mind a bundle wrapped in the do-rag, supposedly containing money, for a few hours. The men spun a garbled story of a non-functioning bank account. Said they would sort out the problem and return for the money. Asked my brother to hand over a couple of hundred dollars as a demonstration of trust. He complied. Memory of the exact chronology of the transaction is lost to me, but at some stage and for some reason, my brother got in a car with the men and off they drove. Eventually they dropped him, unharmed, back at our apartment building. When I returned several hours later, he was still waiting out front for his rendezvous. I took him upstairs and we opened the bundle to find wads of newspaper. Geoffrey had taken the duping well, laughing at his naivety. I was less inclined to laugh. It was the early 90s; New York was not a safe place and I would never have got in a car with two strange men, regardless of their colour.

Seated beside me on the sofa, almost two decades later, Geoffrey laughed with me at the memory as he returned everything to the tin and replaced the battered lid. From the poster container, he extracted a photo, an enlarged copy he'd ordered of one he'd seen and liked in the *West Australian* newspaper.

'It's the expressions,' he said. 'They say so much.'

He unrolled the photo and my heart swooped with joy: it was like gazing through a chink in time to the Kalgoorlie years. Two elderly Aboriginal men stood close, their heads and bodies touching each other as if melded. One man was apparently blind and had his eyes shut. His friend's were open, blue and stern, gaze unwavering, as if he could see far into the distance, well enough for two. The men were spectacular. But what really made my heart swoop was the knowledge that despite the stranger-danger warnings, my brother's childhood had somehow imprinted on him the same way it had on me. When he looked at the photo of the two Aboriginal men, what I saw in his eyes was recognition and love. And suddenly the New York incident years before made sense. It was *because* the men were Black that Geoffrey had got into the car.

Later that night, in the narrow single bed from my childhood, I thought of Robbie as a child, not knowing he was Aboriginal, in a sense growing up in the wrong skin. And I thought of another member of the Stolen Generations saying in his online testimony that he felt like a white man in a black body. And the word tumbling over and over in my mind, like whorls of red dust in a willy-willy, was assimilation.

Some of Them Were Promiscuous

Greg and I had arrived in Kalgoorlie late afternoon the previous day, in the second half of 2013. He had elected to stay with Tony. My usual hotel was full, so I checked into the Palace Hotel. A sign outside the downstairs bar set the tone with an advertisement for the day's 'skimpies': Brooke, Jenna, Saskia and Kayla.

After breakfast, I checked out and set off for Coolgardie. As I drove, crows rose, blackly squawking, from roadside carrion and scattered into the bush. I found myself thinking of how Mr Sercombe had told me our first interview had left him feeling better than he had in a while. On the phone the day before, he'd sounded more frail than ever. Somehow I didn't think this interview would improve his state of mind.

In Coolgardie, Dorothy opened the sliding door to my knock and hugged me. Mr Sercombe was resting in a lounge chair, just inside the door. Sallow and emaciated, he stood, wobbled and looked as if he was going to fall. He steadied himself and greeted me.

Dorothy offered me a cup of tea. Mr Sercombe and I moved to the kitchen table and I set out my notebook. Mr Sercombe gave permission for me to record our conversation. Dorothy asked if he'd taken his medication. He said he would in a while. Dorothy poured a glass of water and placed it in front of him, next to a small bottle of pills. Then she set to work in the kitchen, opening cupboards beneath the bench and removing dishes and pans.

'What are you most proud of from your time at Kurrawang?' I asked.

Mr Sercombe responded swiftly.

'The majority of the people who worked there had a love for the people.'

'Why did you leave?'

'One of the reasons was probably burnout, I expect. It's not always easy working in close relationship with everyone.'

'Can you give me an example?'

'I don't go into that too much. Some things are better forgotten. You can't all think alike. When you're in a managing position, there are bound to be different opinions.'

'With Mr Sharpe?'

'Mr Sharpe was a fairly austere sort of chap but I worked well with him. I took the attitude of respect for those above you.'

'What about regrets? Do you have any?'

'I don't know, really. I don't know if it's any good having regrets. I certainly don't regret going there. And I certainly don't regret what I did. Sometimes I wish I'd carried on a bit longer than I did. My sons say it was the best time of their lives.'

I thought of Robbie, who had spent almost his entire childhood in the Mission. Said nothing. Made more notes.

Then I asked if Aboriginal languages were allowed at Kurrawang. Mr Sercombe shook his head.

'Things were different then. It was the law. A government law. We weren't supposed to speak the language. We weren't even allowed to learn the language.'

'What about the Aboriginal kids? Could they speak in Wongi?'

'They could please themselves.'

Dorothy hadn't spoken, and I wondered what she thought of my questions. I suspected she would disapprove of their more confrontational nature. I looked down at my notes, wondering how to phrase my next question.

'There is one thing that's not such a happy event.' I glanced at Mr Sercombe. He was gazing steadily at me, his expression sober and unchanging. 'Do you remember Beverley Joy Noble?'

Mr Sercombe frowned and thought for a moment.

'Joy Noble, yes. She wasn't called Beverley. She might have been in her teens when I was there. She had given the Queen a bouquet.'

I nodded and paused. Looked up and met Mr Sercombe's gaze.

'Apparently she was raped at the Mission. By four older Wongi boys. They raped another girl too.'

Mr Sercombe grasped the edge of the table and reeled back in his chair, eyes wide, mouth agape. Behind me, Dorothy's clattering stopped.

'That's the first I've heard of that.' He sounded shocked, disbelieving even.

'It may not have been during your time.'

'I know she had a child.'

'While she was at the Mission?'

'No. She left and came back with a child. We took her and the baby into our house. She didn't cope. She left after a short while. She was there by invitation.'

'In your house, you mean?'

'Yes. She wasn't a good mum.' Then he quickly added, 'I shouldn't say that really, I suppose. She didn't have that motherly instinct to care for the baby. Ronnie Noble was fine.' Taking rapid, shallow breaths, Mr Sercombe charged on, his words heading off-course at full tilt, like a spooked horse. 'He went to work on a sheep station. He became a Christian too. His mother's funeral was the first funeral I went to. I went out to the sorrowing area and when they finished sorrowing they were going to punish Ronnie because he wasn't there to look after his mother. No one officiated at the gravesite. I rang the superintendent of Native Welfare and said it wasn't good enough. I decided I would take the funerals. I took many, many of them after that. There was always a respectable burial.'

Dorothy coughed. She folded a piece of foil and stepped closer to the table.

'Have you had your pill?' she asked. 'You said you'd take it in half an hour.'

'I didn't take it.'

'You naughty boy.'

Mr. Sercombe took a pill from the bottle, popped it in his mouth and washed it down with a sip of water.

'A lot of them died. Some of the boys became alcoholics. They could have got it from their parents. I think a lot of it is what they've inherited.'

He seemed unaware of what he'd just said, of his

judgmental tone, of the other possibilities the word 'inherited' implied for boys who'd grown up in institutional care.

'Greg identified the rapists to me. In a photo,' I said.

'Oh.'

'They're all dead now. The older boys made the younger ones watch the rape.'

'I've never heard that.'

'Adrian carries a sense of blame for not having reported the rape.'

Mr Sercombe pressed his lips together and took a breath.

'In those days I don't think much would have been done about it anyway. There wasn't … I don't know how people would have viewed that. I don't know what I would have done. You've got to be in the situation. It must have been before my time. Must have been way before my time it happened. Joy was a working girl when we got there. When we got there Greg had been there four years.'

By working girl, I knew Mr Sercombe meant that Beverley Joy had left school and was helping out with domestic chores, the accepted fate of Aboriginal girls raised in missions. Beverley Joy must have been around 15 or 16, not that age, or gender for that matter, was relevant when it came to vulnerability to rape. As for the timing of Greg's arrival and the rape, I later realised Mr Sercombe's maths were wrong. He arrived in 1966, the year after Greg. Greg remembered the the rape taking place while he was still in primary school, putting the year at 1965 or 66.

Dorothy interrupted to announce lunch; I accepted her invitation to join them. Mr Sercombe and I watched while Dorothy set out knives and forks, and ladled minestrone soup (Bonox added for extra nutrition for Mr Sercombe) into bowls.

Mr Sercombe shook his head. He looked immensely sad.

'I've never heard of it.' He sounded genuinely bewildered. 'Some of them were promiscuous, you know. I couldn't do anything because they never told me. Perhaps they didn't tell anybody out of fear. There was a lot of fear.'

He seemed unaware of the stereotype he'd bought into, of the black-skinned woman as lewd and lascivious – known in America as the Jezebel stereotype. It probably originated with early European colonists when they encountered and misinterpreted semi-naked women in Africa. The other stereotype Mr Sercombe was dancing around was that of the Black man as a rapist.

He failed to elucidate on the possible reasons for Beverley Joy being silenced by fear, but during my previous visit, he'd hinted at the Aboriginal children's fear of dark spirits – yet another example of their 'savage' state. A more likely reason for Beverley Joy's fear is that, having been exposed to a decade's worth of the Brethren's moralistic teaching, she might well have seen the rape as her 'fall from grace', something she'd 'asked for' merely by being present. I have little doubt she feared punishment on disclosure. As I was to discover, the boys weren't the only ones subjected to beatings. And the missionaries' fear of moral turpitude was evident in the way they rigorously segregated the genders, and carefully avoided any discussion of puberty and sexuality. Theirs was an attitude I understood well: my mother had enthusiastically upheld similar principles.

Dorothy served custard, jelly and stewed fruit for dessert, encouraging Mr Sercombe to add cream for calories. His most recent weigh-in had, apparently, revealed a loss. As we ate, he seemed preoccupied and afterwards, while we were clearing away the dishes, he told me that Adrian should visit him. He didn't need to carry guilt, he said. He quoted a bible passage and said that Jesus Christ died for us and would bless Adrian with forgiveness. He broke off to take a call from his daughter. I noticed a painting of Sturt's Desert Peas on the wall.

'They're my favourite flowers,' I said to Dorothy. 'I remember them from when I was little and my parents took us camping in the bush around Kalgoorlie.'

Dorothy said she would show me some real examples. Outside, beyond the patch of lawn, the Hills Hoist, and the inevitable red dirt, we inspected a single, raised bed bordered by wooden sleepers and rocks. The distinctive flowers bloomed among the sprawling sage-green foliage, each flower a miracle of two fiery-red tapers, extending several inches either side of a glossy, black centre.

I asked Dorothy if I could photograph her and Mr Sercombe by the flowers, to which she agreed. Calling for Mr Sercombe, she disappeared inside. She returned with him, nestled under the curve of his arm. In the photo, both gaze directly into the camera. Whether it's the sun in their eyes or the nature of our interview or the future they're facing, neither smiles.

Mr Sercombe said he had something for me. We went back inside and he shuffled through some booklets. He found the one he sought and passed it to me. It was called *The World for Today: Connecting Faith to Life*. Religious paraphernalia was the last thing I wanted, but I thanked him and said goodbye and Dorothy walked me out to my rental car. She looked tired and sad and spoke of the pain of caring for a second terminally ill husband. We hugged and I drove back to Kalgoorlie. I was spending the night at my usual hotel on the site of my former home. Greg rang, saying Tony's house was overcrowded, so I booked him a room too. We met in the foyer, and I repeated what Mr Sercombe had said about the rapes. Greg's face tightened. 'He will die soon,' he said. 'And my land will bury him.'

In bed that night, I opened the booklet Mr Sercombe had given me and turned to the reading for that day, Friday 19 April. Taken from Ecclesiastes 7:9, it read, 'Anger resides in the lap of fools.'

The First Fleet

In the back seat of a white truck, I swaddled a joey in my jacket and pressed it to my chest. In front, Geoffrey Stokes was behind the wheel, driving Greg, Tony and me into the fading light as swathes of pink, yellow and orange washed over the horizon. Geoffrey frequently exclaimed at the spectacle and urged me to take photos, pointing out various cloud formations. From time to time, I removed one hand from my bundle, hauled out my phone and angled it skywards. The movement upset the joey. It had squirmed into an upside-down position by then and would kick out against my arms, its legs surprisingly strong, and its head would emerge in my lap. Whispering, I would lower my chin to my chest, restrain the legs with my jacket, gently tuck the head back in, then gather the bundle closer to me, closer to what I hoped was the soothing beat of my heart.

A couple of days had passed since the visit to Mr Sercombe, and the much-talked about kangaroo hunt had finally taken place, and well before we turned back to Kalgoorlie, the fraught nature of my quest was becoming apparent to me. For starters, in Noongar culture, hunting animals the size of kangaroos was male terrain.

I was still unclear as to my motives. In practical terms, a hunt promised (and would subsequently deliver) the sort of action in short supply during my days at the desk. My real prey, of course, was not kangaroos but Greg's friendship. I somehow managed to ignore the fact that I had bludgeoned him with my requests to go on a hunt. My love for the blue skies, the ever-present sun, the eucalypts and the red dirt was still the only motive I could cop to without a qualm.

My motives in wanting Greg's friendship were even muddier and came from deep within my heart. Just as a complicated and interrelated set of circumstances cause the heart itself to beat – electrical impulses from the sino-atrial node, exercise, emotions, fever, illnesses and medications – so too have a variety of things, some doubtless unconscious, shaped my desire for friendship with Greg. The liberal white person wanting a black friend to prove they're not racist has become a contemporary stereotype. Much as I would like to deny it, I'm unable to completely discount the possibility. From the outset, my stated aim has been a personal reconciliation with the Aboriginal people I grew up with, which by definition involves friendly, non-racist relations with those people. But I realised early on I couldn't allow Greg's Aboriginality to define any real friendship: he couldn't become my 'Aboriginal' friend. Nor could I burden any friendship we formed as representing a general reconciliation between Aboriginal people and me or as emblematic of my non-racist stance. Quite the reverse. As with any positive abstract quality – kindness, generosity, compassion, mercy – my performance with strangers, not friends, would be my true measure. Would I walk past an empty seat next to an Aboriginal person on the bus or take it? Would I offer a cup of coffee to a homeless person on the street? Would I acknowledge their humanity by stopping to chat rather than merely tossing a coin?

But why Greg? As a child, I had known his brother, not him. But of the men I'd spoken to or interviewed, Greg was the one I was spending most time with; the one, by virtue of his single status, most available for friendship. Yet compared with Bronwyn, who had welcomed a renewed friendship, he resisted my overtures, which, in the way of human nature, was why I found myself in the position of chasing it.

Which, I know, is dodging the real question: what was it about Greg that made friendship with him so important? And this is where I was burdening him unfairly with the task of representation. Greg represented for me the male connection to a part of my past I'd lost. Tony, my old school friend, was in a relationship and therefore unavailable in local cultural terms for a close friendship. Without knowing it, Greg also fitted the bill for the close, platonic male friendship I'd always wanted but never found. We shared a passion for the region's past history and for the fight for equality. It didn't hurt that he was good-looking and treated me with gentle respect.

If he had got wind of the stakes, he would have disappeared into that red horizon.

I had met up with the men mid-morning. They greeted me warmly, including Tony, who, on our previous meeting, had said little. Greg told me they'd brought kangaroo tails along to cook in the event of an unsuccessful hunt, but I had my hopes pinned on the real deal. We set off along the road to Kanowna. After about 10 kilometres, the bitumen gave way to gravel. We hurtled along, trailing behind us a maelstrom of red dust. Each time, the car hit a pothole or flew over the crest of a hill, Geoffrey yelled 'Yiha!' and stretched his arm out the open window, hooting with laughter, eventually emboldening me to wind my window down and cautiously stick my right arm out. The sound of rushing air filled my ears and the wind tugged at my skin. But I'm not a rule-breaker by nature, so after a moment, I withdrew my arm and wound up the window.

Geoffrey craned his neck to see me in the rear vision mirror.

'Tell them the story about how your father delivered me,' he said.

We had met at Monty's to discuss the hunt, and I'd told Geoffrey my father's story. Greg had heard it too, but I repeated it for Tony's benefit, describing how my father had delivered Geoffrey in the Kalgoorlie Regional Hospital the same day my younger brother was born. I knew that Mrs Stokes probably gave Geoffrey the same name as my brother to honour my father, a common practice at the time, but it seemed a post-colonial hangover to me. Embarrassed, I'd kept the information to myself.

'Huh!' Tony said.

There was a brief pause.

'What's your brother's name?' Geoffrey asked.

I hesitated.

'Geoffrey,' I said. 'His name is Geoffrey.'

Geoffrey laughed; it wasn't a joyful sound.

'Now I know where I got my name from. I used to think I was named after my Uncle Geoffrey.'

Beside me, Greg stared out the window, giving the impression of paying no attention.

'Maybe you were,' I said.

'No,' Geoffrey said, his tone definite. 'My brothers' names are Elvis and Winston. I'm named after your brother.'

He hummed to himself and then, 'Your brother left-handed?' he asked in the tone of someone looking for a point of connection with a stranger.

'Yes,' I said. 'Only one of three kids. Are you?'

'Yes. Only one in the family.'

A coincidence, I'm sure we both knew, but it was like opening a window to get rid of a bad smell.

After an hour of driving, Geoffrey announced a morning tea stop. He turned off onto a side track, narrow and dustier still, and dropped his speed by a quarter. A couple of hundred metres later, he stopped the car on top of a long, low escarpment, three metres above a plain stretching towards the horizon, the sparse saltbush interrupted only by a dry lake bed, red like the ground, and the occasional withered limbs of a tree.

'There's a waterhole that way.' He pointed to a spot 10 metres to the left, where the land dropped sharply away. 'Don't fall in.'

I climbed out and started walking. Overhead, puffs of cloud hung as if dabbed against the broad blue palette of the sky. At the very edge of the ridge, I came to the waterhole. An important water source for travelling Wongi people in the past, the waterhole was now partly obscured by old wooden railway sleepers and barbed wire. A dank smell emanated from the murky yellow water about two metres below. Not only had white settlers stolen the land, they had contaminated the water through farming and mining practices.

Morning tea was a minimal affair – a few sips of town water each – and then Geoffrey urged us to get back in the truck. He took us first to see fields of ochre – white ochre animal shapes set in a low pink ochre cliff and a honeycombed hillock of yellow, white and pink ochre arising from a pink ochre bed. We returned to the main road and continued until we came to another turn-off, leading to the traditional land belonging to Geoffrey's family. We pulled up under the shade of a willow tree and climbed out of the truck. With a poppet head in the distance behind him, Geoffrey faced Greg, Tony and me.

'Welcome to my country.'

Greg and Tony nodded. I murmured my thanks. In Sydney, I'd attended functions where an Aboriginal person had welcomed us to country or a non-Indigenous person had acknowledged the Traditional Owners, but I'd never been welcomed to country in the Kalgoorlie region, where I was born and spent the first 11 years of my life; where the red dirt felt like an extension of my skin. It was a strange sensation, as if I were a visitor in my own home. I wondered how it was for Greg and Tony.

Geoffrey lifted the canvas covering the tray back and lowered the tailgate.

'Our cooking table.'

The men lifted camping chairs and cooking equipment out. Greg and Tony gathered dry branches and twigs and in no time had a fire going in a freshly dug pit. Greg set out a couple of tomatoes and a pack of sausages. Geoffrey strapped on a metal detector and disappeared.

I wandered off, swatting at swarms of sticky black

flies. Before long, I turned and headed back to the truck. Although I'd come from this country, if I lost my way, I wouldn't survive long.

As I neared the truck, I saw Greg slicing into something long and yellowish on the tailgate. It looked like a baguette. I drew closer and the shape revealed itself to be a kangaroo tail. The tourist's version of bush tucker, I thought. But of course food, like Kurrawang, is another example of the dynamic nature of Aboriginal culture: tails had become a common form of tucker, in the bush and elsewhere.

Using a large, wide-bladed knife, Greg made several long shallow cuts down the length of the tail. Next he peeled back the skin. It took some effort and made a ripping sound. The exposed pink muscle, the surface striped with white sinew, drew hundreds of flies. Not wanting to appear too precious, too white, I did my best to ignore them. Greg cut the tail into segments, liberally salted them, and wrapped each one separately in foil.

'Where did you get the tails?' I asked.

'We bought 'em at the pet food shop in town.'

'Oh,' I said. 'Do some people feed them to their dogs?'

'Only *wadjela*,' he replied.

'Not the Wongi?'

'Oh no.' He shook head. Gave an incredulous laugh. 'That'd be sacrilege.'

The tips of the three other tails on the 'table' protruded from newspaper. Each tail, the Kalgoorlie pet shop owner would tell me the following day, sold for four dollars. Tony picked up one of the whole tails. He draped it over a large branch he'd arranged in an arc across the fire. Acrid grey smoke rose from the flames. After a few minutes, Tony picked the tail up by the tip and scraped the singed hair off the burned side with a knife before returning the tail to the fire to singe off the hair on the other side. He repeated the process with the next tail. I stood back and watched, swatting the flies, my mouth clamped shut. Greg and Tony buried the unwrapped tails and the foil-wrapped segments in the coals.

A loud shout from Geoffrey brought us all running. He swung his metal detector over a patch of earth and it whined. He sent Greg back to the truck for a pick and continued to swing the detector. The whine intensified as the circular disc reached a spot between a cluster of bushes and receded as the disc swung away.

Greg returned and scraped away the top layer of dirt with the pick and then, handful by handful, he painstakingly held the deeper dirt up for Geoffrey to pass over with the detector. Eventually they isolated the gold-bearing handful. Greg licked the end of a finger on his free hand and dabbed at a tiny, dirty lump in his other hand until he uncovered the unmistakable glint of gold, half a centimetre long. He and Tony returned to the car to store the tiny nugget in a jar. I followed. Geoffrey continued his search. I had wondered how the local Wongi people viewed the effect of the Super Pit and the other mines on the landscape. Those I spoke to mostly wanted to share in the profits reaped from their land. Surprised at first, I soon realised how easy it was for financially privileged people to take an environmental stand. For people who struggled to find decent work with fair pay in a racist town, where a king's ransom was being made on what had been Aboriginal land, it was a different story.

When lunch was ready, we all gathered. Greg passed me the tip of a tail wrapped in foil – a delicacy, it would seem. I nibbled carefully, not wanting to break an already damaged crown on a front tooth. The meat tasted gamy and unfamiliar. I balanced my paper plate on my knee and tried to saw meat from the bone with a plastic knife but soon gave up and skewered a sausage for my plate. The men made no comment. They divided the foil-wrapped segments between them and, using their fingers, ate with gusto.

Next, Greg and Tony uncovered the three intact tails, lifted them out from the ashes and laid them crosswise on a bed of white pebbles. An artistic if unappetising (to me at least) display. Greg broke off a handful of leafy twigs from the tree behind me and whacked the tails hard, one at a time, to remove more charred skin. The men demolished one of the tails between them. The other two they wrapped and stored in the truck, under the canvas.

Geoffrey said he had a story to share. Almost immediately he recanted.

'It might offend you.' He looked at me.

'You have to tell me now,' I said. Greg and Tony agreed.

Geoffrey said that a man on one of his bush food tours had commented on the number of flies and asked their Aboriginal name.

'I told him we didn't have one,' Geoffrey said.

The man insisted there must be a name, given the large number of flies.

'So I told him that flies came out with the First Fleet. And that's why we don't have a name for them.'

We all laughed, my laughter partly relief at having kept quiet about the flies. Only later did I consider the possible subtext of Geoffrey's story – that white people introduced all things bad; that a refusal to name something represents a form of resistance.

We stacked our dishes and the frying pan in the back of the truck, folded up the chairs and stowed them. Greg kicked dirt over the coals, and we piled back in the truck. I didn't want to leave and would have leapt at a suggestion of camping. But it was time for the kangaroo hunt.

Once we'd reached a known kangaroo habitat, Geoffrey switched off the engine and he and Tony climbed out to retrieve the rifle from the tray-back. Under Geoffrey's guidance, Tony loaded a bullet and snapped the barrel into place. They got back in the truck.

Before starting the engine, Geoffrey suggested Tony take a practice shot at a branch about 150 metres away. Tony pointed the gun out the window, took aim, and fired. Bark flew off the target tree. He passed the gun back to Greg, who offered it to me.

'Have a go.'

'Me?'

Greg explained how to hold the rifle and pull the trigger. He told me to aim for a discarded plastic bucket less than 100 metres away. I rested the barrel on the window ledge and fitted the rifle butt to the hollow of my shoulder. Bent my head and pressed my cheek to the stock to sight the bucket. I curled my finger around the cold metal trigger and pressed. The rifle bucked as I fired, my aim wide of the mark. Feeling foolish, the white tourist woman handed the gun over the seat to Tony. We set off. Wanting to enter into the spirit, if not the practicalities, of the hunt, I trained my eyes on the landscape, looking for a furry hump or a pair of pointed ears twitching above the long grass.

Geoffrey felled the first kangaroo with a shot to the neck, an effective way to preserve the meat's tenderness because the animal bleeds less. He put the gun down and reached for a foot-long metal bar on the floor. He climbed out of the truck. We followed him to the kangaroo, which was still alive. Geoffrey raised the bar and I leaped back. Geoffrey brought the bar down. The efficient and merciful nature of the killing impressed me. No live animal transport as was the fate of cattle. No abattoir. Instead, freedom right up to the last few moments of life. Greg grabbed the dead animal by its long hind legs and dragged it towards the truck, leaving a bloody trail on the crazy paving of sunbaked red dirt. The men heaved the kangaroo onto the bonnet and wedged it behind the truck's bull bar, and we resumed our search.

Within 10 minutes and after a few failed shots, a second kangaroo was pressed against the first behind the bull bar and any desire to hunt had left me. We reached the main road, which was still gravel, and picked up speed. The car's motion caused the second kangaroo to roll. Its legs flailed up and blood spattered the windscreen. It was a horrifying sight but I reminded myself that this had been a humane killing by any estimation, and there'd be no waste. Every last ounce of meat would be eaten, right down to the tips of the tails.

Geoffrey asked Greg if he would like to shoot the third kangaroo.

'No,' he said.

I glanced at him, surprised. Greg had spoken to me

with great enthusiasm about past hunts. Why pass up this opportunity?

'My right eye's no good and it's my shooting eye.'

I remembered his history of diabetes and high blood pressure; legacies, as I'd come to accept, of his childhood. Both illnesses could have caused impaired vision. Suddenly, his refusal to drive when with me made sense. He must have passed the vision test for his licence, but perhaps he preferred others, with better vision, to drive when possible. His reluctance to take me hunting himself likewise made sense. Why hadn't he told me? Was it culturally related reticence? Or had he considered it simply not my business? I didn't know but knew better than to ask.

Tony took the last shot and a third kangaroo went down. Again, I climbed out of the car with the men but turned away when the bar came down.

'It's got a big joey.' Geoffrey reached into the kangaroo's pouch and extracted a struggling joey, about a foot long, a perfectly formed miniature.

The Ugle brothers seemed regretful at having shot the mother. I felt sickened.

'Can we let it go?' Tony asked.

'No,' Geoffrey said.

Aware from my days as a wildlife carer in the Byron Shire that the joey was too young to survive on its own, I advocated putting it out of its misery. In the end, the men decided to bring the joey with us. Geoffrey thrust it at me, which was how I came to be in the back of the truck with my bundle. The men roped the mother on top of the other two bodies and climbed back in the truck. The hunt was over. Time to go home.

We hadn't gone far when one of the kangaroos rocketed off the bonnet. Nothing, it seemed, was too gruesome for this trip. Geoffrey pulled over and Tony went back for the kangaroo, splayed on the gravel like roadkill. He hauled it to the truck. Geoffrey decided to shift our cargo to the tray back before we hit Kalgoorlie. Tony and Greg helped. Then Geoffrey cleaned the bloodied windscreen and we set off again, towards the point where the road met the horizon and the sun melted into a golden pool in the hollow between the trees.

The drive took over two hours. For a while we listened to a football broadcast – the Eagles versus the Blues. Every so often the men rallied: 'Get it between the posts!'; 'Garn the blues!' At one point, Geoffrey's wife Christine called. Geoffrey said he would be home soon and hung up. He invited us for tea at his place. Greg and Tony hesitated.

'Sure,' I said, not wanting the day to end.

Darkness had settled, warm and soft, by the time we reached the outskirts of Kalgoorlie. At Geoffrey's house, one of his sons held the gate open. Geoffrey reversed in to facilitate unloading the kangaroos, and we got out. A short white woman with a long grey ponytail emerged from the house. Christine looked wary. Her gaze landed on my bundle and hardened.

'That better not be a joey. It's not staying here.'

I introduced myself. Denied responsibility for the joey's presence. Christine appeared to soften and invited me in, unwanted joey and all. I followed her through to the kitchen.

'They're hard to look after,' she said. 'Usually die. I told him no more joeys.'

She disappeared and reappeared a minute later with a pillowslip. Handed it to me.

'They feel safer in a pouch.'

I slid the struggling joey into the pillowslip and passed the bundle to Geoffrey's youngest son, pleased to be unburdened of responsibility for the joey's future.

Christine saw me eye a huge pot of stew bubbling on the stove.

'I never know whether it's going to be four or forty for tea.'

She showed me a film she'd made with Geoffrey's sister, as part of her thesis project to encourage local Wongi people to replace the high-carbohydrate diet many of them lived on with a more traditional – and healthier – diet to combat diseases like diabetes.

Two other health practitioners I spoke to would later outline some of the stark facts: in the Kalgoorlie region, amputations due to diabetic complications are common in Indigenous people in their late 30s and early 40s; deaths from diabetic complications are likewise common in the same age group; Kalgoorlie's 15 dialysis chairs are always occupied. Many patients who need a dialysis chair must travel to Perth. Drugs and alcohol create enormous challenges in the population, and health professionals struggle to get Wongi people to comply with treatment.

After watching the film, I helped set the table on the back porch. We all sat down to eat, the three dead kangaroos laid out on the grass to my right. I found myself unable to eat any of the turkey legs Christine had roasted; their shape too closely resembled that of the legs of the dead animals near us. During the meal, the subject of Indigenous health again cropped up. According to Christine, an Aboriginal male born in Kalgoorlie in 1962 had an average life expectancy of 38 years; that is, many of the Aboriginal men who would have been 51 that year had already died. She urged Tony and Greg to decrease carbohydrates in their diet and eat as much protein as they wanted, preferably from lean meat like kangaroo, as well as plenty of vegetables.

I was helping Christine with the dishes when she noticed Greg and Tony attempting to leave without me. I felt a rush of annoyance: Greg was staying in the same hotel as me, for goodness sakes! I grabbed my things and rushed to catch a lift.

The next morning, I received a text at 7.20: 'Hi Amanda, I am in room 104 and was wondering if you can drop me down Boulder.' Still annoyed about the previous night, wondering why he couldn't call Tony, and feeling more than ever like a probationary friend, I texted back: 'Sure thing, Greg. When do you want to go?'

Five minutes later, the receptionist rang to say Greg was waiting for me downstairs. Not trusting our relationship enough to have it out with him, I picked up my purse and car keys and dutifully trotted downstairs. When I did eventually bring the subject up, months later, Greg looked surprised. He said he and Tony had simply been ready to leave Geoffrey's house, and I was still helping Christine. He hadn't stopped to wonder how I would get back to the hotel. The request the following morning was entirely separate. I'd always been happy to drive him around; why should 7.20 on a Sunday morning be any different? He was right. The incident was nothing more than a failure of communication – mine as much as, if not more than, his.

At the time, we greeted each other amicably enough. As I drove, I wondered aloud at the joey's fate.

'It'll be dead.' His reply was immediate and matter-of-fact.

'I know.' I sighed.

'Either way it would have come into town.'

I knew that too: joey was probably the bush equivalent of veal.

I had the afternoon to fill in, no great plans and only the voice inside my head to listen to, which was not the greatest of company that day. I decided to change my flight to the following morning, a day earlier than planned. Contrary to bringing us closer, the kangaroo hunt had left me feeling further from friendship with Greg than ever. It seemed that we needed a break from each other. After some aimless sightseeing, my only remaining task was to pay Greg the money I owed him for his guide work. To avoid another awkward interaction, I decided to slip it with a note under his door.

I sat at my desk and scrawled a few lines, polite and formal, and then I tore the page up and walked down the hallway to Greg's room and knocked. He opened the door. He was wearing tracksuit pants, not jeans as he usually did. Looking pleased to see me, he invited me in.

Greg sat at the table and I took the other chair. One side of the bed was rumpled, and the TV was tuned to *The Voice*. I gave Greg the envelope of money and my thanks.

'As long as you're getting the information you need,' he said.

I assured him I was.

'Those pages you sent for me to look at? I showed 'em to my son Jeremy and my sisters – June, Gloria, and Delphine.'

'You did?' I sat forward. 'What did they say?'

'They're worried because you're talking to the missionaries too. They think you're going to glorify the Mission.'

I wondered if this was Greg indirectly conveying his own worry. I reminded him it had been his idea for me to speak to Mr Sercombe. I said he and his sisters could all read the Sercombe interview when I had written it up properly. He seemed satisfied and we fell silent, comfortable together, our attention drifting to the television. After a moment, Greg looked at me.

'Want to know what happened to the joey?'

I sat bolt upright. Waved my hands in front of my face, palms outward, fingers splayed.

'No. Don't tell me.'

The small muscles around his eyes flickered, and the corners of his mouth turned up a little.

'I saw it come out of the oven this afternoon.'

'No!' I doubled over, head in hands.

Greg grinned. It seemed he had predicted my reaction, had wanted me to understand the practical and completely unromantic outcome of the hunt. But perhaps his telling me this was about something entirely different. Perhaps it was a subtle redress of power, in which the writer became the hunted instead of the hunter. Or perhaps I've reverted to my old habit of overthinking the matter, and Greg was merely indulging in a little sport and I, the squeamish white woman, was a ready victim. I uncovered my eyes and sat up. Mumbled something about being pleased that the joey's inevitable death wasn't wasted. Waited for my pulse to gradually slow. Greg waited too, silently, his gaze not unkind.

It was getting late. We both stood. I wanted to hug him or shake his hand but it would have felt too intimate in his room, so I did neither of those things. When his door closed behind me, a feeling of loss settled over my heart. Yet I was pleased to be leaving a place where the tectonics of time, the fault line between past and present, constantly threatened to overwhelm me. Kalgoorlie was at once my home and not my home, the land that had grown me, but now seemed hard and unyielding, determined to spit me out. The constant process of recalibration was exhausting. In some ways, I was pleased, too, to be leaving Greg, to be leaving the strain of navigating the subterranean byways of cultural difference, and to be returning to my home and to a relationship that didn't feel like it hung in the balance. To Kevin, who had known and loved me for almost 30 years, and to the accumulation of our shared lives, my bedrock.

A few months passed before I sent the interview transcript to Greg. In the interim, we spoke on the phone and corresponded by email. Any impression I'd had of him being annoyed with me after the kangaroo hunt (for reasons I didn't understand) had passed. Even so, I remembered him saying he'd walk away if he didn't approve of my writing. I opened the return envelope with some apprehension. In the margin next to the paragraph about Geoffrey's Welcome to Country, Greg had written, 'I would like to show you my land.' And next to the description of him and Tony attempting to leave me behind after dinner he wrote, 'I was rude and inconsiderate. But I accept the fact that you do get angry with me and you are my friend.' The dynamics of the night at Geoffrey's were no longer of concern, but the apology and claim to my friendship were important to me. Greg had begun to trust me. He wouldn't be walking away.

Aboriginal Land

My phone rang as I was about to disembark at Perth airport on yet another trip west, only a few weeks after the previous one. It was Nigel Sercombe, Mr Sercombe's son. I'd rung a few days previously, to ask if I could visit Mr Sercombe the following Monday, and Nigel had answered the phone. He'd told me his father had deteriorated, so I should check in a few days' time. Now, when I heard Nigel's voice, I knew what was coming. Mr Sercombe had died. In the early hours of the morning, Nigel said, with three of his children at his side. A peaceful passing.

Greg had set up interviews for me with two of his sisters – Gloria and Delphine. I visited Gloria first. Photos covered every surface in her house – the walls, bookshelves, the bureau behind the table where she offered me a seat. I spotted an old black-and-white photo of her with the bronze statue of Kalgoorlie's official golden hero, outside the Town Hall.

'Ha! Here's you with Paddy Hannan. Do you have other photos of you as a child?'

'I don't like to display photos from Mission days,' she said. She made me a cup of tea and set out a plate of the biscuits I'd brought.

'What do you remember from your childhood?' I asked.

'I remember everything but I don't like to live in the past,' Gloria said. It struck me then how differently each of the Ugle siblings coped with their childhood trauma.

Like Greg and Adrian, Gloria remembered her parents' drinking. But she had happier memories too. She remembered her mother lighting the fire in the mornings to cook the damper they ate for school lunches. When the damper was ready, her mother melted the leftover grease from the previous night's meal.

'She would wipe a piece of damper around the inside of the frying pan and then wrap it in newspaper and give it to a child.'

At the mission, Gloria lived in the girls' dormitory.

'The girls were split between three sections,' she said. 'June was in the older girls' section, I was in the middle, Diane and Delphine got put in the younger girls' section. The older girls were not allowed to talk to the younger girls. But I knew they were there.'

'Who were your dorm parents?'

'At first it was Mr and Mrs Sharpe. They was very strict. Mrs Sharpe was as bad as Mr Sharpe. Not loving or kind at all. But I didn't have much to do with them because there were thirty-eight of us. We just did what we knew we was supposed to do.'

Thirty-eight, I thought, and the Department of Native

Affairs had refused an aunt custody of the Ugle children because she had 11 of her own in the house.

Once, in high school, Gloria and another girl missed the bus home.

'The Comptons were the house parents by then. The other girl and me, we started walking home. The police picked us up along the way and put us in the back of the paddy wagon. They took us back to the Mission. Mr Compton, he beat us with a bamboo stick. See, I still have the scar.' Gloria exposed the inside of her wrist to reveal the thin, pale imprint of that long-ago stick.

She told me another story, of a runaway girl.

'When they got her back, they made her change into her bathing suit,' Gloria said. 'They got all the girls to come to the quadrangle and told them, "This is what happens if you run away." They beat the girl with a strap but she refused to cry. We never cried. What was the point of crying if no parent would come to help? They kept beating her until she fell to the ground.'

So much for the Sharpes' 'kindness and perseverance'.

'What did you think at the time?' I asked.

'I just went to bed and didn't think too much about it,' she said.

I wondered if Gloria had repressed the memory, erecting a mental barrier between past and present, just as the missionaries had erected barriers between her and her brothers and younger sisters. Or if she chose not to examine a memory that evoked complex emotions.

Gloria, like her siblings, left the Mission with just a plastic bag containing a few clothes. Native Welfare drove her to Perth and dropped her at a house.

'They said, "Your aunt lives here." I had to make my own way after that. Some cousins tried to get me into drinking but I remembered my parents and didn't want to go that way.'

Gloria studied at two secretarial colleges, spending a year at each, but was unable to find a job, a situation she attributes to her Aboriginality. She married at 18 and had five children. Since the beginning of the year, with her children all grown, Gloria had held a cleaning job.

'I love it,' she said. 'I love the financial independence and working makes me feel good about myself.'

Of the Mission, she said, 'It was good and bad for me. The missionaries taught me domestic skills and how to dress nicely and look after my appearance. If we had stayed with our parents we might have ended up drinking like them. But the Mission was bad in other ways. The missionaries were brutal and it was very strict and regimented. We was never shown any love. The only time I ever got any idea of how romantic love worked was when Mr Smith and Miss West fell in love and married. We was never given any sex education. I didn't know to expect a menstrual period. The blood just appeared. But who I am now is because of what happened to me. I decided I would make something of my life.'

She said she was angry with her parents for not making a decent home for them. She saw her mother a few times after she left Kurrawang, when she was living in the East Perth Cemetery.

'But she wasn't able to be a mother.'

When I asked if she had any sympathy for her mother, she said she thought her mother could have made better choices. I asked what she knew of her mother's life. She said the missionaries had never spoken to her of her parents.

A number of times through our interview, Gloria reiterated that she didn't like looking back and didn't want to live in the past. I asked if Gloria shared Greg's mantra of *balay wadjela*.

'No. I tell my kids that some white people will like them and some won't. I tell them they have to have the right attitude. I tell my kids and grandkids not to bring A into the house. I tell them to bring N into the house.' She grinned. 'Do you know what "A" and "N" mean?'

'No.'

'"A" stands for attitude, "N" for nice.'

Delphine was four when she was removed to Kurrawang. She seemed to recall little of her Mission days. She attributed this in part to not wanting to remember and in part to memory loss due to health problems. I thought then it was one thing to agree to an interview in the service of truth, and another, entirely, to have to rake over personal and traumatic memories. For Delphine, and probably for any number of other Aboriginal people, it was all too difficult.

Delphine said she didn't like to go out much, passing the hours on her computer. I remember a slim, quiet girl in a shift dress smiling hesitantly under the tree in the school yard. In the intervening years, the quiet and hesitant attitude seemed unchanged but that girl had put on considerable weight, perhaps a subconscious barrier between her and a world that had not been kind. The thing that stood out most to me during our interview was her fiercely protective attitude towards her children.

'You can write whatever you like about me,' she said. 'But don't write about my kids.'

A week after Mr Sercombe's death, on a day of glorious sunshine, his funeral was held at the Christian Aboriginal Parent-Directed School in Coolgardie, where he had been a board member. Greg had left for Melbourne with Robbie and Ruth for a prearranged trip to the races, a gift from his son, so I went alone. Someone handed me an order of service; a thin piece of wire was tucked between the two sheets for people to fashion some sort of tribute to Mr Sercombe to throw into his grave. Inside the hall at least 100 people had already assembled, many Aboriginal people among them, most seated towards the middle or rear behind the white people. Geoffrey Stokes arrived and took a seat off to the left. Mr Sercombe's widow Dorothy, in a powder-blue suit, her usually unruly hair neatly brushed, arrived on a man's arm – Malcolm Sercombe, someone whispered.

The service lasted two hours, conducted mainly by the Sercombe brothers. The sisters played a minor role, in keeping with the Brethren church's rules regarding women. The overall impression was of a deep love for and pride in the father they'd lost.

After the service, I joined the motorcade to Coolgardie cemetery for a further hour-long service. Under the spreading boughs of a eucalypt tree, Mr Sercombe's coffin was lowered into a grave alongside his first wife, Alicia. The occasional cloud drifted in front of the sun. At my feet, an Aboriginal baby played in the red dirt. On the far side of the gathering, a young Aboriginal boy clambered over a headstone.

The voices swelled, lyrical and lovely in the late afternoon light, in a final hymn. I joined in the refrain:

In the sweet by and by
We shall meet on that beautiful shore.

One by one, we all stepped forward to offer our wire tributes, mine a crudely shaped 'K' for Kurrawang. Men grabbed shovels and started to fill the grave.

I knew by now that Mr Sercombe had done wrong at the Mission, in the form of beatings and maintaining sibling separation at the very least. It was also possible that the rapes of Beverley Joy and the other girl had taken place on his watch. Certainly his attitude towards her and the 'promiscuity' of the Aboriginal girls was reprehensible. He had only ever admitted some of it to me, but he seemed to have spent his life attempting to make up for those other wrongs. And perhaps he'd left the Mission, only three years after leaving Queen and country, because he hadn't liked the person he was becoming, the lessons in violence he was learning. Or perhaps this was just my interpretation, arising from my inclination to not point the finger at a man I'd known and liked, who'd left behind a family who had loved him. Or was it me wanting to protect one of my own – a white person? I hope not, but I've learned by now how deeply ingrained lessons learned in childhood can be, and how difficult it is to unlearn them. But I've also learned that the first step forward is in acknowledging the existence of those ingrained lessons.

I found Dorothy and offered my condolences. Surrounded by people, she gave no sign of recognition. I turned and walked towards my car. Before I climbed in, I looked back. Half a dozen men were still shovelling in a swirling cloud of red dust. Crows cawed in the distance. The sun shone softly through the eucalypt leaves above Mr Sercombe's grave. Aboriginal land had buried him.

One of the Last

Side by side, on a cold, clear July morning in 2014, Catherine Noble and I walked along a half-buried car track in the bush on the edge of Coolgardie. The town had grown on me. I'd come to appreciate the wide open streets and the feeling that time had stood still.

'You want to ask me some questions,' Catherine said.

'Yes.' I repeated my usual spiel about the right to refuse to answer questions she considered invasive.

'What's your interest in this?' She gave me a direct look. 'What's in it for you?'

Balay wadjela again. Watch out for the white man. Or in this case, woman. Always. Who could blame them? I gave Catherine my elevator pitch and told her I would not profit financially from the book I was writing.

Ten minutes into our conversation, Catherine turned to me.

'I was sexually abused before I was six,' she said, in the matter-of-fact voice I'd grown to expect during interviews, a voice that indicated too close and frequent an acquaintance with trouble.

'I'm so sorry.'

Unable to undo the past, the words felt as inadequate as they always had. But I know it is important for abuse survivors to be believed, and heard with empathy. The simple offering of one human to another that says, 'I hear you; you matter.'

Catherine said the abuse had taken place at Kurrawang. No one had been there to protect her. Not the missionaries and, of course, not her mother. She'd been too scared to tell anyone. When I commented on her openness now, she told me she had decided to expose the past rather than keep it secret.

'That way I'm free,' she said. 'The bad things that happened to me lose their power over me.'

'How old were you when you were put into the Mission?'

'I was taken off my mum and put in there when I was a baby.'

'So you were Stolen Generations too?'

'The tail end, one of the last,' Catherine said, her voice still calm.

I thought of Bowee voluntarily handing over Beverley Joy and Ronnie and then losing the next two children to illness. Catherine, I thought, must have been her youngest child. I wondered how Bowee would have coped with that final loss.

'You had a sister at the Mission, didn't you?'

'An aunty,' Catherine said. 'Louise Noble. I used to hang around her. I said, "What that girl got the same name as me for?" But she was a big girl, too busy hanging round with her friends to talk to me. Them missionaries, they never told me she was my aunty.'

'Louise?' Confused, I could feel myself frown. 'What about Beverley Joy? Wasn't she your sister?'

'She was my mum.'

I stopped abruptly. Faced Catherine.

'Beverley Joy was your mum?'

Catherine nodded. 'She give flowers to the Queen.' A note of pride in her voice.

I gaped at her. If Catherine had been sexually abused at Kurrawang, and I had no reason to doubt her word, then both mother and daughter had suffered the same fate. Catherine talked about the two infants – her uncles – who had died of pneumonia and gastroenteritis. And about her grandmother, Bowee, who had died near my family's home, and whose funeral, I now knew, was the first Aboriginal funeral Mr Sercombe had attended. Bowee had died in a hit and run accident, Catherine said.

She gave no indication she knew of her mother's sexual abuse. The aunt, Louise Noble, who had lived at Kurrawang, was, I would later learn, a child of Giddum, Beverley Joy's father, born after the death of Bowee, Beverley Joy's mother, and subsequently relinquished to mission care.

'Did you ever see your mother?' I asked.

'I remember she brung me a doll once. No one encouraged me to spend time with her.' She sounded regretful. I couldn't even begin to imagine how she must feel about not taking one of her few opportunities to spend time with her mother, who would soon be stolen again, this time by death.

Eventually her mother had moved to the east coast, where she had lived with an older white man, who, according to Catherine, had not treated her well. Beverley Joy died – an alcohol-related death, Catherine thought – aged 32. The nature of Beverley Joy's death was unsurprising to me, given her trauma. She died seven years younger than her mother Bowee had been at the time of her death. Estelle Sharpe's prophecy, when Beverley Joy arrived at Kurrawang, of 'all the new wonders in life that were to be opened to her' fell tragically short.

Catherine and I resumed the slow rhythm of our walk. Recent rain had swollen the crazy-paving soil here, making it spongy underfoot. Catherine wore thongs, and every so often she would pause and stoop to rub between her toes, removing a stone or twig. She observed her surroundings keenly, stopping to point out the delicate shape of a young plant, its partially unfurled leaves like the fingers of two cupped hands facing each other.

'Do you have many memories of the Mission?'

Catherine nodded.

'One good thing that come from the Mission was my love of reading. Miss Smith encouraged me,' she said. 'I found the joy of being able to escape into another world.'

I remembered the Sharpes' memoir: 'Whither should they flee?'

'Do you have other happy memories of the Mission?'

'No.' Her voice sounded hard.

We reached a metal viewing platform next to a fenced-off, disused open cut mine, the excoriation in the earth's skin exposing a wound at least twice the size of a football field. We balanced opposite each other on the metal skeleton of benches with the wooden planks missing.

'What else do you remember about the Mission?' I asked.

'I used to piss the bed,' she said. 'They made me have cold showers.'

'As punishment?'

She nodded.

'When I had me own kids, I found meself doing the same thing and then one day I thought, "What am I doing? These kids are me own flesh and blood. Why am I doing what them mob did to me?"'

She told me how important her children were to her and how she had tried to be a good mother. She wanted to protect her children, she said, and warned them about abuse, a theme she would return to a number of times that day.

'There were other punishments at the Mission,' she said. 'They made us eat a teaspoon of salt or Tabasco for lying. Another time I got made to eat a mouldy sardine sandwich. Miss Smith told us we weren't allowed to throw our sandwiches out or she'd know, so I left mine in my schoolbag. On Monday morning Miss Smith found it and made me eat it. I was sitting at the table crying.'

The track had circled around and we were heading towards my rental car. Catherine stopped and bent to scrape a stick along a patch of soil, pale orange amid the darker red dirt. She told me she liked to paint and made her own colours from natural ochre her partner collected for her in the bush. One of her paintings was exhibited in the entrance to the Kalgoorlie Court House. We talked some more about Catherine's abuse, and the conversation opened up.

'Did you know your mother was abused at the Mission?' I said, slowly and carefully.

Catherine halted and stared at me with her dark eyes.

'No.'

I told her about the rape Greg and Adrian had witnessed. I said the missionaries had either not known of or not taken any action over the crime. Catherine listened quietly. She shook her head.

'That's terrible.'

She fell silent and we walked on. When she spoke again, she told me she wanted to make a piece of art. She said she would cut her mother's photo into nine pieces. Using barbed wire, she would shape a noughts and crosses board on the canvas and reassemble her mother's picture. I was reminded yet again of how hard the people I'd met worked to overcome the negative effects of trauma, their refusal to become passive victims.

'I've never been able to find out the name of my father,' she said.

Several months later, I paid Catherine another visit.

'Last time you mentioned not knowing who your father was,' I said. 'How do you feel about that now?'

'I don't want to find out,' Catherine said. 'I am who I am.'

'Have you ever tried to find out?'

'I asked an old aunt once. She did this.' Catherine assumed a sad expression, bent her head and shielded her eyes with a hand, in the attitude of someone who knew better than to look at something she wouldn't want to see. 'She said she knew that this day would come. She told me a name. But I never knew him.'

The following day, on our way to the swimming pool in Kalgoorlie, Catherine, her youngest daughter and I stopped in at the Court House to admire Catherine's painting. A couple of metres square, it depicts the Seven Sisters, one of Catherine's ancestral stories, in an intricate network of dots in circles and wavy lines. The painting also depicts bush foods and Catherine had encouraged her children to place handprints around the circumference, symbolising, to my mind, their orbit around Catherine, the central influence in their lives. The paints were all made from ochre or charcoal. As we drove back towards Coolgardie through Kalgoorlie's streets, Catherine noticed Wongi fringe dwellers clustered on street corners.

'I grew up afraid of the Wongi,' she said. 'I went to piano lessons at lunchtime, behind Sheed's grocery, and if I saw Wongi, I crossed to the other side of the street. Uncle Ronnie, he would call out to me, and I would cross the street, away from him. I reckon I learned to be scared of the fringe dwellers when I was in the Mission. We're still jigsaw puzzling our families back together again.'

To Be a Friend

The simple fact that friendship depends on give and take took me a while to figure out. Several weeks after Mr Sercombe's funeral, I invited Greg to stay with me at the Mullumbimby cottage Kevin and I owned. On the day of Greg's arrival, I was standing on a desk scrubbing mould from the top of a wall with a sharp-smelling mix of water and vinegar. On finishing, I rose to my tiptoes, ready to leap down, and accidentally hyper-flexed my right forefoot. I heard a sickening snap and felt a stabbing pain.

X-rays at the hospital confirmed a broken bone, requiring a boot and crutches. The following day, I handed Greg the keys to go sightseeing and grinned.

'It took a broken foot to get you to drive.'

Greg laughed and climbed into the driver's seat.

A couple of days later, I left Greg at the cottage and joined my husband for a long-planned getaway for our thirtieth wedding anniversary. Three days later Greg met up with us at our Sydney house. He fitted in easily, questioning my son about his university course and chiding Kevin on his lack of sporting knowledge. It was un-Australian, Greg said, to not know the footy score, and unnatural to go surfing: didn't Kevin know the ocean was a shark's kitchen?

In between trips to the zoo, to Redfern and to the Blue Mountains, I asked Greg if, culturally, he found it strange going 'out and about' with a married white woman.

'Well, I wouldn't be here if my missus was alive,' he said. 'But you're my friend, and I wouldn't do anything to mess that up.'

It occurred to me then that for quite some time we'd had our sights set on the same thing – friendship. Of course it was a friendship with borders. Greg had lived through experiences I would never fully comprehend, and he faced down preconceived opinions and lowered expectations on an almost daily basis, something I would occasionally find a window into but for the most part never saw.

During another conversation, Greg told me of a visit he, Adrian and a couple of cousins made to Kurrawang not long after Greg first arrived in Perth, to visit Tony and Robbie. To Greg, the Mission still felt like home compared to the inhospitable outside world. He approached Robert Smith, the missionary he knew best, and asked permission to stay.

Mr Smith seemed dubious. After checking that Greg neither smoked nor drank, he said he would discuss it with the other missionaries. Greg, Adrian and the cousins continued on into Kalgoorlie, where they camped for the night. The next day, they returned to Kurrawang and Mr Smith granted Greg permission. Greg fetched a denim jacket and his spare pair of jeans from the car, waved goodbye to Adrian and the cousins and settled back into the boys' dormitory. Mr Smith rummaged up more clothing for Greg. Knowing him to be a responsible and keen worker, the service station Greg had worked at while still a state ward was happy to take him back. To enable Greg to get to work more easily and in one of his more fatherly gestures, Mr Smith started teaching him to drive. Before he got his licence, Alison Sercombe, one of Mr Sercombe's daughters, drove him to work each day, a huge privilege, apparently, as she was beautiful and all the boys envied Greg his private time with her.

Eventually Mr Smith organised a partition next to Greg's bed to afford him some privacy. Greg stayed at Kurrawang for 18 months, his return probably simultaneously indicating the relative safety the Mission represented to him and how ill-prepared it left the residents for independent life, turning them out without secure family relationships or adequate skills, and no money at all. When the Smiths moved to Pukulari with Robbie and the other boys, Greg moved too, staying six months. Only after his departure did Mrs Smith's pampering sessions begin.

Yet another conversation between Greg and me took place at the kitchen bench over steaming cups of tea.

'A couple of weeks ago, this old guy, Alf Taylor, asked me when I was going to forgive my mother,' Greg said. 'He was an elder. He knew my parents. And then in them pages you give me to read, you made a quick reference to her. You said how it wasn't her fault. How she was Stolen Generations too. It's not something my brothers and sisters and me ever thought about. It's like old Alf was preparing me to listen to what you said.'

I asked Greg if he'd like to read what I knew, from the document in his book and from searching online, about his mother.

'That'd be good,' Greg said.

I handed over the pages, precious few because there was so little to work with, so thoroughly had Native Welfare worked to eradicate Aboriginal pasts. Greg put his glasses on and started to read, not stopping until the end.

'I didn't know any of this. None of us did,' he said slowly, wonderingly, as if he'd finally ventured up a hill he'd always known existed, only to be astonished by an unexpected view. I thought how strange it was that he should learn some of the details of his mother's life, years after her death, from me, a white woman who had never known her. Details that should have been made available to him by Native Welfare a long time before. His voice hardened. 'The only thing I want you to change in these pages is her name. Call her Miss Ugle. She wasn't married. Native Welfare wouldn't let her.'

As is often the case with Aboriginal people born before 1970, there is some confusion about Miss Ugle's age. A Native Welfare document gives her age at the time of her mother's death in 1939 as 10. Someone, presumably an official, later discovered an error and, after crossing out the original number, changed Miss Ugle's age to six. She went to live with her grandmother Mrs William McKenzie at Badjaling Mission. Imagine Miss Ugle's distress a year later, when, having adapted to life with her grandmother, she was removed by Native Welfare and sent to East Perth Girls' Home because 'it was thought she would do better', this girl with a 'half-caste' or '3/4s black' mother and 'half-caste' father and the lighter skin they bequeathed her.

The infamous Commissioner AO Neville, formerly Western Australia's Chief Protector, went on long service leave on 28 March 1940, prior to his retirement in October of that year; Miss Ugle's removal on 17 March would have been one of the last he authorised.

From the East Perth Girls' Home, perhaps because she was younger than first realised, Miss Ugle was sent to the Moore River Native Settlement, the mission immortalised in Doris Pilkington's *Follow the Rabbit-Proof Fence* and the subsequent film, and known for its severe conditions. In his Stolen Generations testimony, Sam Dinah, a former resident, describes being locked in his dormitory each night from 6 p.m. until 6 a.m. without adult supervision, unable even to access a toilet. In *Broken Circles*, Anna Haebich writes of residents, 'They ate in silence under the watchful eye of the Aboriginal police who ruled "by the strap". With no cutlery they were obliged to eat with their hands.' Moore River existed to train 'half-castes' for the workforce. Imagine a seven-year-old girl waking in the night, surrounded by other children she barely knew, no family in sight. Not even a pillow to muffle her sobs as she lay on a hard pallet, desperate to go to the toilet, possibly wetting the bed before the doors are unlocked, only to receive a scolding and, according to former Moore River resident Lewis Wallam (Catherine Noble's partner), the punishment of being locked up. Miss Ugle received no schooling. She suffered chronic ear infections, requiring several hospitalisations in Perth and an operation. She likely never saw family members.

In 1942, Miss Ugle's grandmother appealed to the Department of Native Welfare for care of her granddaughter; her request was denied. The following year, Miss Ugle, aged 10 according to the altered document, was sent to Mount Rupert, a large wheat station owned by Sir Eric

Fleming Smart and his wife Lady Jean Constance. She lasted two weeks before being returned to Moore River for unspecified reasons. Perhaps Lady Jean saw through any attempt to pass the girl off as 14. Or perhaps Lady Jean saw the young girl's extreme vulnerability to men on the station. One year, 30 of 80 girls sent into domestic service from Moore River returned pregnant. It's thought that some of the babies from such unions were murdered by authorities, or by the white fathers if the girl remained in service. If there were more sinister reasons for Miss Ugle's return, I was unable to find them – which doesn't mean they didn't exist.

Miss Ugle subsequently absconded several more times, being caught and returned to the Mission each time. 'She was a runner, my mum was,' Greg said, seemingly pleased to find evidence of her systematic rebelliousness. On one occasion, she ended up 'in the company of Allied Negro servicemen', which must have struck horror into the Native Welfare officers, intent as the department was on breeding out blackness. The last time she absconded, Miss Ugle was sent to Carrolup Native Settlement.

In 1947, the Settlement submitted a 'Notice of Intention to Marry' form on behalf of 14-year-old Miss Ugle and a man called Phil Donaldson. Permission was denied, reportedly because Donaldson was already married. The following year, Miss Ugle gave birth to Greg's half-brother Roger, whom Greg only ever saw twice, once as a child, once later.

Despite all the traumas she lived through, Miss Ugle went on to establish a relationship with Greg's father, with whom she lived for at least 14 years. For an undetermined number of those years, she struggled with domestic violence and alcohol dependency. Who wouldn't want to numb the pain of her background? She received no help, no rehabilitation, no pension to ease the poverty of John Jackamarra's periodic unemployment. In 1965, she attempted suicide and two weeks later, received a jail sentence of 42 days when really what she needed was medical care. On her release, her children were gone, made state wards until the age of 16, their whereabouts unknown to her.

On his final day in Sydney, Greg and I were again on stools at the kitchen bench. He said his son Ben had found Miss Ugle's grave.

'He rang me from the cemetery one day and said, "Dad, I've found Nanna." I didn't know who he meant but he told me he meant my mum. I could talk to the others and maybe we could all visit the grave together.'

Greg, it seemed, had his own reconciliation business to attend to, and that, I understood by then, would be a private affair, for the family.

I returned to Catherine Noble during a time of searing heat. She and her 10-year-old daughter lifted an old wooden table into the shade of a eucalypt, and Catherine pulled up several chairs. While I read the chapter I'd written about Catherine and her mother Beverley Joy aloud, Catherine's daughter played on my laptop, quizzing me every so often about my photos. Catherine assured me she wanted her daughter to hear. A couple of Catherine's young grandchildren interrupted from time to time to show me a water pistol, or try on my sunglasses. At one point, I stopped to ask Catherine if she was doing okay with what I'd written.

'Yes,' she said quietly. 'It's taking me back to that day we had.'

At chapter's end, Catherine said she wanted no changes. 'It's what happened. It's good to tell my story.' She paused. 'What was her real name again? My mother? You said her real name. I never knew it.'

'Owatta,' I said.

'Owatta.' She repeated the name several times. Again I thought how odd and wrong it was that it fell to me to deliver information about a mother to an Aboriginal person. Aboriginal people can access their Department records, but perhaps the onus shouldn't be on the Aboriginal person. Perhaps government departments and churches should join forces and set about locating Stolen Generations people and their descendants and offering them the option of being given all available information pertaining to their families. Catherine fell silent, a look of wonder on her face, and then said, 'I never knew.'

Adrian met me a second time, on the front verandah of his house, with his wife Audrey and two adult sons. We sat in a mismatched assortment of chairs. Adrian's health had not been good. He was still recovering from a stroke before Christmas 2014. A few months earlier, he'd been admitted to hospital for heart problems. Three of his sisters were admitted at the same time with similar problems, the four of them ranging in age from their early 50s to early 60s.

One of Adrian's sons said he'd been unable to finish the transcript of his father's interview with me. He found the story too sad, hated to think of his father and uncles as anything other than strong men. He said they never talked about the Mission. His comment prompted Adrian to start talking, telling his sons stories of their grandparents and the Mission. It felt like a moment of profound sharing.

Adrian walked me out to my rental car.

'I've been wanting to talk to you about the rape,' I said. 'It wasn't your fault. You were too young to stop those boys. It was a violence against you too, you know, being forced to watch.'

The sun beat down on the concrete driveway. Adrian stopped and looked at me, and when he spoke, his voice seemed to come from a deep, hidden place, a raw and elemental core stripped of all artifice, like the engine room in a ship, that he rarely visited himself and likely spoke of even less.

'Amanda, when I left the Mission, I come to Perth. I took up boxing. Every time I was in that ring, every single time, I was fighting those rapists.'

My immediate reaction was to think how heartbreaking and sad, and then I thought how great it was that Adrian had figured out a safe way to express his anger, had escaped the intergenerational violence that affects so many Aboriginal people. But of course it was all more complicated. Many Aboriginal men turned to the boxing tents for a ready source of income. You could earn up to $40 a fight. It was one of the few readily available avenues of employment, performing in a ring in a tent, often for the enjoyment of white men. And boxing had failed to ease Adrian's sense of guilt.

During my most recent visit to Adrian, we were once more sitting on the front porch, gazing out over a lawn browned by a recent heatwave. An athletic teenager in a basketball shirt bicycled up the driveway – one of Adrian's 13 grandchildren. After a brief exchange between Adrian and his grandson, Adrian and I got to talking about the Mission.

'You've had some hard times, haven't you?' I said.

'You don't know the half of it," he said, sounding disbelieving himself, rather than angry or accusatory, as I might have expected when we met.

'I know some of it.' I looked Adrian right in the eye.

'You know about Henry and Grace?' He sounded surprised.

'How do you survive a loss like that?' I said.

According to Greg, Adrian's wife Audrey had refused a smoking ceremony, traditionally performed to drive away the deceased's spirit. I could imagine doing the same thing in her position.

'They're still here, Amanda. Those thirteen grandchildren? Whenever one of them walks in, I see a little of Henry or Grace in them, in the way they look, what they say, the way they move.' Hard-won words, spoken with conviction.

Adrian still visited his children's graves several times a week, Greg said. At the time of the accident, Greg was quoted in the media as asking where the police were the day Henry and Grace died. Only one police car had been chasing the stolen car that ploughed into Henry and Grace's car, which Greg thought insufficient to safeguard other drivers on the road. On the other hand, when the police had questioned Greg's son near a police station over the ownership of his bike, a crowd of policemen had gathered to watch the spectacle.

Adrian took me inside, showed me photos on the wall. Two beautiful teenagers, their smiles easy and natural, as if they knew where they came from and could face the future with confidence. I wanted but couldn't even begin to imagine the sound of their laughter and running feet filling the house, or the sight of a young arm thrown casually around a parent's shoulder. Adrian pointed to Henry's photo. 'He was an actor. Was in lots of TV ads.' And of Grace's photo: 'She was a brainbox.'

Adrian and I returned to our seats on the front verandah. When we'd talked a while longer, an hour and a half in all, Adrian paused.

'I've taken up enough of your time,' he said.

But it was me who had taken up Adrian's time, and he had given me the most generous gift of all in inviting me into his life and sharing such personal details.

Chain Reaction

My ongoing friendship with Bronwyn is complicated. She is homeless and lives on welfare, a combination of circumstances that make it difficult to get ahead. The inevitable happened, and Bronwyn asked for more financial help.

I remembered my American friend telling me to donate through charities. I knew Professor Judy Atkinson, the author of *Trauma Trails*, believed bureaucratic intervention to cause dependency and increased feelings of victimisation. Atkinson is scarcely a voice in the wilderness, and wouldn't giving money privately have the same outcome?

Greg told me Bronwyn was my friend and if I could help, I should, and allow her to spend the money as she liked. I both agreed and disagreed. While I didn't want to be yet another white person dictating terms, neither did I want to be part of a chain reaction leading to liver disease or lung cancer. Bronwyn said she'd drunk heavily at times, although was drinking less now. When she had the money, she smoked up to a packet a day, although she was trying to cut down and would eventually start using nicotine patches. And while I sometimes found it tempting to think she should spend any money she had on food, I could see that a homeless person with a history of severe trauma might well be tempted to self-medicate. I also knew there were next to no culturally sensitive facilities available in the Kalgoorlie region for an Aboriginal person wanting to give up any kind of substance abuse. During a morning spent in court, I saw two Wongi mothers pleading with the magistrate to keep their sons in custody and therefore off the streets and away from drugs. One parent had seen her child go through the only available local treatment options, only to have nothing change for them.

The deciding factor was my love for Bronwyn. If muscle memory exists, then so too does soul memory. We talk often on the phone, and spend hours together when I visit. We laugh, we tease, sometimes we scold. Like the day in Kalgoorlie recently, prior to my visit to Adrian in Perth, when I arrived a couple of hours late to find her sitting in a chair on the footpath, crocheting as she waited for me. I'd texted several times to alert Bronwyn to my delay, but she must have come down from her son's Homes West flat, where she'd been staying, ahead of time.

'I've been sitting out here two hours,' she fumed. 'Where have you been?'

'I'm sorry,' I said. 'I won't do that to you again.'

'Where have you been?' she repeated. *Account for yourself.*

Her anger reassured me as to how she viewed our relationship. Where I'd been was my business, not hers, but next time we met, I was early.

To ignore a friend with less than enough seems wrong, so when Bronwyn has asked, I've helped, unless I've thought she'd asked too often – more a measure of my confusion over whether giving money to someone who would most likely buy cigarettes and alcohol was the right thing to do than her need.

Of course, the money thing was bound to run into complications. A little over a year ago, my husband and I bought Bronwyn a secondhand Holden Commodore. Not long afterwards, an ongoing argument between Bronwyn's family and another family came to a head. One of the people involved rammed Bronwyn's stationary car; she wasn't in it but one of her grandsons, who had no licence, was. Fearing for his life, he drove off in her car. He was stopped by the police and charged, and the car was impounded.

Months passed before I visited Kalgoorlie again. I took Bronwyn to the impound yard. She didn't have the registration papers and was unable to recall the number plate. A person who knew Bronwyn served us and told Bronwyn no record of a car belonging to her existed. Bronwyn and I went to the Transport Authority to check the registration. A woman told us, not unkindly, that Bronwyn needed personal identifying information from Centrelink to access information. We drove to Centrelink, where Bronwyn queued with others, many of them Wongi, while the security guard unlocked a 'public' bathroom for me to use. When I exited, the door of the not-so-public bathroom relocked itself.

We returned to the Transport Authority. They held records of other cheap cars Bronwyn had owned, all ancient, unwanted vehicles that inevitably broke down, but the car we'd bought Bronwyn seemed to have vanished into thin air.

Back in her son's Homes West flat, Bronwyn searched her personal belongings yet again. This time she found the third party insurance certificate. It gave the registration number and indicated that registration had been up to date at the time of impounding. We returned to the impound yard. An assistant checked their records and, lo and behold, was now able to tell us that a letter had been sent to Bronwyn saying, in effect, that her car had been released by the court and she was free to collect it. The woman told us the car was taken to the tip when Bronwyn didn't turn up.

'The tip?' I said. 'So you're telling me you didn't receive any money for the car?'

'No,' the woman said. 'It went to the tip.'

'Is that even legal?' I asked.

The woman shrugged, said it was, suggested I speak to the Impound police.

Under the impression that any type of policeperson could be found at the police station, I took Bronwyn there. We rang the bell at the untended desk. Ten minutes later, we rang it again. The door opened and a policeman emerged. I could see into the back room, to a couple of policemen chatting, another munching a doughnut. The policeman suggested I ring the bell again. I did. This time, an administrative clerk emerged. She clearly knew Bronwyn, and wrote down the name of Bronwyn's deceased partner without asking.

Between us, Bronwyn and I repeated the story. The woman disappeared into the back room. A policewoman emerged, a tall woman of heavy build, clipboard in hand. She asked Bronwyn the whereabouts of another Aboriginal woman. Bronwyn gave her the information; the Wongi grapevine works efficiently in Kalgoorlie.

By now I needed the bathroom again, so I asked the

policewoman to unlock the supposedly public bathroom. When I emerged, she had taken over from the clerk regarding Bronwyn's car. Bronwyn was getting frustrated; her voice was rising. The policewoman told her she'd have to leave if she didn't calm down. Bronwyn turned away, pressed her lips together, folded her arms across her body.

'Are you listening to me?' the policewoman demanded.

No reply.

'She's listening,' I said.

To my right, a man with a young child was reporting a missing wallet. He needed to buy nappies for the child, he said.

The policewoman asked another question or two, which I answered, then she disappeared into the back room and returned a couple of minutes later. Red-faced, she glared at me.

'You already know you have to call the Impound Unit.' She sounded livid. Wrote down a number on a card and handed it to me. So now I knew: you can't find all types of police at the police station.

'Thank you for your help.' My voice was overly polite. 'And what was your name?'

The policewoman's eyes bored into me. At that moment, she was her uniform, and her uniform was a bully. Seething, she turned her badge over, so I could inspect her photo. She ground out her name through clenched teeth, inadvertently guaranteeing that I'd remember it.

I'd given up for the day. It seemed inconceivable that Bronwyn's car could be impounded even though she hadn't been the driver. But of course, if you own a car, you're ultimately responsible for who drives it and how. Fair enough. I want my children to be safe on the roads too. However, it seems to me that the Kalgoorlie police know how to tap into the grapevine when they want to. When it came to letting Bronwyn know she could collect her car, they didn't bother.

Charges against Bronwyn's grandson were dropped because he was attempting to flee the assailant. The letter to Bronwyn went to a relative's house, the address that Bronwyn, homeless, used for official purposes. The relatives, who were going through an ordeal themselves, mislaid the notice. But we found out that Bronwyn's car was not taken to the tip, as we'd been told. Bronwyn's son told her he'd seen another woman driving the car. The police confirmed that the car had been sold.

Blaming Bronwyn is the easy option here: she didn't check on the car, and somehow her grandson had access to the keys and was able to drive without a licence. But with her car impounded, Bronwyn had no transport. It was a good hour's walk in hot temperatures from her temporary accommodation to the impound yard. Besides, the car was damaged and she had no money to repair it. And I had been across the continent and clueless as to how to deal with the situation. It was difficult enough when I finally made it to Kalgoorlie. And it was difficult enough with my white skin, well-educated accent and air-conditioned rental car.

Later that day, I accompanied Bronwyn to the Goldfields Indigenous Housing Organisation in Kalgoorlie. A helpful woman with an Irish accent tried to explain a new scheme to Bronwyn. Her debt could be halved and she would be eligible for housing while repaying the debt over time. But Bronwyn wouldn't listen. Her ire having already been raised at the police station, she ranted at the woman about the injustice of not being given a house when her other house had burned down. Bronwyn had been out of town, 500 kilometres away at a funeral. When she returned to Kalgoorlie, her house was gone, everything lost except for a bed and a green tin of photos. Bronwyn claimed to have been $3000 ahead in rent at the time. Eight thousand dollars of furniture belonging to her daughter went up in smoke. Nothing was reimbursed.

I tried to calm Bronwyn.

'Let her speak,' the woman with the Irish accent said. 'She needs to be heard.'

The woman, one of the few people we'd encountered who carried out her job in a kind and helpful manner, was right. Bronwyn did need to be heard. But Bronwyn was all steamed up and unable to stop, taking her anger out on the woman in a personal way. Eventually the woman shook her head.

'You're not being fair, Bronwyn,' she said. 'It's not my fault, and I'm trying to help. Come back when you're ready to be fair.'

Afterwards, in the car, Bronwyn looked contrite.

'I need to go back and see her,' she said. 'I need to apologise.'

So Bronwyn may yet get a house.

Bringing Them Home – to Where?

After a failed previous attempt, I made contact with former Kurrawang missionaries Doreen and Robert Smith, using Facebook, that most modern of research tools. Doreen suggested we meet at a coffee shop – 'neutral territory' – and told me to look for a woman with a pearl-entwined walking stick, a large woman, 'so don't go looking for a little lady'. Her self-deprecating description made her immediately likeable to me.

With coffees and toasted cheese sandwiches on their way, Doreen, Robert and I settled down to talk. Yet again the wheeze of coffee machines, the scrape of chairs on tile and the echoing babble of hundreds of voices formed the backdrop for my interview. Doreen reminded me of my mother and any number of women I'd known through my mother's church association, easy to talk to and well-intentioned.

Robert appeared to regard me with a little more suspicion. He started to tell their story. He arrived at Kurrawang in 1966. Planning to stay six months to work on the construction of the new boys' dormitory, he stayed 25 years with a year's break early on, after his marriage to Doreen, who had arrived in 1967.

When the Smiths first became house parents, they looked after 25 boys, with the assistance of Mr McGeorge.

'Often the parents would visit,' Robert said. 'But not the Ugles' parents. Mr Ugle came once. He lost his leg. In the Midland area, I think. He was drunk. Was run over by a train. There was little government communication about the children. We never knew exactly where they came from and usually didn't know where their parents were.'

Writing as fast as I could, I nodded, not bothering to correct him: Greg's father was John Jackamarra; he wasn't called Mr Ugle.

'We had no training, no qualifications; we wouldn't get away with it now,' Doreen said.

'I was a carpenter,' Robert added.

'And I was an office girl. We always knew we were substitute parents. That's why we got them to call us "Aunty" and "Uncle". It's Aboriginal tradition, you know, to call your elders by those names,' added Doreen.

'Robbie said he had to call you "Mummy" and "Daddy".'

'No. The Sharpes were called that. We called them "Mummy and Daddy Sharpe" too. And we had to call each other "Mr Smith" or "Mrs Smith" or whatever in front of the children.'

'Mr Sharpe's rules?'

'Yes.'

The Smiths denied that siblings had been separated intentionally, claiming it was an age and gender matter, a decision made by Mr Sharpe so he could manage them more efficiently.

'But they were all like family, even though they were too big a group to be a family,' Doreen added.

'I used to take the boys bush every Saturday, on the back of the truck,' Robert said. 'Then we'd walk for three or four hours. They could do what they wanted. Be boys. Go hunting. Collect things, like quandong nuts to take back and make flour.' He paused, laughed. 'We went bush one day and when we came back the other couple that helped look after the boys had packed up and left. No one knew they were going. They were harsh, very British in their attitude.' Another pause. 'Not Mr Sercombe.'

They declined to name the couple, unsurprising given the close-knit nature of the Brethren community. Initially, Robert assumed the role of cook, and then Mr Sercombe took over, as he himself had told me.

'Why did Mr Sercombe leave?' I asked. 'He gave burnout as the reason but I got the impression there was friction between him and some of the other missionaries.' I remembered him saying that you can't get on with everyone, and that some things are best forgotten.

'He felt unsuited to the task of manager,' Robert said. 'He had come to help the old people, not the children. And he had no real control. Any changes he tried to make were undone.'

'By Mr Sharpe?' I said.

Robert nodded.

'I don't want to criticise him. But when he retired to Esperance, he still wanted to control things. Good pioneers are not always good team players. He had drive, tenacity and the strength to stick with things. But he couldn't let go.'

This struck me as being at odds with the Open Brethren practice of shared authority. The word 'Esperance' jogged my memory.

'I remember taking Bronwyn Newland to Esperance for a holiday,' I said.

Robert and Doreen both looked agitated.

'Ah. For Christmas, was it? That happened once.' I could hear derision in Robert's voice. 'Native Welfare said they wanted the children to have a good Christmas. They had a good Christmas! They never missed out. People sent presents from all over. But Native Welfare wanted the children to be billeted out with local people.'

The children were sent out two days before Christmas. Apparently Tony Ugle was unhappy with his 'family'. On Boxing Day, they rang Native Welfare and arranged for him to return to the Mission. According to the Smiths, the missionaries told Native Welfare that it would be all or none from then on: there could be no favourites regarding who went out and who didn't. And that was the end of the billeting experiment.

The missionaries had other issues with Native Welfare, saying they'd sent three young boys who'd been found guilty in the court system to the Mission. One was 13.

'We got him when my parents were staying with us. The first night, my dad was doing the washing up and the boy was drying the dishes. He had a carving knife in his hand.' Doreen held her hands 12 inches apart to indicate the knife's length. 'He said, "I stabbed my dad with one of these." Lucky my dad was calm. He asked the boy why he stabbed his father. The boy said, "Because my dad was belting my mum."'

'Native Welfare never told us anything about those boys,' Robert said. 'The boys told us themselves. We had them among our other boys. They could have been a bad influence on them. We did a three-for-one trade – a boy from a hostel in Kalgoorlie who used to wag school in exchange for the three boys. The hostel had a locked area.'

The Smiths grumbled some more about Native Welfare – the lack of communication, the inexperience of university graduates who posed as experts. I murmured sympathetically as they talked: imagining the frustration of dealing with a top-heavy bureaucracy hundreds of miles away wasn't difficult. I checked my watch: if I wanted to ask the tough questions, I'd need to do so soon. But I knew by now to cover some easier territory first, a technique that could be seen equally as softening up before going in for the kill, or allowing the interviewee to present their best side first. Interviewing ethics, I was finding, were as muddy as human motivation.

'Greg told me you changed the fashion,' I said to Doreen.

'What do you mean?' She sounded worried, looked defensive.

'He said you got rid of outdated clothing.'

'It was first in, best dressed when we arrived,' Doreen said. 'Whatever they could find. Baggy clothing. Those silly shoes.'

'Jellies?' I asked.

'Yes. I changed it so they had their own clothes, labelled with their names. And proper shoes. We raised money for new bedspreads too. We saw Greg recently and he said, "When we were little, they meant a lot to us."'

'That's another thing I want to ask you about,' I said. 'Why did you take him back after he'd left?'

'Two cars of Aboriginals turned up that day,' Robert said.

'We're Christians,' Doreen said. 'Our fellow workers said not to take him back because he'd been out in the world and would be a bad influence on the others. We had half an hour to make up our minds. We sat on our bed and prayed and looked at each other. When we first started, we'd prayed that we would make a home that they'd want to come back to. So we decided to let Greg come back.' Their story only departed from Greg's in the time they spent deliberating: not half an hour but overnight, according to Greg.

We discussed Greg's return to work at the service station and then I said, 'You taught him to drive?'

'Yes,' said Robert. 'His first car was in my name. He used to stay out past curfew. I used to have to go looking for him.'

'Robert was always going out to look for him,' Doreen said. 'Greg stopped out until midnight. Sometimes all night.'

'What did you say to him?'

'Well, I couldn't force him to come back,' Robert said. 'He was nineteen. He was usually at Sherma's house. I'd say, "Don't you think it's time to come home?" He needed some sleep to get to work the next day, you see.'

I gave a perfunctory nod, and grinned. Greg's behaviour sounded pretty normal for a young man with a girlfriend who would become his wife. Over time, Greg had taken to mentioning Sherma's name in passing, when telling a story, but we still never discussed their marriage. It was good to hear that he'd stayed out late and occasionally stole a few dollars from the missionaries (money that probably came from the substantial portion of his pay packet he handed over each pay day). His misdemeanours made the pedestal I'd come to place him on a little shaky, brought him closer to my flawed self.

'Tony was thirteen or fourteen then,' Mr Smith said. 'Unsettled. One day I heard Greg through the wall. Tony was saying he wanted to leave. Greg went crook at Tony. "You don't know what it's like out there," he said. Taking Greg back was the best thing ever. He used to help with those boys. Greg and Sherma did more to help Aboriginal people than any other Aboriginal couple I know. They were always helping Aboriginal people. They had them in their house. Greg helped them with their cars.'

I needed to leave soon to catch a flight home. My mind was racing while I scribbled away: I still had my more difficult questions to ask and I didn't want to sound accusatory.

'What sort of punishment did you use?'

'They used to get a hiding,' Robert said.

'That was before we had television,' Doreen said. 'After we got television we could withdraw privileges.'

I pressed further about the beatings. Said Adrian had described a specific incident with Robert. Robert said Adrian was the only one he couldn't catch.

'They were fast, the Ugles,' Doreen said.

'Adrian was very specific with details.' I said. 'He said you sent him to Mr Sercombe. He described the stick. Said the beating took place in the store.'

Robert shrugged, said he didn't remember.

'That was the punishment back then,' Doreen said. 'They used to get caned at school. At the Mission, if someone had to be beaten, someone else had to witness the beating and it had to be recorded in a book. I know because

I did the recording. Native Welfare could inspect the book. I don't feel great about it. I can't watch the *Rabbit-Proof Fence.* It's too close to home.' She pursed her lips, looked more upset than she had through the whole interview. 'We weren't perfect. We did things we regret. We didn't have the training. We didn't know what we were doing.'

'I remember clipping teenagers over the ears.' Robert spoke quickly, giving me the impression he was eager to unburden himself of a wrong he'd carried in his heart a long time, and he sounded genuinely remorseful. 'I wouldn't do that now because I know the damage that can cause. You didn't know what to do, how to punish them, in those days.'

'Robbie said you used to beat them with a hose at Pukulari.'

'It was probably the nearest thing to hand.' Robert said, with a pleading smile, head tilted to the side. He shrugged, hands out and palms up, as if to say *what do you do?* 'It was a twenty-four-hour job, seven days a week. No such thing as rosters.'

Finally I mentioned Beverley Joy Noble. Doreen said she'd known her as a friend.

'Before I lived at Kurrawang,' she said. 'I visited a couple of times. Beverley Joy and I were the same age. We got on really well. I was fifteen or sixteen then. When I came back she'd had the baby. She was an alcoholic.'

The Smiths said they'd known nothing of the rape until a few days previously, when Greg had told them. They gave no indication of understanding that the sexual abuse might have contributed to her alcoholism.

'Catherine came to live with us as a baby,' Doreen said. 'She was abused by her mother. When she got older, I used to get her to help me with my own baby daughter, so she'd learn how to look after a baby herself. I always knew she'd do well.'

We finished up and said goodbye and I returned to the overheated interior of my rental car, baking in the sun. On the way to the airport, I felt torn by the need to tell the truth, and a desire to not cause harm to any of the living. The responsibility of deciding if I'd even been told the truth weighed heavily, as it always did. But really, I chose that responsibility when I took on the task of writing this story, just as the Smiths chose the responsibility to care for those children. And when you take on a responsibility, you are accountable.

I admired the Smiths for agreeing to meet with me, although I also suspected their capitulation came from realising the inevitability of the book and wanting to put forward their views. I admired too their admissions of guilt, incomplete as they might well have been, and their remorse. It takes courage to admit mistakes when you were acting within the guidelines of a faulty system you didn't fully comprehend, and when you hadn't realised you were placing yourself in a position that would be judged openly and harshly by history.

Caning was indeed common in Western Australia in the 60s. Still, Native Welfare did not dictate the form of punishment and the missionaries could have chosen more enlightened methods. I have to remind myself they were probably under more duress than most white parents, who also had smaller numbers of children under their care. And in fact some of the white children would have experienced similar violence within their own families.

Regardless of how their actions are viewed, the Smiths, like the Sercombes, were endeavouring to do what they thought was best for the children, right or wrong, and narrow as that vision might have been, unlike most non-Indigenous Australians, who consciously or unconsciously chose not to see Aboriginal people's lives playing out on the streets or as reported in the news.

Our conversation confirmed the extent to which the Brethren feared the influence of the outside world on the Aboriginal children and how, like the Chief Protectors, they questioned the moral fibre of Aboriginal people in general. Sadly, apart from dispensing substantial doses of fairly rigid Christian values to the children in the hopes of keeping them on the straight and narrow, the missionaries did little to prepare the children for that immoral outside world. Instead, they set them adrift, more or less severing ties, Greg being the notable exception.

On a more personal level, our conversation cast my holiday with Bronwyn in a different light. While I'd been tickled pink to have a playmate for the holidays, and I do recall asking for Bronwyn specifically, Bronwyn had not had a choice. Granted, she seemed to have good memories of the time; even so, we took her away from her second family, her 'Mission' family, the friends with whom she lived, ate, played and travelled to school, making me more complicit than I'd thought, even if I hadn't known it at the time. Viewed from another angle, by a strange quirk of fate, a Native Welfare decree had thrown Bronwyn and me together, deepening our friendship in the process, and deepening my sense of responsibility now.

When I asked Greg's opinion, he said he was impressed

with the Smiths for not trying to hide behind the Bible, for admitting that the beatings were imperfect human solutions for what they saw as problem behaviour.

In a subsequent email exchange with Doreen Smith, I discovered a hitherto unknown connection I had with William and Marjorie Sharpe. The Brethren Church is actively involved in Scripture Union, a non-denominational Christian organisation that runs holiday beach missions for children. In Esperance in the 60s, I attended a fortnight-long day mission every Christmas holiday. It was a highlight; the missions offered bible studies, singing, prayers and sandcastle-building competitions (my castles never won a prize!). Kurrawang Mission children took part, too, although I have no memory of their presence. Mr and Mrs Sharpe, Doreen said, were often in charge.

The news came as a surprise, and emphasised the layered nature of so many aspects of my childhood. I remember the beach mission leaders as benign, gentle people, who preached a message of love and joy. No canes in sight. No separation of genders in the sandy tents that I can remember. If the beach mission was the antechamber to heaven, then Kurrawang led to some kind of hell, either while in residence or later.

I'd thought Greg might be unique in having wanted to return to a mission, but then, near the end of my research, I met Nicki Gordon, in the town of Leonora, where she was visiting family. Welfare removed Nicki, who was a baby, and her three sisters after their parents left them unsupervised at Tea Gardens, on the outskirts of Kalgoorlie. The children were sent to Norseman Mission. Nicki remembers children crying day and night. She remembers stealing biscuits because she was so hungry and being rapped over the knuckles. She remembers wetting the bed and being made to shower in cold water, wash the sheets and drag the mattress outside. She remembers chores like washing, cleaning and polishing shoes, which she enjoyed because they gave her a chance to be on her own and think.

When Nicki was seven or eight, the children were returned to their parents. The family lived on a reserve out of Kalgoorlie. After her father died, her mother 'lost the plot' and began drinking. One of Nicki's older sisters had left her three young children with their grandmother so she could live in Perth. During this time, Nicki's mother disappeared, leaving Nicki to care for her sister's three young children, alone on the reserve. They were sleeping in gravel pits and red diggings from mine shafts and had no food. Nicki was unable to attend school.

Nicki still remembers the name of the welfare officer who rescued them – Mr Budge. He suggested Kurrawang to Nicki and she thought it sounded like a good idea. She could be relatively close to another sister who lived in a hostel in Kalgoorlie and worked.

She felt secure in Kurrawang. 'The Comptons were really good to me. I was never abused or ill-treated. Mrs Compton was about as old as me oldest sister.'

Nicki spoke of having her own clothing and bed. She said she felt at home in Kurrawang and didn't want to leave, but was forced to before she turned 18. This was when she started to realise how ill-prepared for life outside the

Mission she was. She'd been encouraged to leave school at the end of year 10, and had no skills.

'I had no idea where to go. I didn't know who was out there for me.'

She stayed in the working girls' hostel with her older sister for a while. When Welfare sent a letter to say she was no longer a 'welfare kid', Nicki ripped the letter up and threw it away. For her, it was like being told she was no longer part of the family.

Eventually, Nicki found work as an Aboriginal liaison officer in the pre-primary system, but she is now too unwell to work. She dreams of owning a new bed with plenty of blankets – 'not those old grey prickly blankets. I want soft snuggly ones with a hint of lemony smell. And crispy white sheets and a bedspread of patchwork colours.'

'I've had a miserable life, and I'm just trying to make it better for my grandchildren,' she said. 'I went from squatting over a hole in the ground, to sitting on a pan that we used to empty. I still don't own a toilet.'

It took me several years to tease out the most recent sequence of events in Kurrawang's history. On 2 October 1970, a 99-year 'peppercorn lease' over native reserve 23648 had been given to the Kurrawang Christian Aboriginal Community, which was still functioning as a mission. At the end of the year Mr Sercombe left and another missionary, Mr Grenville Compton, took over. He oversaw a change from dormitory to family-style accommodation for the children. In 1974, Pukulari opened as family-style accommodation under the Smiths. In 1981, an Aboriginal

Child Care Agency was established in Perth. From then on, Aboriginal children in need of care were placed with Aboriginal families where possible. Gradually, children were withdrawn from Pukulari. According to the Smiths, the last child left Pukulari in 1986. The Smiths say they remained in the Burt Street premises until 1988. They say the government reclaimed the property in 1991 because Aboriginal children no longer lived there. How the Burt Street property was used between 1988 and 1991 remains unclear, although I suspect Brethren missionaries remained in occupation, free of charge.

With no more children to care for, the Brethren decided to develop Kurrawang into a place where Aboriginal families could live more independently and as 'a nucleus in which a spiritual work could be carried on'. Essentially, in order to maintain their Christian vision, the Brethren invited Christian Aboriginal families from Kalgoorlie's People's Church to live at the Mission. These families came primarily from the Mount Margaret Mission area, north-east of Kalgoorlie.

In 1984, a community-based executive was formed to administer the Christian Aboriginal Community. A number of white Brethren served alongside Christian Aboriginal representatives.

Then in 1993, the *Native Title Act* was passed. A slew of claims in the Kalgoorlie region ensued, a number of different family claims overlapping and including Kurrawang. By then, the Kurrawang community had started a thriving emu farm. Community leaders saw the writing on the wall. In conjunction with the Aboriginal Land Trust, the community now sought and succeeded in having the cancellation of the reserve proclaimed in December 1994. This paved the way for negotiations with the State government, apparently in conjunction with the Aboriginal Land Trust.

The following year, on 21 March, in a landmark move, the Western Australian Aboriginal Affairs minister handed over the freehold title for the Crown reserve land to the Kurrawang community, although technically the land was no longer a reserve. Kurrawang was now owned by Aboriginal people who, although they'd been mission residents as children, were not from Kurrawang. Nor did they necessarily have rights to the land through native title. Kurrawang was specifically carved out of surrounding native title land for the purpose of protecting the Brethren-assembled community.

In a submission to the House of Representatives Standing Committee dated 11 October 2000, Les Tucker, Chairperson of Kurrawang Aboriginal Community, referred to a recent $3 million NHAS grant for improvements. While every Aboriginal person in Australia has the right to a decent living standard, it seems unfair that the survivors of Kurrawang should witness such largesse extended towards their former home, yet receive so little themselves.

A year later, the Human Rights Royal Commission *Bringing Them Home* report recommended:

> That churches and other non-government agencies review their land holdings to identify land acquired or granted for the purpose of accommodating Indigenous children forcibly removed from their families and, in consultation with Indigenous people and their land councils, return that land.

In my initial enthusiasm, I'd thought the recommendation meant the land should be returned to people who had lived at the Mission as children. But this was not the case. The land would be subject to Native Title claims, which need to prove an ongoing connection to the land. A difficult task for Stolen Generations people.

The other complication, written about in the *Bringing Them Home* report, was that some people or their descendants lived in ex-Mission communities that were not on their traditional lands. The Kimberley Land Council refers to these people as 'the historical people'. In working with Traditional Owners, the Kimberley Land Council had, by the time of the report, helped create islands of such communities within larger Native Title claims.

In submissions to the 1997 National Inquiry into the Separation of Aboriginal and Torres Strait Islander Children from their Families, a number of churches such as the Anglican Church of Australia, Diocese of Perth, acknowledged that they'd contributed to the losses of the Stolen Generations through the Missions. Some churches agreed with land restitution. The Brethren Church was not listed in the appropriate appendix as having made a submission. But in having handed over the land to Christian Aboriginal families, they had, in essence, already complied with the report's recommendation.

A further recommendation of the report was for churches and other non-government agencies to arrange for the preservation, indexing and access of all records, which must surely include photographic records. Robert Smith has sorted all of his photos of Kurrawang and is happy to email copies to former residents on request. It is to be hoped he will eventually hand over the original copies for preservation. Max Jefferies and the Sercombe family also hold photographs, and it's likely that families of other former missionaries do too. Perhaps they, too, will see fit to allow access.

Lucky

In some ways, this is a story with no ending. It's the story of people who lived on this continent for tens of thousands of years before white people came, and who will prevail. In other ways, this story has a happy ending, but it hasn't happened yet. It will happen in change authored primarily by Aboriginal people; change to which the hearts of white people need to be open. Someone in the future will write the last chapters, a Ugle grandchild perhaps: the young woman who recently became the first Ugle to graduate from high school, or the girl with the winning smile and talent for art and science who drove with her grandfather and me to Kalgoorlie, for example. When Australia's Aboriginal peoples have equality, when every Aboriginal person has a roof over his or her head, when private home ownership becomes a reality for Aboriginal people now living on communal land, when all Aboriginal families have food on the table, access to education and healthcare, employment opportunities and the same life expectancy as non-Indigenous Australians. When no Aboriginal person has to say, as Nakkiah Lui, writer, actor and Gamillaroi and Torres Strait Islander woman has, 'It's hard to put into words how incredibly worthless this country can make Aboriginal people feel.'

'Why should we be trying to make amends for things that happened in the past?' a friend said to me recently. 'My mother's family came out from England. They lived alongside the Thames. I imagine they were about as pleased to come here as the Aboriginal people were to have them. What about my family's claim to land on the Thames?'

Here's why it's not the same, my friend: you're sitting at a table in a café having spent the last hour surfing with your friends. You need do no sums in your head to see if you can afford a coffee because you're a doctor, so you know you can. Tomorrow you'll go to your work in a hospital, a job you have because of the education you received; a job you like and have no fear of losing. Probably no one will comment on the colour of your skin. If you go to the cafeteria for lunch, you won't wonder if the server is going to refuse to serve you or serve you last. If you complain about some aspect of the service, you're unlikely to be asked to leave. Likely no one other than your children will call you derogatory names, and even they will do so infrequently and without any real venom. You're not especially traumatised, because while some family member, guilty of a crime like petty theft, might have been forced to migrate to Australia, you don't come from a family of two or three or more generations of children who have been removed and placed in care for no better reason than the colour of their skin.

The day after I arrived back in Sydney, Greg called: his eldest brother Alfie had died. I'd never met Alfie, but knew from Greg that he lived in a nursing home. That he'd been an alcoholic, and had been ill since a recent stroke. Greg told me Alfie's Stolen Generations compensation money, held by the Public Trustee, was sufficient to cover funeral costs. If Greg saw any irony in how 'lucky' that was, he wasn't letting on. He invited me to attend the funeral. He wanted Alfie acknowledged.

And so, on a hot Perth day with business-as-usual blue skies, I stood in the vestibule of an overflowing funeral chapel, the only white person in a crowd of Noongar people. A parlour employee passed out attendance cards for everyone to write on. A couple of children passed out leaflets for the service. Through the doorway, I could see Alfie's coffin, light pine against a charcoal-grey wall. On top of the coffin stood a photo of Alfie, a larrikin smile on his face. Beside the photo a bouquet of yellow and red flowers. On the floor to one side, a wreath of yellow and red fresh flowers and black silk flowers. Death is political as well as personal in this Aboriginal community.

Air conditioning hummed in the background. A strip of fluorescent lighting illuminated a room of grieving family members, the men dressed in black trousers, white shirts and black ties, the women in similarly formal attire, the red, black and yellow colours of the Aboriginal flag present in the occasional badge or hat band. Almost everyone present was either a member of the Stolen Generations or related to someone who was.

A niece read the eulogy, a simple outline of Alfie's personal history along with messages from immediate family members. When she spoke of the night Alfie and his siblings were removed, her voice broke, and she stumbled over her words, pausing frequently to try to regain her composure. In the congregation, people bowed their heads and, shoulders shaking, silently dabbed at their eyes. Two older women hurried from the room. The sense of collective grief over the past, over a wound that had yet to properly heal because it had yet to be properly addressed, was tangible.

Afterwards, we drove to the Midland Cemetery, to a waiting crowd of several hundred Noongar, Wongi and other Aboriginal people. Robert and Doreen Smith also turned up, Robert pushing Doreen in a wheelchair. After a brief message from the pastor, Alfred Ugle's body was laid to rest not far from Greg's wife Sherma and Adrian and Audrey's children Henry and Grace, all dearly beloved and gone too soon.

Afterwards, I stood near the Smiths in the shade of a tree. Gloria Ugle came up and thanked them for all they had done for her. Then Greg's son Ben appeared. With tears in his eyes, he thanked Doreen for being a 'mother' to his father, and then he hugged her. The complicated and enmeshed relationship between the missionaries and their charges struck me once more.

The following day, Greg drove one of his granddaughters – Ben's oldest daughter – and me to Kalgoorlie. A beautiful girl with Ben's high-wattage smile, she carried with her a stack of books to read, and work to complete for the advanced science course she was taking at school. Greg had cleaned the floor of his car and the back was piled high with luggage and pillows. His granddaughter and I took turns in the front seat. When it was my turn in the back, I leaned against the scrunched-up car seat cover, turned my face to the window and watched the clouds skim past, in the huge skies of my childhood, above the changing colours of the soil. Loud music filled the car – country and western and 70s rock hits – and there seemed to be no barrier between my brain and the sound. It filled my head and swept me along, and as we travelled towards the land that had grown me, I felt more at peace than I had in a long while. Without being morbid, I knew then that I wanted my remains to be returned to Kalgoorlie when I died.

We stopped in Welbungin in the wheat belt, where Greg was living with his family when he and his siblings were removed. Greg drove off the main road, down a dirt track, and parked the car. We got out and walked over pale pink dirt, not grey as I'd imagined and Greg remembered, paler than the Kalgoorlie dirt, through patches of prickles, to a clearing. A soft breeze shushed in the stands of ti-tree that infused the air with their distinctive smell, and flocks of pink and grey galahs rose squawking into the air.

A couple of pieces of wood, weathered grey and uneven, marked the breadth of what was once a small hut. Greg recalled catching the bus to school in the mornings and returning in the afternoons. The children would scramble to get off and be first home. He remembered running around the hut, tapping on the tin and listening for a hollow echo. He showed us where the cooking fire was made, pointed to where the beds were positioned and showed us the rusted but recognisable chimney. He reeled off the names of other families and pointed to where they had lived. Pointed to the upturned, rusted hulk of the family's Ford Prefect, spoke of piling in with all his siblings while their father drove into Bencubbin, the car making a noise like a chaff-cutter, to buy 'plonk' from the back of the pub because he was not permitted inside.

A couple of crested pigeons lifted from the high branches of a tree and flew off into the bush. Greg remembered chasing them along the ground and whacking them with a stick. His mother would get the children to pluck the feathers, and then she would see to the cooking. Greg's voice drifted off and his eyes took on a distant look, as if he were seeing things invisible to his granddaughter and me. 'It was a happy time,' he said. 'Chasing cockies and twenty-eights too. Messing around with the other kids.'

He smiled gently and picked his way between pieces of corrugated iron with varying degrees of rust, and the past he always carried with him seemed, for once, to soothe him. We returned to the car and continued on. Greg drove at the speed limit, smoothly and confidently.

'Why did you make me drive you around all the time?' I asked, somewhat miffed.

'You can tell a lot about a person by the way they drive,' he said. 'Your man, he's a fast driver, doesn't hesitate.' *Not like you,* the unspoken words.

'I didn't realise it was a test,' I said. But of course, our whole friendship was in many ways a test, for him and for me.

In Kalgoorlie, I arranged to meet with Greg, to clarify a few points. We met in the lounge area of my hotel room, while his granddaughter watched TV.

'I want to talk about our friendship,' I said.

Greg sat up straighter, both feet flat on the floor, his facial muscles tight.

'Last time I came to Kalgoorlie, you hugged me,' I said. 'At Alfie's funeral, you hugged the Aboriginal women but you shook my hand. Do you really see me as a friend?'

For me, this was not merely a matter of bruised feelings. As a non-Indigenous Australian, I would share in the responsibility for the official Reconciliation process for the rest of my days, a responsibility that would be highlighted sooner than I'd thought, when revelations of abuse of juveniles in custody in the Northern Territory came to light, a responsibility that would be measured in social, political and economic change. One measure of personal reconciliation, on the other hand, was friendship. It would indicate a willingness to accept my commitment to a two-way process, with the possibility of future positive outcomes in areas we hadn't yet explored. What I didn't fully understand then was that there existed a depth of connection between us that defied simple definition and, with our cultural differences, was easily misunderstood or overlooked. I might have seen Greg's handshake as relegating me to the role of neutral observer or family storyteller, when really the fact of him inviting me to Alfie's funeral in the first place signified the special place I'd come to occupy in his life. But it would take me months to figure that out.

Back then, when I raised the issue of friendship, Greg frowned.

'You're my friend.' He sounded surprised, as if I had questioned a foregone conclusion. 'I ring you when something's going on in my family. I just need you to listen without trying to solve my problems. That's what friendship means to me. If your man was over there,' he pointed to a space near the door into the bedroom, 'I would hug him, but not you. You're his *yorga*. You don't want to go causing problems. It's cultural. People here in town, they don't hug. They nod.'

'Do you have many white friends?'

'Oooh, no!' Greg was adamant; astonished, even, at the suggestion. He relaxed a little, bent one leg at the knee and folded it under him, pale sole facing up. 'When you invited me over to stay with you, I thought you'd put me up in a motel. But you didn't. That surprised me. When you put me up in your house, we became brother and sister.'

Knowing that Greg had even thought I might put him up in a motel saddened me: I knew it came from a multitude of past experiences that influenced our current friendship.

'I don't always like answering your questions,' he continued. 'And I don't always give the full answer. Like when you asked what my sisters thought. They were worried. "What you goin' around with that married woman for?" they asked. They were protective of me, I think. The blackfella always gets left behind. It happened with the *Rabbit-Proof Fence*.'

I read Greg a dedication I intended to put inside the front cover of the book.

'No,' Greg said. 'Put your name on the cover. You did the writing. You put it all together. Put the dedication at the end.'

So here it is:

If ever a community produced a book, this is it. Bronwyn Newland, Catherine Howard, Geoffrey Stokes, Ben and Cheryl-Lee Ugle, Adrian and Audrey Ugle and family, Robbie Ugle and Ruth Bonney, Tony Ugle, Gloria Phillips, Delphine Ugle, the other Ugle siblings whose stories lie within these pages even though I didn't interview them – Alfred (now deceased), June, Diane and Susan – and especially, and with enormous gratitude, my dear friend Greg Ugle, this is *our* book.

Epilogue

There were many factors to consider in writing this story. First and foremost was the question of telling someone else's story, particularly fraught when that someone comes from a less dominant group. An easy second was how to tell one's own story – especially one of privilege – within that story (without dwelling on the question of white guilt). After that my ranking system fails, the level of difficulty of the other concerns being impossible to distinguish from each other: the responsibility of a researcher to her interview subjects, the question of money, the right to privacy, and the unreliability of memory. The list is by no means exhaustive.

Helen Garner, speaking to the question of 'who owns the story?', has stated that stories are not found objects. You don't just walk along the street, stub your toe on a story, pick it up, polish and publish it, and then sit back and wait for the money to roll in. The writer has to find raw material, shape it, and turn it into art. Usually over a long period of time. With great effort. And the money rarely rolls in.

Garner's words are reassuring. However, it remains controversial for white Australians to write stories about Aboriginal people. The 'A' word – appropriation – hovers, like an apparition. In any case, my main subject, Greg Ugle, had already written and self-published his story. But as with many self-published books, it did not have the advantage of access to editing and distribution that I have. Nor did I merely want to repeat his story. As I've already mentioned, what interested me was the gap between my perception, in childhood, of my friends' lives and their reality; my responsibility as someone who'd grown up in the same place at the same time; and the possibility of personal reconciliation. So, putting aside Garner's view on ownership, I belonged to the story and the story belonged, at least in part, to me.

But here's the thing: my Aboriginal interviewees' stories were my raw material. Without them I didn't have a story. Was it fair, then, that I should financially benefit, not them? To complicate matters, I'm fortunate to be financially secure, whereas my Aboriginal friends live constantly on the brink of poverty.

The downsides to paying my Aboriginal interviewees are obvious. I risk being seen as buying their stories, with an element of coercion involved. Of greater concern is the way the payment of money tips the balance of power in favour of the interviewer – me. I assumed the upper hand in an ongoing story in which white colonial upper-handedness is a root cause of problems. (Although in some ways that power was an illusion; my interviewees ultimately retain ownership of my raw material.) Money could also have influenced my interviewees in negative ways. It could have persuaded them to tell stories they'd rather not, or it might have tempted them to embellish the truth in an attempt to make their stories more saleable.

Despite these concerns, I found myself returning to a common refrain among writers: 'We should be paid for our work.' Shouldn't interviewees be paid for their time, effort and stories?

Perhaps timing makes a difference. I thought that money might complicate the dynamic less if the subject agreed to the interview before the issue of payment arose. I hope this is so.

My personal involvement in the story – my position, in historical terms, on the side of the exploiter – convinced me that I should not profit from any published work.

Paying one subject, even if he is the main interviewee, and not others is potentially problematic unless the agreement is kept secret, yet surely transparency is important when money changes hands. To this end, I decided to offer all interviewees a small lump sum payment on publication. To minimise the risk of coercion, I elected not to tell the relevant individuals ahead of time.

I say all interviewees but I mean all *Aboriginal* interviewees. Why? Because at the heart of this story is the wrong done to Aboriginal people by white settler Australians – the taking of land, the killing, the removal of children, the subjugation. If anyone should benefit from the telling of this story, it's the Aboriginal subjects.

The other way I worked to negate any downsides to payment was to give my Aboriginal friends the right to read transcripts of our interviews and correct any errors or remove details they don't want published.

The other reason I gave them the right to edit our interviews is because I believe the interview process is inherently unfair. A knee-jerk response, in medical terms, is a tendon response to a short, sharp tap with a hammer. It involves a local neural circuit, not higher neural processes. Similarly a verbal knee-jerk response doesn't engage higher thought and doesn't necessarily reflect deep-seated opinions. The writer has the opportunity to edit his or her opinions at leisure before they are published. The interviewee, on the other hand, is potentially hung out to dry with opinions or statements given without forethought, and sometimes with unintended meaning. The TV crime show scenario of the criminal who accidentally blurts a confession in response to questioning under pressure doesn't necessarily hold true for an interview. A given response may indicate hunger or confusion or boredom with the interview process. Or the question might have been poorly worded. Giving the interviewee the opportunity to edit seems only fair.

A separate issue arises with interviewees who are knowingly or unknowingly on the same side as perpetrators of past injustices. I'm talking here about the missionary Mr Sercombe. I gave him the opportunity to review the transcript of my notes from our first interview, but because the second interview was recorded, I didn't. From time to time since his death, I have found myself wanting to edit his harsher comments. I'd caught him off guard; he hadn't known about the rape and was visibly shocked. He hadn't had time to consider the factors that might have contributed to the girl's lack of skill as a mother. My initial thought was to include his comments – they make good copy, after all. Then I thought I might have some responsibility to delete spur-of-the-moment comments he might well have regretted, or at least put them in context. Creative nonfiction, after all, should be the domain of activist, not vigilante, writing. But spur-of-the-moment or not, his comments, I believe, reflect a belief shared by Chief Protector Neville that Aboriginal people suffer from a lesser morality, and this belief underlay the gender segregation at the

Mission that splintered families and caused much suffering.

In a similar vein is the issue of dead people, who have no comeback to our writing. After Mr Sercombe died, his children found a copy of the transcript of our first conversation and a son called me. I could hear the anxiety in his voice: What was I planning to do with this material? Was there a later draft? But Mr Sercombe agreed to the interview and consented to the tape recorder. His testimony stands. Similarly, my grandfather accepted a government position, funded by taxpayers' money, and, in his official capacity, submitted a report to council that was later published in the local newspaper. I'm merely giving the Hill's Hoist a spin; my grandfather hung himself out to dry.

The case of a dead person who was a victim of an unreported crime raises other issues. I told myself that this part of the story reveals a truth of Mission life: the adult-to-child ratio was hopelessly inadequate. The children couldn't possibly have received quality care. In the case concerned, the system let a girl down. Badly. But perhaps this is another example of the vigilante in me trying to get out. Perhaps I'm conducting a kangaroo court on the page, looking for justice for the girl who went on to live an unhappy life and died prematurely. Would she have wanted it? And what of the dead perpetrators who cannot defend themselves in a court of law? On the other hand, what of the then-underage witnesses who seem to want to relieve themselves of the burden of secrecy? Aside from corroboration of witness statements – here the unreliability of memory is a particular concern – and permission from the woman's daughter, there are no easy outs. There never are.

Reading List

Malcolm Allbrook, *Henry Prinsep's Empire: Framing a distant colony*, ANU Press, Canberra 2014

Judy Atkinson, *Trauma Trails*, Spinifex Press, Melbourne 2004

James Baldwin, 'A Letter to My Nephew', first published in *The Progressive* magazine in 1962, and later as an essay in the collection *The Fire Next Time*, Vintage Books, New York 1993

Edwidge Danticat, *Brother, I'm Dying*, Vintage Books, New York 2007

Stephen Gray, *The Protectors*, Allen & Unwin, Melbourne 2011

Anna Haebich, *Broken Circles: Fragmenting Indigenous Families* 1800–2000, Fremantle Arts Centre Press, Fremantle 2000

Melissa Lucashenko, *Mullumbimby*, University of Queensland Press, St Lucia, 2013

Russell McGregor, *Indifferent Inclusion: Aboriginal People and the Australian Nation*, Aboriginal Studies Press, Canberra 2011

Kim Mahood, *Craft for a Dry Lake*, Anchor, Sydney 2000

Barack Obama, *Dreams from My Father,* Text Publishing, Melbourne 2008

Doris Pilkington (Nugi Garimara), *Follow the Rabbit-Proof Fence*, University of Queensland Press, St Lucia 2002

Rene Powell and Bernadette Kennedy, *Rene Baker File #28/E.D.P.*, Fremantle Arts Centre Press, Fremantle 2005

William and Marjorie Sharpe, *What an Experience*, Boolarong Press, Salisbury, 1989

Gregory Ugle, *Forced Exile*, Xlibris, Gordon 2011

Perhaps timing makes a difference. I thought that money might complicate the dynamic less if the subject agreed to the interview before the issue of payment arose. I hope this is so.

My personal involvement in the story – my position, in historical terms, on the side of the exploiter – convinced me that I should not profit from any published work.

Paying one subject, even if he is the main interviewee, and not others is potentially problematic unless the agreement is kept secret, yet surely transparency is important when money changes hands. To this end, I decided to offer all interviewees a small lump sum payment on publication. To minimise the risk of coercion, I elected not to tell the relevant individuals ahead of time.

I say all interviewees but I mean all *Aboriginal* interviewees. Why? Because at the heart of this story is the wrong done to Aboriginal people by white settler Australians – the taking of land, the killing, the removal of children, the subjugation. If anyone should benefit from the telling of this story, it's the Aboriginal subjects.

The other way I worked to negate any downsides to payment was to give my Aboriginal friends the right to read transcripts of our interviews and correct any errors or remove details they don't want published.

The other reason I gave them the right to edit our interviews is because I believe the interview process is inherently unfair. A knee-jerk response, in medical terms, is a tendon response to a short, sharp tap with a hammer. It involves a local neural circuit, not higher neural processes. Similarly a verbal knee-jerk response doesn't engage higher thought and doesn't necessarily reflect deep-seated opinions. The writer has the opportunity to edit his or her leisure before they are published. The intervie other hand, is potentially hung out to dry with statements given without forethought, and som unintended meaning. The TV crime show sce criminal who accidentally blurts a confession to questioning under pressure doesn't necessari for an interview. A given response may indicat confusion or boredom with the interview proc question might have been poorly worded. Givi viewee the opportunity to edit seems only fair.

A separate issue arises with interviewee knowingly or unknowingly on the same side rators of past injustices. I'm talking here about t ary Mr Sercombe. I gave him the opportunity tc transcript of my notes from our first interview, l the second interview was recorded, I didn't. Fr time since his death, I have found myself want his harsher comments. I'd caught him off guarc known about the rape and was visibly shocked. had time to consider the factors that might ha uted to the girl's lack of skill as a mother. My init was to include his comments – they make g after all. Then I thought I might have some r ity to delete spur-of-the-moment comments he have regretted, or at least put them in context nonfiction, after all, should be the domain of a vigilante, writing. But spur-of-the-moment or no ments, I believe, reflect a belief shared by Chief Neville that Aboriginal people suffer from a les ity, and this belief underlay the gender segregat

Reading Lis

Malcolm Allbrook, *Henry Prinsep's Empire: Framing a* Canberra 2014

Judy Atkinson, *Trauma Trails*, Spinifex Press, Melb

James Baldwin, 'A Letter to My Nephew', first pul magazine in 1962, and later as an essay in th *Time*, Vintage Books, New York 1993

Edwidge Danticat, *Brother, I'm Dying*, Vintage Boo

Stephen Gray, *The Protectors*, Allen & Unwin, Mel

Anna Haebich, *Broken Circles: Fragmenting Indigenous* Fremantle Arts Centre Press, Fremantle 200

Melissa Lucashenko, *Mullumbimby*, University of Lucia, 2013

Russell McGregor, *Indifferent Inclusion: Aboriginal Pe Nation*, Aboriginal Studies Press, Canberra 2

Kim Mahood, *Craft for a Dry Lake*, Anchor, Sydne

Barack Obama, *Dreams from My Father*, Text Publis

Doris Pilkington (Nugi Garimara), *Follow the Rabb* of Queensland Press, St Lucia 2002

Rene Powell and Bernadette Kennedy, *Rene Baker* Arts Centre Press, Fremantle 2005

William and Marjorie Sharpe, *What an Experience,* Salisbury, 1989

Gregory Ugle, *Forced Exile*, Xlibris, Gordon 2011

Acknowledgments

My heartfelt thanks to many people:

To early teachers and readers: Rebecca Solnit, Ana Maria Spagna, Kyle Minor, Steve Almond and aunt extraordinaire Val Kermode.

To Tom Reynolds from the WA State Records Department.

To teachers from the short-lived but stellar City University of Hong Kong MFA program – Xu Xi, Luis Francia, Suzanne Paola and especially Robin Hemley. May the program's spirit remain alive in alumni work.

To my Mullumbimby writing group – Sarah Armstrong, Hayley Katzen, Jesse Blackadder and especially Emma Ashmere.

To Melissa Lucashenko for her generosity and timely advice.

To my Varuna gang – Alice Nelson, Leah Kaminsky and David Carlin. Catherine Therese, let's meet at Venice Beach.

To Kathryn Heyman for her magical touch and critical feedback for the final draft.

To Christobel Botton and Kevin Skelton for casting keen eyes over the final draft.

To my father Stan Webster and my brothers Geoffrey and Graham for their generosity in allowing me to tell our family story.

To my wonderful agent Lyn Tranter for believing in the story and finding it the perfect home.

To the award-winning team at NewSouth Publishing, Phillipa McGuinness, Paul O'Beirne, Josephine Pajor-Markus , Rosina Dimarzo and Vivien Valk, for believing in the story and bringing the book into the world.

To Jocelyn Hungerford, who had my back. Thank you. It was a privilege to work with such a talented editor.

And to Bronwyn Newland, Adrian and Audrey Ugle, Tony Ugle, Robert Ugle and Ruth Bonney, Gloria Phillips, Delphine Ugle, Ben and Cheryl-Lee Ugle, Geoffrey and Christine Stokes, Catherine Howard and Nicki Gordon for sharing their lives and their memories with me. Thanks, too, to Alfred Ugle (now deceased), June Ugle, Diane Ugle and Susan Ugle: it's your story too.

To Greg Ugle, without whom there'd be no book, thank you and happy wandering.

And to my children Rick, Andy and Louise, ever-patient and ever-encouraging. You guys are the best!

www.ingramcontent.com/pod-product-compliance
Ingram Content Group UK Ltd.
Pitfield, Milton Keynes, MK11 3LW, UK
UKHW041353190726
13851UKWH00014B/94